SYMBOLS IN SOCIETY

HUGH DALZIEL DUNCAN

OXFORD UNIVERSITY PRESS

London   Oxford   New York

To Kenneth Burke, Master Symbolist of Our Time,
and George Herbert Mead,
Founder of the Chicago Tradition in Symbolic Analysis

OXFORD UNIVERSITY PRESS

Oxford London New York
Glasgow Toronto Melbourne Wellington
Cape Town Ibadan Nairobi Lusaka Addis Ababa Delhi
Bombay Calcutta Madras Karachi Lahore Dacca
Kuala Lumpur Hong Kong Tokyo

PREFACE

Shifting from analytic to dogmatic writing is a chastening experience. The aphoristic quality of propositional statement leaves little room for rhetorical charm and the joys of soliloquy in footnotes. Readers of propositions expect explanations, not arguments. But, as all skilled rhetoricians know, an explanation is often simply one voice in argument. We "explain" during the silence of our opponent who, in turn, waits for our moment of silence to "explain" his view. My opponents are the mechanists, and particularly those whose signatures appear at the end of the "General Statement" of *Toward a General Theory of Action*. I do not believe roles should be studied as "mechanisms," nor that symbolic systems "gear" and "mesh." Many sociologists (certainly many American sociologists) are mechanists. I point this out not to stir up further argument, but to place the voices in argument. What I am arguing against is summed up in "Some Fundamental Categories of the Theory of Action: A General Statement," which serves as an Introduction to *Toward a General Theory of Action*. The reader can (and should) turn to what my opponents have to say.

I hope I have done more than repeat in sociological jargon what has already been said, and well said, by Mead and Burke. Since my previous books and articles deal at length with the traditions of symbolic analysis and the relevance of this tradition to sociological analysis, I have decided here to avoid the usual scholarly apparatus of footnotes. There is, however, ample discussion of each proposition. Some of these attempts at clarification will repeat what I have said elsewhere, especially in *Communication and Social Order*. But in any attempt to make a systematic statement out of past work this cannot be avoided. It may be, indeed, that I have been too elliptical in my explanations of the propositions. Readers who think so are advised to turn to my previous works.

Mead, Simmel, Cooley, Malinowski, Weber, Dewey, Freud, and Burke have supplied many of the ideas used in this work. But if my argument is determined by my friends, we must admit too that my opponents have much (perhaps, indeed, in some ways even more) to do with what I say. Scientific discourse is like a heated discussion; we cannot avoid the dispute if we choose to stay in the company of the disputants. We listen for a while to find out what is going on, and as we listen we are not sure how to reply to those who seek to enlist us on their side. But soon we are engaged and, as we commit ourselves to the discussion, find that we have opponents as well as friends in the gathering. And even in the objective discussion of science, we often share the heat as well as the light of argument. We take sides, and argue with friends against opponents. And as we argue we discover that our opponents determine us, as we determine them. So while my opponents are the mechanists, at present what I think of as the "Harvard Mechanists," I respect them as any student respects an opponent who makes him think hard about his own point of view. And since, at one time or another, I have gone to school to both Professors Shils and Parsons, they are responsible, if only in a highly negative way, for much of what I say.

It has taken me some years to develop my own system, and as I have done so, I have grown to admire the success of Professors Parsons and Shils in achieving such a high degree of consistency in their system. So I hope that they will realize my indebtedness to them. In the heat of argument, I may have said things which told much more about what was wrong with behaviorism than how to correct the faults I discovered. But, as I have said before, if we know what is wrong with a method we must know this from the practice of some right method of our own. Fortunately, many of my castigations of behaviorists have found their way (with gentle nudging from friends) to my wastebasket. But if some sharpness remains, or if my occasional teasing of the mechanists for their sudden leaps, or (to bring images up to date), sudden thrusts into the mystical realm of mechanics where what is moving determines its own motions, seems to violate scholarly decorum, I hasten to say that my disagreement is not intended as ridicule, but as a voice in argument.

Those who try to say something about the reciprocal relations between symbols and society work in a rich tradition. Many good things have been said about the social function of symbols in both the humanities and the social sciences. There is no need for the modern sociologist to start from scratch in the study of symbolic interaction, or to confuse ignorance of a field with its non-existence, but it is true that the observations on symbolic interpretations which exist in classic sociological theory have not been the subject of much study in America. I have argued in previous works that classical sociological and anthropological theorists have said many useful things about symbolic interpretation. I hope that my analyses of what has been said in social science about the social interpretation of symbols will do something to create a bench mark in sociological communications theory. This is badly needed. Too many of us are repeating each other (and ourselves), just as too many symbolists are discussing communication in society as if there were no tradition at all.

Many good things have been said about communication. The cause of sociology will be advanced if we fashion this rich inheritance into a body of sociological propositions. We must create a sociological model of communication, and while we cannot yet work with any great sense of finality in this, we ought to try to create propositions that can be tested. The series of propositions offered here will be subject to much refinement as they are used by others. As I have pointed out in my previous works, I owe much to Kenneth Burke's theory of "dramatism." This book, like all my books on symbolic analysis, could not have been written without his help, and the help of other social theorists whose work is discussed elsewhere in my writings.

I owe thanks to my students in sociology and English at Southern Illinois University. Through discussion in seminars and classes I have had an opportunity to test these propositions and bring them into their present form. Southern Illinois University has been generous with time and resources. A grant from the National Institute of Mental Health (MH 10266-01) made it possible for me to get this book under way. Earlier versions of some of my propositions appeared in *Communication Theory and Research: Proceedings of the First International Symposium*, edited by Lee Thayer (Springfield, Illinois: Charles C Thomas, Publisher, 1967) and in *Human Communication Theory: Original Essays*, edited by Frank E. X. Dance (New York: Holt, Rinehart and Winston, Inc., 1967), and I thank them for permission to quote from their publications.

I should also like to thank the following individuals and companies for giving me permission to quote from copyrighted material: Basic Books, for *Sociology Today: Problems and Prospects*, edited by Robert K. Merton *et al.*; Basic Books, Sigmund Freud Copyrights Ltd., Mrs. Alix Strachey and the Institute of Psycho-Analysis, The Hogarth Press Ltd., and Allen and Unwin Ltd., for the *Standard Edition of The Complete Psychological Works of Sigmund Freud;* The Free Press, for *Theories of Society: Foundations of Modern Sociological Theory*, edited by Talcott Parsons *et al.* (Copyright © 1959 by The Free Press of Glencoe), and *A Selected Bibliography on Values, Ethics, and Esthetics in the Behavioral Sciences and Philosophy, 1920-1959*, by Ethel Albert and Clyde Kluckhohn (Copyright © 1960 by The Free Press, a Corporation); W. H. Freeman and Co. and *Scientific American*, for Kenneth Boulding's Review of *Communications and Social Order*, by Hugh Dalziel Duncan, in *Scientific American*, 203, 1 (January 1963), 157-60 (Copyright © 1963 by Scientific American, Inc. All rights reserved); Harper & Row, Publishers, for *Contemporary Sociological Theories*, by P. A. Sorokin; Oxford University Press, for *From Max Weber: Essays in Sociology*, translated, edited, and with an introduction by C. Wright Mills, and *The Sociological Imagination*, by C. Wright Mills; and Robert E. Spiller and Carl Winter Universitätsverlag, for "Value and Method in American Studies," by Robert E. Spiller, in *Jahrbuch für Amerikastudien*, Band 4, Heidelberg 1959, Carl Winter Universitätsverlag.

CONTENTS

I INTRODUCTION

1. Confusion over the social function of symbols in American sociology, 3

2. The neglect of communication theory in American sociology, 8

3. Structure and function in social action: a dramatistic model, 16

4. The problem of function in symbolic analysis, 21

5. Time in American social thought: the destruction of the past by the future, 25

6. Tradition and debate in sociological analysis of symbols, 30

7. Sociodrama as a source of power in modern society, 33

8. Sociological jargon, 35

9. Democratic bias of this book: equality as a form of social order, 36

10. Hopes and fears, 39

II AXIOMATIC PROPOSITIONS

1. Society arises in, and continues to exist through, the communication of significant symbols, 44

2. Man creates the significant symbols he uses in communication, 46

3. Emotions, as well as thought and will, are learned in communication, 47

4. Symbols affect social motives by determining the forms in which the contents of relationships can be expressed, 48

5. From a sociological view motives must be understood as man's need for social relationships, 49

6. Symbols are directly observable data of meaning in social relationships, 50

7. Social order is expressed through hierarchies which differentiate men into ranks, classes, and status groups, and, at the same time, resolve differentiation through appeals to principles of order which transcend those upon which differentiation is based, 51

8. Hierarchy is expressed through the symbolization of superiority, inferiority, and equality, and of passage from one to the other, 52

9. Hierarchy functions through persuasion, which takes the form of courtship in social relationships, 53

10. The expression of hierarchy is best conceived through forms of drama which are both comic and tragic, 59

11. Social order is created and sustained in social dramas through intensive and frequent communal presentations of tragic and comic roles whose proper enactment is believed necessary to community survival, 60

12. Social order is always a resolution of acceptance, doubt, or rejection of the principles that are believed to guarantee such order, 61

III THEORETICAL PROPOSITIONS

1. Social order, and its expression through hierarchy, is a social drama in which actors struggle to uphold, destroy, or change principles of order which are believed "necessary" to social integration, 63

2. Social differences are resolved through appeals to principles of social order believed to be ultimate and transcendent sources of order, 66

3. The structure of social action involves five elements: (1) the stage or situation in which the act takes place; (2) the kind of act considered appropriate to upholding order in group life; (3) the social roles which embody social functions; (4) the means of expression used in the act; (5) the ends, goals, or values which are believed to create and sustain social order, 67

4. All explanations which ground social order in "conditions," "environments," "the body," "forces," or "equilibrium," are situational explanations, 70

5. Social institutions are the most directly observable units of action in society. Eleven such basic units may be distinguished: these are (1) the family, (2) government, (3) economic institutions, (4) defense, (5) education, (6) manners and etiquette (pure forms of sociability), (7) entertainment, (8) health and welfare, (9) religion, (10) art, (11) science and technology, 71

6. In analyzing social roles we ask: what function is supposed to be performed in what role, and how is this role played before various au-

diences? what style of life is involved in role enactment, and how is this style used to legitimize beliefs in certain forms of social order? 72

7. Symbolic means of expression, the media in which we express ourselves, must be analyzed for their effect on what we communicate, 72

8. Social action cannot be analyzed solely in terms of situation, institution, role, means of expression, or beliefs in certain principles of social order, but only in a synthesis of all five elements, 74

9. Superiors, inferiors, and equals must expect disobedience, indifference, and disloyalty, and while those who control social order must teach us to feel guilt over the commission of such hierarchal "sins," they must also provide us with ways of ridding ourselves of fear and guilt, so that we can act with confidence in the efficacy of the principles of social order under whose name we act, 75

10. All hierarchies function through a "perfection" of their principles in final moments of social mystification which are reached by mountings from lower to higher principles of social order, 78

11. Five types of audiences are addressed in social courtship: these are, first, general publics ("They"); second, community guardians ("We"); third, others significant to us as friends and confidants with whom we talk intimately ("Thou"); fourth, the selves we address inwardly in soliloquy (the "I" talking to its "Me"); and fifth, ideal audiences whom we address as ultimate sources of social order ("It"), 81

12. The general public ("They") is a symbolization of the whole community, 93

13. The community guardians ("We") symbolize the conscience of the community, 95

14. The significant other ("Thou") is symbolized through dialogue in which the self is created and sustained, 100

15. Soliloquy, like inner dialogue between the "I" and the "Me," is the symbolization of role conflict in society, 105

16. Principles of social order are grounded in ultimate principles of order which serve as the final audience in social address, 110

17. Social order is legitimized through symbols grounded in nature, man, society, language, or God, 116

18. Social order, and its expression through hierarchy, is enacted in social dramas in which actors attempt to uphold, destroy, or change the principles of that social order, 123

19. Hierarchal communication is a form of address (courtship) among superiors, inferiors, and equals, 127

20. Disorder in society originates in disorder in communication, 130

21. Social disorder and counter-order arise in guilt which originates in disobedience of those whose commandments are believed necessary to social order, 135

22. Society must provide us with means to expiate guilt arising from sins of disobedience, 140

23. Victimage is the basic form of expiation in the communication of social order, 144

24. Victimage of the self is determined by social victimage, 147

IV   METHODOLOGICAL PROPOSITIONS

1. All statements about the structure and function of the symbolic act must be demonstrated to exist in the symbolic context of the act, 151

2. Sociological explanations of symbols must be grounded in the analysis of social drama as a drama of hierarchy, 155

3. The staging of an act in society is a social drama of authority which we analyze by asking: where, or under what conditions, is the act being presented? What kind of act is it? What kind of actors are selected for what kind of roles? What means or instruments do the actors use to communicate authority? And how is the expression of hierarchy related to a principle of social order? 161

4. Stage, act, role, means, and the principle of social order invoked as a determinant of social order, are linked in various ways in social drama: ten types of linkage may be distinguished, 166

5. In symbolic analysis of social drama we ask: in the struggle for power within an institution, who evokes what symbols of authority? In what kind of action? By what means? Under what conditions? And in the name of what transcendent power is authority legitimized? 169

6. Themes and plots in social drama may be studied by noting moments of transformation as well as fixed moments of belief in the drama of social hierarchy, 170

7. The ways in which audiences are addressed in social drama offer many clues to the distribution of authority, 171

8. There are seven basic forms of social drama: these are games, play, parties, festivals, ceremonies, drama, and rites, 173

9. Childhood play is the first experience of social address, 176

10. Games teach us the power of rules as a form of social order, 177

11. In parties and social gatherings we learn to relate on a purely social basis through manners, 179

12. Festivals increase social integration by creating joy in fellowship, 181

13. Ceremonies are social dramas in which we seek to uphold the dignity and majesty of social roles believed necessary to social order, 183

14. Rites are social dramas in which collective sentiments are fixed through communication with supernatural powers who are believed to sustain social order, 185

15. Drama depicts social action as symbolic action to be judged by principles of order believed necessary to order in society, 189

16. The staging of an act in society is a social drama of authority in which the relationship between ends and the means must be kept under constant review through criticism, 191

17. Relationships between authorities, symbol manipulators, public, and critics, may be determined by asking to what degree communication between and among them is open or closed, 193

18. The primary type of relationship between authority, symbol manipulators, critics, and audiences exists within face-to-face groups, 194

19. A second type of relationship occurs whenever a status group, class, institution, or society seeks to monopolize communication, 195

20. A third type of relationship occurs whenever critics judge in terms of craft principles, 196

21. In a fourth type of relationship the critic conceives of his role in terms of communicating directly to the public, and acts as a delegate of this public to the artist, 196

22. In a fifth type of relationship, authorities, artists, publics, and critics assume a mutual responsibility for the creation, distribution, and use of what they consider to be the best kinds of symbolic expression, 197

23. Basic functions in society must be dramatized before they can be communicated as actions, 199

24. Authorities relate family life to social order through the depiction of courtship, marriage, and parenthood as a preparation for citizenship in the community, 201

25. Symbols of government must be dramatized as symbols of social order, 202

26. Authorities must create and sustain ways of making, distributing, and consuming food, clothing, and shelter, according to beliefs in right of superiors, inferiors, and equals to share in these services, 206

27. To understand authority we must observe what kind of social drama is mounted by the military, the police, and the intelligence services used by each, 208

28. The basic function of education is the transmission of traditions, customs, and sentiments which are believed necessary to social order, and at the same time, the creation of methods of inquiry which will help us to solve problems we must solve if the community is to survive, 211

29. Forms of sociation in themselves become transcendent ultimates in social relations, as we see in manners, etiquette, and play, 212

30. In play we learn to subordinate ourselves to rules, and to "internalize" the meaning of roles, 214

31. Health is symbolized by authorities as a means to increased group participation, 215

32. Religious invocation of the supernatural, the ways in which we communicate with our gods to infuse social order with supernatural power, is a basic form of social integration, 217

33. Art creates symbolic roles which we use as a dramatic rehearsal in the imagination of community roles we must play to sustain social order, 223

34. Science raises problem-solving to an ultimate value by making methods used in problem-solving a guide to social action, 228

35. The final and most powerful moment in the drama of authority is the invocation of the ultimate power which upholds social order and thus wards off threats to the survival of the community, 234

IV CONCLUSION

Sociodrama and Power in Modern Society, 236

The Modern Sociodrama of Victimage, 237

The Confusion of Social Integration with Religious Integration in European Social Thought, 239

The Protean Power of Mystification, 242

Art as the Home of the Critical Spirit, 243

In Sociodrama Man Becomes the "Maker and Molder of Himself," 246

Index, 249

I

INTRODUCTION

We hear everywhere in the social sciences that the relatedness of men in society is determined by economics, politics, sex, technology, urbanization, or religion. Little is said about how symbolic forms shape our social life. As we read in Sorokin's *Contemporary Sociological Theories:* "In this field [the social role of arts] our scientific knowledge is especially small, making particularly great our need of beginning to study these phenomena more carefully. . . ." Of the nearly eight hundred pages in this standard review of sociological theory only one page is devoted to a discussion (entitled "Other Cultural Agencies") of the "social role of arts, morality, fashions, and other cultural agencies."[1] What Sorokin said in 1928 could be said with little change today. In his *Sociology of Language,* published in 1965, Joyce O. Hertzler says that while there has been increasing reference to communication in the sociological literature of the past thirty years, notably among sociologists who call themselves "symbolic interactionists," sociological writings on language have been superficial and unsystematic.[2]

There are many reasons for the inability of American sociologists to think well about symbols in society. One of these is the confusion of the symbolic with the subjective. As Max Scheler said: "All modern theories of value share the premise that values as such, and moral values in particular, are only *subjective* phenomena in man's mind which have no independent meaning and existence. Values according to this view, are but the projections of our desires and feelings."[3] Sub-

3

stitute the word "symbol" for "value," and we have a good statement of the problem confronting sociologists who try to deal with the social effect of symbols. In American social thought, acts are "integrated," their patterns "maintained," or their structure "organized," but when we examine closely how this organization occurs we soon discover that integration is being assumed, not demonstrated. As we shall stress, a structural description is *not* a description of function but only a formal abstraction. Form must be shown to exist *in* the content of the form (just as content must be related to the form in which it is expressed) and, above all, form must be described as a *sociological* form.

To say that symbols are locked up within a self we cannot observe, or that they are abstractions which have no reality yet "point to," "reflect," or "represent" reality, makes little sense. A symbol such as a proverb is hardly private and subjective. It is used because it *is* public. When I use a proverb I am not saying what I alone think, but what others think. The proverb is not "mine" but "ours." Yet when we say that desire cannot be fulfilled socially until it is given a form which enables it to be communicated, that, in short, the fulfillment of desire is dependent on the communication of significant symbols (as in art), symbols which must have a public content if they are to be used as social symbols, we are saying something unacceptable to American sociologists. We are told by some sociologists that literature, and all public forms of expression, cannot be studied by "scientific" methods because we must gather our own data. What this really means is that we must prefer very bad literature, called "case histories," or "life histories," to good literature. A young delinquent who is telling us his life story cannot invent a unique and original *way* of telling his story. Not even Tolstoy could do that. What he does, and what we all do when we narrate anything, is to make use of the forms available for such narration in our society.

Even the wildest dream has a form. The absurdity of the dream, like the "ravings" of the lunatic, or the "silence" of the mute child, is not formless. The dream has plot, the lunatic "raves" in quite specific ways, the autistic child expresses his withdrawal from normal communication in forms which do not differ from those used by other similarly afflicted children. Dreams, like all fantasy, are not simply random gatherings of images; they have very definite forms. Yet these symbolic forms which are so basic to all experience have not been studied intensively by social scientists. Content analysis, as the very name implies, is a study

4

of symbolic content based on the belief that what we are expressing tells us more about motivation than how we express it. As sociologists we study the content, but not the style, of life, even though our greatest sociologist, Max Weber, held that status and class must be studied as a style (as well as a content) of social experience. He argued, notably in his discussion of the Chinese literati, that how we express ourselves determines what we express, just as what we are trying to express determines how we express it. Unfortunately Weber did not develop a sociology of style. The same is true of Freud. He taught that the meaning of a dream must be derived from its form, as well as its content, but the content "sex" often is used to explain very diverse forms of the dream. If we know before we analyze the imagery of the dream that the images are sexual, we reduce form to content. The form need not be taken seriously because, at best, it is but a mask, a screen, an embellishment, a play of the content (what "really" goes on behind the mask of symbols).

American sociologists think poorly about communication because of their "trained incapacity" in the use of non-mechanistic models. The reduction of all science in sociology to research models derived from the physical sciences makes it all but impossible for the sociologist to deal with meaning. Sociologists of the behavioral persuasion (and this includes a large number of American sociologists) must, if they are consistent, do away with consciousness, intention, and meaning, in their research models. In place of "harmony," "order," "integration," we hear of "process," "equilibrium," "homeostasis," and "gearing." Order and disorder in human relationships are caused not by individuals enacting roles, but by "processes" which "occur" in "patterns" or "systems." Even those in the United States who style themselves "symbolic interactionists" often seem happier when they talk about "interaction patterns" and "structured responses," and employ other kinds of mechanistic imagery that ground social theory in the spatial (but seldom the temporal) aspects of the physical environment.

It is impossible to talk about human relationships without saying *something* about meaning. And meaning, even when it is called "pattern maintenance," is usually studied through the interpretation of symbols, for it is only in symbols that meaning (as attention and intention) can be observed. Thus Weber tells us that the spirit of capitalism is what Benjamin Franklin (among others) said it was in his various handbooks of advice on how to become a successful businessman in

5

American society. Now either we deal with such meaning through sociological methodology which allows us to interpret symbols in their social categories, or we disregard symbols and assume that they are but "reflections" of some kind of extra-symbolic reality. We "know" (like Pareto) that behind the mask of the symbol there lie interests—economic, political, sexual, as the case may be—which "really" determine human relationships. This, of course, reduces symbols to epiphenomena which exist on the surface of a social system whose "gearing" and "meshing" (in modern mechanistic parlance) really determine human motivation.

The description of symbols as "masks" or "reflections" of economic, political, religious, or sexual "realities" is not new. Dualisms between mind and nature are very ancient in social thought. It has long been realized that any mode of social analysis will produce at least two types of entities: first, analytical elements called "social facts," which can be observed easily enough; and second, the entities (not so easily observed) that arise in a system because analysis was made in the particular way in which it was made. In more specific terminology, the easily observed elements are called relata, while the elements "underlying" the system are called relations of those relata. What is peculiar to these relations as social relations is that they take place in and through symbols whose forms make possible intention or purpose. That is, we cannot intend to play a game of baseball unless the form of the game, its rules, already exists prior to our intention to play the game. As we shall argue in the following pages, we cannot intend to enact a role which does not already exist in the kinds of symbolic personification common to all forms of communication.

The definition of a symbol as a sign which "denotes" something other than the symbol itself is another source of confusion. In Professor Hertzler's *Sociology of Languages* we are told that there "is nothing *in the nature* of any of the signs . . . used as symbols that gives them the meanings they carry; these meanings we human beings bestow upon them by agreement or convention. . . . [Symbols] are the instrumentalities whereby men codify experience, or create a 'map' of the territory of experience. Their utility depends upon the fact that all group members are conditioned to react more or less uniformly to them."[4] But how do we "bestow" meaning, or "codify" experience, or create a "map" if not through symbols? And if symbols function as a "carrier of meaning" and the source of meaning is not symbolic, just what is the source of meaning? This is not to imply that an event, such as making love, can be explained wholly as "symbolic." But neither can we explain the human experience of love by sexual "drive." Love is *both*: it is sex *and* symbol.

Relationships between symbol and event are determined by *what* we are trying to do, and *how* we do it. And since both what and how take place in communication, the data of communication are prime social data. In human relationships "relatedness" is the kind of relatedness we experience in communication. Man is a trader, as he is a politician, parent, child, or worshipper of supernatural forces, but in all his roles he is a communicator. As businessman, parent, soldier, lover, artist, scientist, or priest, he communicates, and *how* he communicates, the forms in which he enacts these roles, determines success or failure in them. In sum, if needs, wants, desires—religious, economic, political, sexual, as the case may be—are to be accepted as motives for conduct, how we communicate these motives must be studied. If an act has a content or a function it must have a form or a structure of this content. Sociologists need not concern themselves with the philosophical problems of the relation of form to content. But when we accept the humanistic position that form determines content (that is, that *what* we do in social relations is determined by *how* we do it) we must still earn our keep in the human studies by saying something *sociological* about form. We will not do this by paraphrasing in sociological jargon what has already been said by physicists, astronomers, biologists, botanists, biochemists, embryologists, zoologists, psychologists, neurologists, artists, or students of religion, but by developing sociolinguistic models of our own.

There are, of course, symbols whose social meanings are difficult to grasp. The images in night and day dreams, the language of the schizophrene, the sudden enfolding of memory and the visions of the future, like the grotesque, caricature, nonsense, and other highly fantastic genres in life, literature, and art, are obscure and ambiguous. But obscurity and ambiguity must not be explained away as meaningless, either because of difficulty of interpretation or subjectivity. A symbol is "meaningless" only because we do not know how to interpret it, just as the dream was "meaningless" until Freud gave us clues to its interpretation. And perhaps it is the ambiguity of symbols which makes them so useful in human society. Ambiguity is a kind of bridge that allows us to run back and forth from one kind of meaning to another, until we take firm resolve to cross the bridge into new, and fixed, meanings. Doubt thus becomes a kind of experiment in which we weigh the social consequences of action. When doubt is difficult, fearful, or sinful, it must hide behind grotesque and absurd masks. Freud called this "outwitting the censor." But doubt can always be used as a method for *assessing* relationships between means and ends in conduct.

2. THE NEGLECT OF COMMUNICATION THEORY IN AMERICAN SOCIOLOGY

Systematic explanations of human relationships as determined by communication of significant symbols are not much in vogue now in American sociology. We have, so we hear, a "scientific" technique for the study of human relationships. In *Sociology Today: Problems and Prospects*,[5] published "under the auspices of the American Sociological Society," the problem of communication is reduced to some thirty pages out of 599, and even then is discussed simply as "mass communication." The term "symbol" does not even appear in the index. The implication in these official sociological pronouncements is that all sociologists need to do is to apply certain techniques to "social data" and we shall have a science of human relationships.

In his talk, "Value and Method in American Studies: The Literary Versus the Social Approach," delivered to the *Deutschen Gesellschaft für Amerikastudien* in Cologne on May 21, 1959, Professor Robert E. Spiller indicates the difficulties in communication between mechanists in sociology and humanists in literary studies. In reporting on a joint seminar given at the University of Pennsylvania by Professor Thomas C. Cochran and himself, he says:

> [We] had not been in session more than a month before a deep schism appeared, and as the year progressed, the group split more and more definitely into two parties: those who were primarily concerned with the nature of society itself as the embodiment of a culture and those who were concerned with the expression of the culture in mass media or individual art. This difference might well have been and remained little more than a division of effort toward a common aim, the one group describing the culture through the evidences of social data and the other through those of various media expressions, had not the split become final in the refusal of either group to admit the validity of the methods of the other. That which we may call the "social" group maintained that the method of content analysis could be

applied with complete objectivity to public documents, advertisements, literary works, and all other forms of expression, without allowing any hierarchy of values other than that of their degree of abstraction; whereas the "literary" group maintained that the element of discrimination in, say, a first-rate novel, lifted it and all the values in it to a different plane from those found in, say, the advertisements of a brand of toothpaste to be found in the three top mass-circulation periodicals of a given year. The "literary" group were of course at fault because they were violating one of the basic assumptions agreed upon at the start: namely, that the principle of relative evaluation should not be applied to values themselves. Their error had been to agree to any such proposition because, by doing so, they relegated all art to the role of social documentation and eliminated the subjective elements of intuition, insight, imagination—call them what you will—which are the very essence of all aesthetic expression and without which art as such is non-existent. How, then, could a culture be described if its students were forbidden to deal with art as art?[6]

Professor Spiller believes that the power and prestige of the physical and natural science fields has become so great that there is danger that "American Studies may well become a branch of sociology and move with the purists in that field into severely limited and definable areas of research. . . ." The other alternative seen by Professor Spiller is equally grim; the American Studies "may dissolve with the New Criticism into the vacuum of pure literary analysis." For Professor Spiller sociological purism seems to begin and end with the work of Professor Bernard Berelson and the school of content analysts. These sociological "purists," as Professor Spiller calls them,

> would not approve such formulations as Malinowski's imaginative as well as scientific study of the mind and habits of the primitive Trobriand Islanders, Constance Rourke's attempt to probe the roots of American culture by exposing folk elements which underlie a complex and rapidly changing modern civilization on the move, and the broad revelation of a national character in the generalization of David Riesman and his associates that modern times have witnessed a shift of emphasis from the "inner" to the "other" directed man. All such speculative studies are suspect by the purists among research scholars because their hypotheses cannot be submitted to factual and quantitative validation; but it is just this quality which allows them to impinge on the realm of the human imagination and thereby provide possible meeting grounds for the sudents of the arts.[7]

9

If we agree that "scientific" symbolic analysis is the kind practiced by Professor Berelson and his colleagues there is no escaping Professor Spiller's conclusions. As sociology becomes more quantified it tells us less about literature—and all symbols—as a social fact. As the study of literature becomes more "textual" it tells us less about what such literary texts do to people who read them. The gap between art and sociology, which seemed to be closing a generation ago, widens daily. But in the study of literature and art, as well as in the study of society, there are growing signs of uneasiness over this lack of *rapprochement*. Few sociologists now argue against quantitative studies of symbolic expression. Artists may be studied as members of an institution. Their work is a product whose distribution and consumption can be studied by techniques commonly employed in all such studies. The artist's public is also a population which can be studied by quantitative techniques used so successfully in all population study. In short, all questions of who uses what kind of art, when, and where, like the question of who reads what, can become questions of quantity. And until such questions are answered accurately, and some relationships among quantified variables are established, we cannot think well about art in society. Those of us who have tried to make rigorous statements about the relationships between art and society are keenly aware of how little is known about the production, distribution, and· consumption of symbolic material in our society—or any society, for that matter.

The view that art is a kind of inferior sociological inventory of society, which will be corrected when a sociological "breakthrough" occurs, creates further difficulties. C. Wright Mills tells us that

> In the absence of an adequate social science, critics and novelists, dramatists and poets have been the major, and often the only, formulators of private troubles and even of public issues. Art does express such feelings and often focuses them—at its best with dramatic sharpness—but still not with the intellectual clarity required for their understanding or relief today. Art does not and cannot formulate these feelings as problems containing the troubles and issues men must now confront if they are to overcome their uneasiness and indifference and the intractable miseries to which these lead. The artist, indeed, does not often try to do this. Moreover, the serious artist is himself in much trouble, and could well do with some intellectual and cultural aid from a social imagination.[8]

Hopes for a sociological breakthrough should not be discouraged, but the confusion of faith with performance is no more enlightening in sociology than in any cult (for too often it *is* a cult). Freud warned human scientists that creative writers are valuable allies of the scientist. Their writings must be prized highly, "for they are apt to know a whole host of things between heaven and earth of which our philosophy has not yet let us dream." In their knowledge of the mind, Freud continues, they are "far in advance of us every day people, for they draw upon sources which we have not yet opened up for science."

The "ridiculous swagger," as William James called it some sixty years ago (in his discussion of religion and neurology in *The Varieties of Religious Experience*), of those who would reduce all psychic phenomena to measurable units has become no less ridiculous with the passage of time. This is recognized now by creative workers in the human sciences. It is not those investigating human motives who warn students against the arts. Few, if any, serious students of social motivation would argue that sociologists know more about familial interaction than our novelists. How many top-ranking sociologists and anthropologists would argue that *Crime and Punishment* gives no "real" understanding of the criminal and his motives? It may be that someday we will know more than Dostoevsky, but until we do, it would be better for the advance of sociology not to make ignorance of the arts (or of any source of knowledge) a virtue.

The student of symbols who thinks there is a brave new world of American sociologists who can supply him with needed tools for inquiry on the social aspects of symbolic experience soon faces disillusionment. Of the 1033 research projects under way in American sociology, as listed in the official bulletin *Current Sociological Research, 1962: A Listing of Research in Progress as Reported by Members of the American Sociological Association*,[9] only six are listed under the section entitled "Sociology of Science and the Arts." Few current textbooks in sociology deal with art, and although there is a vast sociological literature concerned with communication, this has little to do with communication as a symbolic act. *Sociology Today: Problems and Prospects* lists only four page references to "contemporary studies in literature." These occur in an article "The Sociology of Art" by James H. Barnett, who concludes that for "the present, sociologists of art need to undertake a great many frankly exploratory and descriptive studies in order to ascertain the over-all dimensions of this field. Only then will it be possible to formulate and test hypotheses that will yield generalizations applicable to all or to certain types of arts. And only after this stage in turn has been reached will it be possible to extract from our knowledge of the artist, the work of art, and the art public conclusions that will contribute to scientific knowledge of society and culture."

In Albert and Kluckhohn's bibliographical study, *A Selected Bibliography on Values, Ethics, and Aesthetics in the Behavioral Sciences and Philosophy, 1920-1958,*[10] which lists 429 sociological studies, only five are listed in the "Guide to the Bibliography" under the heading, "Language, Symbols and Signs in Relation to Values." This bibliography fails to clarify the basis on which items were selected, and, indeed, states quite openly that to "the surprise of the compilers there was little agreement between them as to which writings were so good that inclusion was imperative, which so poor that exclusion was obvious." Although no criterion of quality was established, there was a basis for selection of items. This "was that of mapping the various areas of inquiry in the behavioral sciences and philosophy." Now if judgments of quality did not affect selection ("neither inclusion nor exclusion represents our opinion of the quality of a publication"), exactly on what basis were items selected? Somebody must have had *some* basis for selection. And if "mapping the various areas" is the basis, where is the map? Who decided its known and unknown territories? Who drew it? What school of thought and inquiry does it represent? We are told that it has "been considered the sufficient goal of the bibliography to collect a fair and representative example of what has been written on values in recent years in the behavioral sciences and philosophy and to arrange some two thousand entries selected in as orderly and useful a way as the present state of the subject permits." But how can one sample a population he has not defined? In answer we are told "authoritative definition for general use is not the task of the bibliography. If a writer has chosen to call his subject 'values,' his decision was respected and the work included when it fell within the defined objectives of the bibliography in other respects."[11]

It is not only the preoccupation with techniques borrowed from the physical and natural sciences which makes *rapprochement* between symbolists and sociologists difficult. *What* American sociologists study, as well as how they study, also adds to the difficulties. In his selection of "leading representatives of the classic tradition of sociology," that is, those who "represent the nineteenth century sociologists, and remain directly relevant to the best work that is being done today . . . ," Mills selects in his *Images of Man,*[12] Walter Lippmann, Herbert Spencer (two excerpts), Karl Marx and Friedrich Engels (two excerpts),

Gaetano Mosca, Robert Michels, Vilfredo Pareto, Joseph Schumpeter, William I. Thomas and Florian Znaniecki, Georg Simmel, and Émile Durkheim. The majority of these writers (or at least the majority of the selections taken from their work by Mills) believe that the constituent facts of society are economic and political. And since even political facts are subordinate to economic it is accurate to say that Mills's basic image of man in society is an economic image. It is also a Marxist approach, as Mills makes clear by saying that if he had included selections on the sociology of literature, he would have chosen the work of Georg Lukács, the distinguished Marxist student of literature.

Mills's image is really part of a very deeply rooted tradition in American sociology, as we see in the contributions of William Fielding Ogburn to *Recent Social Trends*, which was prepared in the 1930's. Ogburn made economic factors so central to his theory of society that he defined "cultural lag" as the failure of social institutions and attitudes to keep abreast of technology. The question of *why* people accepted one economic way of life and not another, the social problem of demand which so engrossed Max Weber, is not asked by Ogburn in his empiric studies. He applied economic images of production, distribution, and consumption to social phenomena, and even then selected only those phenomena which were amenable to quantification. That technological growth might be considered as a kind of social *pathology* was never considered.

In the American sociological tradition of James, Mead, Dewey, Park, Cooley, and Burke, the tradition of the "act" is very different from the European tradition of "culture" analysis. Little is said in this work about Burckhardt, Cassirer, Dilthey, and other Europeans who have taught us so much about the nature of symbol systems in religion, art, science, philosophy, and the whole range of culture. The propositions offered in this work should be read for what they are intended to be, namely, a record of the search for answers to questions on how to think of symbols in relation to the act as the act has been defined in American social thought in the work of Cooley, Mead, and Burke. Obviously there is much more in Cassirer, Dilthey, Burckhardt, Sorokin, and Weber than concern over communication theory as social theory. Action theory is very different from culture theory. Art, science, religion, and philosophy in the European tradition are systems of knowledge (how we "apprehend" the world); in the American they are systems of action (how we "act" in the world).

Our leading American theorist in sociology, Talcott Parsons, says that neglect of the study of the interrelationships between art and society

> was the major sin of omission committed by the early theorists of evolution in the cultural and social fields. The fact that they [the interrelationships] are inevitably complicated is, however, no basis for asserting categorically that their analysis has no place in social science. On the contrary, taking them into account will prove to be one of the main bases on which social science can advance beyond its present state—which, in certain theoretical respects, seems to be stuck on a dead level.[13]

Parsons makes his own theoretical position clear when he says: "*Communication* is the action process which is the source and the bearer of cultural creation and maintenance."[14] To indicate what he means by the social study of symbols, Parsons offers a selection from Kenneth Burke's *Permanence and Change*,[15] in which Burke shows how the comic and the grotesque in language (and indeed all art) opens up social perspectives ("orientations") which help us to reach the kind of social integration we must have if we are to act together. References to Burke's work on symbolic analysis is not limited to Parsons.[16] As Parsons suggests, the study of symbolic action is *necessary to the development of sociological theory as well as to the study of symbolic expression*. A consensus is developing that any model of society developed to serve as a working model of the structure and function of the act as a communicative act is a false model if it omits art.

But while Parsons stresses the need for sociologists to study symbolic action, he offers few clues to ways in which this might be done, and the few he does offer are heavily steeped in mechanical imagery. In his discussion, "Language as a Groundwork of Culture," he says: "Language is the most general and elementary mechanism of communication, and so of social integration, at the cultural level of the organization of action. Language constitutes the most important single matrix from which other generalized mechanisms have been differentiated. . . ." How then are we to think about this "matrix"? And if language is a "mechanism," what mechanical model should be applied in its study? In reply Parsons says: "Language should, therefore, have a structure directly comparable to the structure of other such mechanisms, which in this connection, are better known to sociologists—e.g. money."[17] But the classical economic model of money (as Kenneth

Boulding tells us), "deals with the quantity of money, its velocity of circulation, the various forms and species of liquid and other assets, the rates at which they are created and destroyed, and the reciprocal impacts of this system on interest rates, prices and incomes."[18]

American sociologists who think of communication as a "map," a "pattern," or a "net," seem to do so under the illusion that the use of mechanical models will remove symbols from "expression," which is subjective, to some realm of "process," which is objective. As Parsons tells us: "Commonly, language is considered to have two primary functions, expression and communication . . . communication clearly has priority over expression. Because language is the primary medium of cultural-level communication, it can also serve as a medium of expression. Communication is primarily a function in social systems; expression, a function of the personality as a system."[19] What Parsons seems to mean is that communication can be likened to the function of money on a market where money functions as a medium of exchange. As he says: "An actor inevitably spends his store of things utterable. . . . Messages, therefore, constitute a kind of 'circulating medium.' But the 'language' is not 'consumed' by its use. In this sense it is not a resource."[20] But, as Boulding points out, the scientific virtue of mechanistic models of the circulation of money is gained at the price of ruling out the symbolic uses of money. "As we move into other areas of social life—politics, war and peace, religion and so on—we find that the mechanical models by and large fail us. . . . Even at the level of the theory of war and peace, even though we have mechanical models of a sort, the symbolic elements are so woven into the system that we cannot abstract from them without grave danger of a lack of realism."[21]

The "break-through" in communication theory that will advance social theory cannot come so long as we reduce communication to an event which must be studied by existing methods of research. For, obviously, if these methods were sufficient, the break-through would not be necessary. Sociologists are just being admitted to the scientific community, and, like the courtiers of feudal times who were often more royalist than the king himself, they sometimes feel themselves to be proper scientists only when doing research by methods used in the physical sciences. But the questions physical scientists ask and answer so brilliantly are about motion in time and space, not about man in society. Questions about communication must be about communication as a social, not a physical, event. It may be that we cannot answer the

15

questions we ask, and that we must await the advent of a great sociological mind who can. But even with our limited capacities we do not serve the cause of sociology by refusing to ask how symbols create and sustain social integration. For this is the question we *must* ask if language and all symbolization is of such importance in social integration. Great minds distinguish themselves by great answers. Still, there is virtue in keeping great questions alive until the advent of the genius who can solve problems that tease and haunt lesser men.

Media of communication, which are beginning to bemuse so many students of communication, are (as we have said) only one element in the act of communication. In most schemes at least two others—the originator of the message and the audience—are used. But unless purpose is taken into account we are left with a "communication net" which tells us little about the use of the "net." Communication is an attempt to persuade others (and hence ourselves) to certain courses of action that we believe necessary to create a given social order, to question it, or, finally, to destroy it. Beliefs in various forms or order cannot be explained solely by the "environments" or "conditions" in which they occur. For, as American social theorists such as Dewey, Mead, Cooley, Park, and Burke remind us, environments are symbolic as well as physical. The physical alone cannot generate the psychic content of symbolic experience.

3. STRUCTURE AND FUNCTION IN SOCIAL ACTION: A DRAMATISTIC MODEL

In great and established sciences such as physics, we do not need to ground every methodological statement on a theoretical base. But in a new science such as sociology, where we do not yet possess models of sociation which can match the classical models of motion in space and time, we must be careful to ground our methodology in some coherent body of theory.

Our concerns here are with the structure and function of the act considered as dramatic in form and social in content. The *form* of the act consists of five elements, namely, the stage (situation or environment) on which the act takes place, the kind of act it is (its social function), the roles involved in the action, the ways in which communication occurs within the act, and the kind of social order which is invoked as the purpose of the act. The *content* of the act exists in social interests as these are expressed in the basic institutions of society. Eleven such contents of social experience are distinguished. These are (1) the family; (2) ruling, being ruled, and reaching common agreement, as in political modes of action; (3) economics, or the provision of goods and services; (4) defense, or the means ranging from force to the apologetics and propaganda we use to defend ourselves from enemies within and without the community; (5) education, or the creation and transmission of culture; (6) sociability, or the purely social forms we use to court each other as superiors, inferiors, and equals; (7) play, games, entertainments and festivals, in which we learn to act together under rules, and in joy so that our social bonds will be strengthened in the euphoria of "togetherness"; (8) health and welfare; (9) religion; (10) art; and (11) science.

If we say that roles are "enacted" in their basic institutions, we must define what we mean by "enacted." Is "enactment" a "process," a "transaction," a "performance," a "pattern of expected behavior," or a "position"? And whatever definition we select we must construct a model whose structure and function are derived from the same field of experience. If a role is a "performance," it is not a "transaction." If actors "cathect" to "patterns of behavior" they do not perform roles within an institution. Theoretical models, like metaphors, cannot be mixed. The theoretical monsters produced in modern American sociology almost rival the chimeras of antiquity; firebreathing monsters, with a lion's head, a goat's body, and a serpent's tail, have been matched by grotesques with mechanical heads and symbolic bodies. Actors, we are told, are being moved by mechanical processes which are the expression of patterns in which norms are cathected. Even if we know what this means, how do we observe it? What, in short, are the *data* of "process," and "pattern," and *how* is a norm "cathected"?

We must take into account what was communicated, the situation in which the communication occurred, the kind of person who communicated (that is, his role), the means he used, and the social purpose of his communication. If we stress media, or any of these five elements, to the exclusion of others (as does the Toronto school led by Marshall McLuhan), we make our special view so general that it risks loss of meaning, or, at least, loss of precision in meaning, as we have seen in Freud's use of "sex," or Durkheim's use of "society." We ascribe all kinds of affects to media, and then "derive" various effects from our ascription. The same may be said for all mechanistic theoretical constructs which reduce language to a series of signals. Signals do not set, create, or criticize themselves. The pattern within which they function was created by someone to serve a certain purpose.

Kenneth Burke, I. A. Richards, Bronislaw Malinowski, and George Herbert Mead differ in their models of symbolic action. But, in one sense, this is a difference in degree, not kind. In *The Philosophy of the Act* (1938), which is a compilation of unpublished papers Mead left at his death in 1931, and which is a mature statement of views foreshadowed in his early essays, notably "The definition of the Psychical" of 1903, Mead distinguishes four stages of the act, namely, impulse, perception, manipulation, and consummation. In *Mind, Self, and Society* (1934), he discusses the emergence of the self in role enactment, in *The Philosophy of the Present* (1932) he describes the temporal qualities of symbolic action. In *The Meaning of Meaning: A Study of the Influence of Language Upon Thought and of the Science of Symbolism* (in which the authors state, in 1923, the date of the first edition, that some of the pages were written as long ago as 1910), I. A. Richards and C. K. Ogden describe three factors in symbolic action, namely, "mental processes, the symbol, a referent—something which is thought 'of.'" The theoretical problem of symbolic analysis, as they see it, is how to describe the relationship between these three elements.

In his famous Supplment I to *The Meaning of Meaning*, "The Problem of Meaning in Primitive Languages," Bronislaw Malinowski distinguishes between languages as a "mode of action rather than as a countersign of thought" by the elaboration of his concept of "context of situation." In his view there are three fundamental uses of language; active, narrative, and ritual, which are analyzed through a model composed of three elements—symbol, act, and referent. In Kenneth Burke's works, notably *The Grammar of Motives* (1945) and *The Rhetoric of Motives* (1950), we find a synthesis of many views on the structure and function of symbolic action. Burke holds that while symbols are part of a communicative context which is not wholly symbolic, they do have a nature of their own. His task in the creation of a model of the symbolic act, as he sees it, is to conceive of symbols as "acts upon a scene" so that we give due importance to the structure of the act as well as to the relationship between the symbolic act and environment of the act (which, Burke feels, has been stressed far too much in environmentalist schools). In his model there are five terms: scene (the situation), act (what was done), actor (the kind of person who performed the act), agency (the means of instruments used in performing the act), and purpose (why the act was performed).

Burke's pentad can be adapted to a sociological model of action easily enough if we think of the scene as a social stage, the act as the basic social contexts of action we find in social institutions, such as the family, government, economics, defense, education, entertainment, sociability, health, religion, art, and science; the actor as the various social roles enacted in these basic social institutions; agency as the medium in which communication takes place; and purpose as the struggle to achieve the concensus necessary to integration in social action. This is only a structural statement, of course, and if this theoretical approach is to be reduced to a sociological methodology, we must describe how this structure functions in social relationships, and, conversely, how those elements of social action which are based in communication are affected by their symbolic structure.

Freud, Malinowski, and Burke offer us many clues here. The basic sociological question on symbolic function is: How do symbols create and sustain order in social relationships? Mead taught sociologists that the self emerges in role enactment. We assume the roles of others to become aware of our self. When playing at being someone else, the self realizes its own nature at the same time it realizes the nature of the person whose role is being played. The self is born in gestures, and especially in vocal gestures since we hear our own vocal gestures as others hear them. In Mead's model the self arises out of a parliament of selves in which the self takes into account the attitudes of other selves toward the self. This is necessary because in situations which are problematic the self cannot act without the help of other selves. To act with others we need to put ourselves in their place, as they need to put themselves in our place. We can do this because we possess a common stock of public images made available to us in the various symbols we use in communication. For without such public images, what Mead calls "universals" there could be no communication, and, hence, no community.

Granted then that the self arises in communication, what is the specific sociological component of this process? If the structure of the act is dramatistic, as Mead, Cooley, and notably, Burke, teach, what is the specific social nature of this drama? In short, how does the dramatistic structure function to achieve social integration? Of all questions asked in symbolic theory this is the most important to the sociologist. For, if we cannot explain *how* symbols function to achieve order in social relations, we cannot invoke "symbolic action" as a constituent element of the "social." Instead we must reduce symbols to "referents" in non-symbolic elements such as sex, work, or religion. If we say (as I have said in my works) that social structure (hierarchy, in my terminology) is created and sustained in symbolic action, we must say something about how all this happens.

All this seems obvious enough. For, how can we conceive of structure unless we reduce our abstractions to concrete social functions? Sociologists often neglect this question, and when they do, symbolic function within the act is explained not through structure as it functions in action in society, but as in thought within the mind, or as an "element" in some kind of "patterned" process. There is thought in the act, to be sure, but analogies of symbolic action derived from models of thought must be used with great care. Used carelessly they reduce all symbolic action to cognition (how we "perceive" or "apprehend" the world). How then are we to think about emotion, will, desire, affect, or attitudes, unless we consider them to be an inferior kind of thought, or as the "beginnings" of acts which end in cognition? Another source of confusion in thinking about symbolic function occurs when function is reduced to structure. The anthropologist Lévi-Strauss does this in his discussion of Indo-European languages when he says: "The languages have simple structures utilizing numerous elements. The opposition between *the simplicity of the structure* and *multiplicity of elements* is expressed in the fact that several elements compete to occupy the same position in the structure."[22] Marshall McLuhan's dictum that "the medium is the message" is another example of this.

Sociologists are aware of the dangers of echoing what has been said by synchronic linguists (who study languages as autonomous systems without reference to anything except other linguistic systems), and of talking about "structure," "pattern," or "form," as a way of avoiding the problems of talking about the function of language. They know, if others do not, that grammar cannot be separated from rhetoric. Inferences about symbolic function drawn from grammar must be made carefully. As Malinowski said in 1923, in his Supplement to *Meaning of Meaning:* "The lack of a clear and precise view of Linguistic function and of the nature of Meaning, has been, I believe, the cause of relative sterility of much otherwise excellent linguistic theorizing."[23] Even in 1923 the problem of relating linguistic form to function was not new. As J. R. Firth points out in his essay, "Ethnographic Analysis and Language with Reference to Malinowski's Views,"[24] Philipp Wegener had already developed a "situation theory" by 1885. In his first lecture in *A Treatise on Language: or the Relation Which Words Bear to Things*, published in 1836, Alexander Bryan Johnson, the founding father of American semantics, declared that words must be understood as the "expositors of nature."[25]

4. THE PROBLEM OF FUNCTION IN SYMBOLIC ANALYSIS

How do symbols create and sustain social integration? Granted a dramatistic model of symbolic action, how does their structure function? If we abandon mechanical models based either on classical mechanics (in which symbols "gear" and "mesh") or on the new biophysical world (in which symbols "cathect"), what replacement do we propose, and why?

Symbolic integration is achieved through naming. We march to death in the name of God ("In this sign we conquer"), country, ideology, destiny, or way of life. We organize our creative lives in the name of wisdom, holiness, or beauty. We discipline our daily lives in the name of family, work, or what we owe (our social responsibilities) to others. In the name of status honor, we uphold styles of life as expressed in the drama of hierarchy. As Weber says: "The way in which social honor is distributed in a community between typical groups participating in this distribution we may call the "social order."[26] Social order (in Weber) depends on "status honor." "In content, status honor is normally expressed by the fact that above all else a specific *style of life* can be expected from all those who wish to belong to the circle."[27] A style of life, like any style, is an expression through symbols of appropriate and inappropriate ways of acting. These "ways" are carried out under names which are not simply significations of "patterns," "triggers" to "latent forces," "indicators of attitudes," or "evocations" of archaic memories, but *goads* to action.

Honorable names give power because they endow actions with dignity, radiance, and glory. Dignity, as Weber argues, "is the precipitation in individuals of social honor and of conventional demands which a positively privileged status group raises for the deportment of its members."[28] This sense of dignity "is naturally related to their 'being' which does not transcend itself, that is to their 'beauty and excellence'. . . . Their kingdom is 'of this world.' The sense of dignity of negatively privileged strata naturally refers to a future lying beyond the present, whether it is of this life or of another. In other words, it must be nurtured by the belief in a providential 'mission' and by a belief in a specific honor before God."[29] Symbols, then, create and sustain beliefs in ways of acting because they function as names which signify proper, dubious, or improper ways of expressing relationships. As we are taught in religion, we act *in the name of* the Father, the Son, and the Holy Ghost.

Men believe that as they uphold the purity of sacred names they uphold social order. Whoever or whatever threatens this purity must be destroyed. There are, of course, many kinds of purity. We are moved deeply by invocations of holiness, beauty, or wisdom, but every social institution seeks to relate its particular symbols of order to universal symbols of social order. The sociological function of the dramatic structure of action is, therefore an act of organization. If symbols are to become, and to remain, powerful in organizing social relationships they must inspire belief in their capacity to consecrate certain styles of life as the "true" source of order in society. For it is because of this "purity" that they can be used to consecrate actions believed necessary to social solidarity. When a king is consecrated, a debutante "comes out," a student is given his doctorate, a woman is married, they acquire a social role which they did not have before. In doing so the individual must leave a less worthy (or even a sinful state) and raise himself to a state of grace. Consecration is the apogee of an "upward way." We are familiar enough with religious consecration, but we forget that this is not the only form of consecration. Status consecration is another. Our social position may depend on religious consecration (as in cult membership) but our religion also may depend on status consecration for its worldly power.

In so far as symbolic action is social it is an act of identification with good, dubious, or bad principles of social order. The *structure* of such actions is dramatic, but from a sociological view the *function* of this drama is the creation and sustainment of social order. Style, how we express ourselves, is an identification with a social order. Such identifications are both positive and negative. As we respond to the manners of others we are aware that they have *not* acted improperly as well as that they *have* acted properly. Often, indeed, we honor people for what they have *not* done. Purity may be born in innocence (the "pure in heart") but it is preserved in struggles against the temptations of impurity. Principles of social order are kept alive in the glory of roles we use to sustain positions of superiority, inferiority, and equality in social position. So long as we believe that individuals err but that certain kinds of hierarchal roles are necessary to social order, there will be order. As John Dryden said in 1699 (in the introduction to his *Fables, Ancient and Modern*): "The scandal that is given by particular priests reflects not on the sacred function. A satirical poet is the check of the layman on bad priests. When a clergyman is whipped, his gown is first taken off, by which the dignity of his office is secured."

Symbols reach their highest state of power in struggles between good and bad principles of social order as personified in heroes and villains, Gods and devils, allies and enemies, and the like. As we say in vulgar American, the "good guys" and the "bad guys" must "shoot it out." The "bad guy" is called various things. In art he is the villain; in government, the enemy (within as well as without); in religion, the devil; in democratic debate, the "loyal opposition." But in the most profound and moving dramas of social life the "bad guy" is transformed into a victim whose suffering and death purges the social order. In art this is called "catharsis," in religion "purification." As we read in Webster, purification is "the act or operation of cleansing ceremonially, by removing any pollution or defilement; hence, a cleansing from guilt or the pollution of sin; extinction of sinful desires or deliverance from their dominating power; spiritual or moral purgation; as, *purification* through repentance."

Symbols are kept pure through victimage or sacrifice. The pure symbol is used as an intermediary between the sacrificer (the hero), the person or thing which is to be socialized in the sacrifice, and the sacred principle of order to whom the sacrifice is addressed. Thus, all social order depends on consecration through communication, or, as we have said in more specific sociological terminology, through *naming*, and as our generation knows only too well, much blood is spilt in our world over the control of names. Names must be kept holy, sacred, honorable, dignified, and proper; for if they are not, we cannot apply them to ways in which we relate and create order in society. Those whose acts are named "communistic" must be killed by those whose acts are named "democratic." What is a "communist" or a "democrat"? Often, indeed, whoever we name so. What do these names "really" mean? Few know. They are simply god and devil terms, and as we all know, devils must be "driven out" of the community, as of the self, if law and order are to prevail.

We punish, enslave, torture, and kill in the name of principles of sociopolitical order. As the smoke of battle clears, and the cries of the wounded die out in the silence of death, we ask: What was this battle about, for what did we fight? The answer is always the same: We fought to preserve a name whose radiance and glory make life worth living. This is not to say that *all* the misery of war is to purify a name. We fight for food, clothing, shelter, territory, and other materials of life. We may even fight for life itself, just as we may refuse to fight in the hope that we may preserve life ("I'd rather be Red than Dead"). But as we plunge into battle, we cannot fight long and hard unless we fight in the name of some great principle of social order, for it is such names which give our relationship the glory and radiance we need to stave off the pressing horrors of decay and death.

Much has been said on the function of victimage in religion. In their brilliant monograph, *Sacrifice: Its Nature and Function,* Henri Hubert and Marcel Mauss, following in the tradition of W. Robertson Smith, E. B. Tylor, and James G. Frazer, define the nature and social function of sacrifice as a procedure which establishes "a means of communication between the sacred and the profane worlds through the mediation of a victim, that is, of a thing that in the course of the ceremony is destroyed.[30] As they point out, a victim does not come to sacrifice with sacred qualities already perfected and clearly defined; "it is the sacrifice itself that confers this upon it."[31] They conclude that religious sacrifice integrates worshipers because in appealing to power beyond the self we enhance the powers of the collectivity, and, at the same time, the drama of sacrifice makes possible continuous and intensive communication with powers which are sustained in group life.

Purgation through tragic victimage is not the only kind of purification. The comic victim in art stands beside the tragic victim in the purification of social order. As we laugh at him, we laugh at ourselves. In his degradation and suffering we *confront* the many incongruities that beset us as we try to live together in love and hate. Unlike the tragic victim, who puts us in communication with supernatural power capable of great evil as well as good, the comic victim keeps us within the world. We talk to *each other,* not to our gods, about the social ills that beset us. In doing so we bring into consciousness the hidden and dark mysteries of supernatural realms. Consciousness rises in discussion. When talk is free, informed, and public, there is hope of correcting our social ills because in such talk reason can bring to light much that is hidden in the dark majesty of tragedy.

Two great dramatic forms are struggling for audiences in our world. Communism is essentially a tragic drama of victimage in which enemies within the state are killed in solemn and awful rites called purge trials. The communist victim, like all tragic victims, must suffer and die because it is only through his suffering and death that the community is purged of weakness and evil. Democracy is more a comic drama of argument, bickering, disputation, insult, beseechment, and prayer. We elect our leaders, after long and heated discussion; but no sooner are they in office than we attack them furiously for all the incongruities which we recognized but could not cure as we voted them into office. Democratic leaders fall from power because they fail to measure up in discussion, debate, and all the forms of argument which make up the great public drama of politics in a free society. Whether the tragic or the comic will prevail cannot be decided here. But if the argument in the following pages points up any lesson, it is this: Failure to understand the power of dramatic form in communication means failure in seizing and controlling power over men. An opponent becomes a victim when his disagreement shifts in our minds from ignorance to heresy. When this heresy becomes sin and this sin in turn becomes "original" or "categorical" the first terrible step has been taken to war and to the kind of mass victimage Hitler's Germans created in their camps of torture and death known as concentration camps.

5. TIME IN AMERICAN SOCIAL THOUGHT: THE DESTRUCTION OF THE PAST BY THE FUTURE

As I have indicated in my previous writings, I make no pretense whatever of writing without bias. I, and here of course I am typically American, would rather have acts determined by a future than a past—especially when it is assumed that knowledge of the past is blessed as "real" while our knowledge of the future is damned as "subjective" and "imaginary." The past may be pregnant with the present, and even with the future, as Tönnies, Spencer, Maine, Sumner, and the social theorists of the "organic" schools would have us believe. But if this is so, there have been far too many monsters born of these "irrevocable pasts" (as in Italy, Russia, and Germany) to take much comfort in this depressing doctrine. Like Ward, Dewey, Mead, and Cooley in American sociology, I hold to the future because the future can be treated purely as an image or an "idea" and is, therefore, open to criticism. Plans for the future are not always considered "sacred" or "inexorable," or if they are, it is because they are invented by people so steeped in historicism that they cannot conceive of a future different from the past. As Hitler taught his orators of evil, always begin addressing German audiences with a historical review which "proves" that present evils are "caused" by "deviations" from the past which the proposed future will "correct." In Hitler's prophecy the future is always a "return" to a hallowed German and Aryan past.

I do not think anyone needs to admonish Americans about the dangers of finding sanctions for every action, no matter how vile, in some kind of future, where, in proper Hegelian fashion, all the horrors of the present will be "transcended" in a future good. Our treatment of Indians, *American* Indians, is evidence enough of what happens when weak and defenseless people get in the way of "manifest destiny." Social action based on beliefs in Edenic myths of the future, as well as action based on "returns" to a sacred past, are marked by horrible and revolting crimes. Nothing is more painful to endure in American life than our blind belief in the "tradition of the new." Beautiful buildings are torn down to be replaced with parking lots. Meadows, streams, great sand dunes where earth and sky meet, are poisoned and ripped up, to make way for "progress." Whole populations are "dislocated" by urban "planners" to replace "substandard" housing with huge steel and concrete boxes (in "penal-modern" style) whose only virtue seems to be their newness. And our cities, the bright and shining hopes for a new world, are now choked and congested with traffic until movement within them has become almost impossible, and life and health are endangered as we breathe the poisoned air of "progress."

The European suffering from shock over the horrors of historicism now has a brother in America. We have each in our way learned to our sorrow that all forms of "inexorable destinies"—whether of the past or the future—are evil destinies unless they are submitted to critical inquiry. Men must be urged to belief, for we must believe to act, but they must also be urged to criticize, for reason lives in criticism. Admittedly, this places great burdens on reason, and, perhaps, merely supplants one "inexorable" law of society with another. And like all guardians of order who are placed above the order they themselves create and control, there are temptations to the misuse of power lurking in the leadership of those who have blind faith in reason. The melancholy spectacle of modern technicians, who confuse manipulations through instruments with manipulations of reason in critical inquiry, should warn us of this. But with all its dangers, critical reason, as free, open, informed, and widely communicated inquiry, still seems the best hope of men. Perhaps this kind of communication is our last hope, a hope which may exist only in the memory of future beings of another planet who will remember how we used to destroy each other. But if so, this is still a better memory than the memory of those who ended as slaves cowering before masters they despised. Americans may not survive, but the vision of a community where every man could walk in dignity will never die.

This vision of a community guided by critical inquiry, a community where sociology is used as a *method* of social diagnosis, is, admittedly, a vision of a commonwealth which lies far in the future. But it is a vision, not a dream, and as a vision formed by the minds of man it is subject to his will. Social scientists believe that this will, can, indeed, *must*, be guided by reason because it is only when we reason that our love for each other can be trusted. This is not a comforting doctrine, and certainly social science offers no fixed dogmas for those who fear change. But neither does social science offer shelter to those who find in their visions of a future justifications for the injustice and evil of the present. The social studies are essentially studies in how to face the incongruity between ends and means in social action. As sociologists we hope to create better ways of facing the many incongruities which beset men in their attempts to act together for the common good. We seek, in short, to create a *method* of criticism which can be applied to action *in* society.

We hear on all sides that Americans have no understanding of the tragic sense of life. We lack roots, we have no organic feeling for human relationships, we are materialistic, our lives are dominated by money, etc. All this may be true, but at the same time, it must be pointed out that many of us in America live in a world where no bombs have fallen, and no great armies have swept the land leaving hunger and death in their wake. We have seen no one walk in rags, or stiffen and die of cold and hunger. True, we have seen race riots, and we have heard members of minority groups villified and cursed. We have seen the poor sicken and die. We have seen lives wasted for want of help. We still treat the symptoms, but not the causes, of poverty. When our unemployed are broken and sick, we treat their illness, but we do not yet train them to stand on their own as citizens of a free commonwealth. No one is more poignantly aware of America's broken promises to her people than those who must face daily the consequences of our failure. Poverty in the midst of plenty is not new to human experience. But to an American it *is* new, and it is horrible, for in America, thanks to modern communication, it is no longer possible to hide our failure in ignorance or false illusions.

What social theorist in Germany, Italy, Russia, France, *really* believed that authority could exist in a society of equals governed by rules? What have Marx, Darwin, Freud, Pareto, Durkheim, Michels, Sorel, Tönnies, or even Weber, contributed to our understanding of peer relationships? What do theories of social order based in custom, tradition, charisma, law, or primitive religion, have to tell us about a society where beliefs and laws are treated as *rules* of conduct? Much of European social theory is simply irrelevant to American life. This does not mean we should disregard it. On the contrary, we should study it carefully, if for no other reason than to understand how the great civilization of Europe could end in Hitler's death camps. If we reach such understanding we may never know a Dachau. We would be fools to assume that what happened in Birmingham, Alabama, is any different than what happened in Hitler's Germany. Fire hoses and dogs turned on American children dispel any illusions that "it can't happen here." It is happening, here and now, and we cannot be too sure that the battle of civil rights will be won in discussion and debate instead of riot and blood.

Sociological man in Europe is determined by his past, not as in America, by his future. This does not mean that we have no history in America. On the contrary, we have a great historical tradition in America, but it is the history of the future, not the past, which concerns us. There are few historical societies in American small towns (especially the newer ones), but few are without a chamber of commerce which busies itself with plans for a "greater" village. Babbitt, the prophet of a "greater" Zenith, still dwells among us. That he now promotes "culture" as well as real estate and commerce indicates a change of costume, not of heart or mind. Like the Chicagoans of 1890 who were planning the World's Fair, we are determined to "make culture hum." Beauty has left the groves of Academe and workshops of our artist to dwell among politicians. Few cities are without plans for a "Culture Center." These new urban visions of the "City Beautiful" now match the older visions of the village Athens so familiar to us in the work of Frank Lloyd Wright, Vachel Lindsay, and other visionaries of the Middle West who saw an American "Athens" arising out of the bogs and swamps of the Great Valley.

These visions of the future should not be confused with formless dreams or fervent wishes, any more than the European love of history should be confused with obscurantism or blind traditionalism. As Mead points out in his *Philosophy of the Present,* imagery drawn from *both* the past and the future must be used to organize activity in the present. The future and the past exist because they are always the past and the future of a specific present. Action in the present is always problematical, and we use futures, as we do pasts, to create images of perfected acts, not so we can dream, but so we can act. These may be drawn from the past, as when we invoke tradition, or from the future, as when we invoke images of perfected acts (ideal commonwealths, an ideal marriage, etc.), but in so far as they both serve as guides to action they serve a similar function. This American view of the act, on both philosophical and sociological levels, is blessed (or cursed) by adherents of the various schools who find their locus of social reality in the act. The problem of how we know the truth of the future or the past which we are using as a guide to action need not (fortunately!) be answered by the sociologist. But this does not mean that he need not concern himself with how people *think* they are arriving at the truth when they use such "truths" to create order in their relationships.

"Think" may be translated into "act" (as in the American pragmatic tradition), and the sociological data of "acting" reduced to symbols of relationship, as in role theory based on dramatistic view of social relationships (as in the work of Mead and of Burke), but the problem of *how* people think it proper to reach order in their relationships must still be faced. We may talk about "legitimation," "integration," or "consensus," but unless we say something about *how* integration is reached we have not said anything to justify our role as sociologists. American sociologists have been aware of this, and the attempts to face this problem have produced some of our finest work. Two seminal ideas of the "act" have emerged in American sociology. The first stems from the work of Mead, whose model of social integration was taken from the game; the second originated in the work of Kenneth Burke, who taught us that social relations are dramatistic. "Game" and "drama" as models of interaction are peculiarly American.

It is by the rules of the game, as well as by dramatic rules of action, that we achieve and sustain consensus in American society. Tradition, law, charisma, and usage, as Weber taught us, function in our society as they do in every society, but Americans integrate through rules to a far greater degree than any known society of the past or the present. As Tocqueville pointed out some hundred and thirty years ago, Americans are unique in their ability to form voluntary associations that are governed by rules. So while we accept Weber's forms of legitimation, we add another, the power of rules. Rules, it should be noted, are subject to agreement, and in the creation of such agreements those making them become equal. Rules are used to regulate games and contests in which opponents of varying skills struggle against each other to win, but to achieve honor they must win according to the rules. For if tact is the touchstone of sociability in purely social moments in group life, rules are the determinants of honor in games, play, and all forms of contest which are not determined by brute force, appeals to supernaturals, and other forms of relatedness among superiors and inferiors determined by charisma, tradition, convention, or "sacred" law.

6. TRADITION AND DEBATE IN SOCIOLOGICAL ANALYSIS OF SYMBOLS

The following propositions are a summary of my views about communication in society. In my previous works I have grounded my way of thinking about symbols in classical traditions of social thought. In *Language and Literature in Society,* as in *Communication and Social Order,* I have given many references to what has been said in the human studies on the social effects of symbols. These references could be expanded greatly, and, indeed, when the history of sociolinguistics is written, it will be clear that my discussion of precursors in symbolic analysis has not done justice to the traditions of communication theory as it exists in even so limited a field as sociological theory.

The problem facing symbolic interactionists who use dramatic images as models for sociological theory has shifted from struggle over the right to be heard to the necessity of saying something coherent now that we are being heard. The question is no longer one of how to think about social relations as drama, but, assuming the model of drama as our paradigm for a model of social relations, how do we distinguish between drama as art and drama as social? It is possible, of course, to assume no difference, just as our dedicated behaviorists assume that models of spatial relations in physics are adequate models for social relations in sociology. Those of us who follow in the great tradition of symbolic analysis and who desire to do more than repeat what has been said before, must ask: What is involved (for sociological theory) when we use theatrical analogies (such as the familiar social concept of role) for thinking about social relations? What, specifically, is a dramatic model of social relations? What form of drama do we select or create, to explain the social use of symbols? And, finally, what is *social*, as well as dramatistic, about it?

The following propositions are stated in answer to the questions which govern this study. These questions are simple enough. How can we think of communication as a *constituent* element in the creation of order and disorder in human relationships? What is the specific social function of communication institutions as compared with those of the family, religion, politics, or economics? If it is true that communication determines social order, how can this be demonstrated? Few theorists deny the importance of communication, yet, as I have argued, sociological theory fails as symbolic theory because it fails to deal with the effects of communication on social integration. Almost every major social theorist uses some theory of symbolic interpretation to substantiate his system, but his rationale is often very weak, and, indeed, sometimes non-existent.

The theorists reviewed in *Communication and Social Order* make heavy use of symbols. Yet a curious paradox haunts their work. Even though there is constant use of symbolic data, the social functions of symbols are often explained by non-symbolic contexts of experience. The social meaning of a symbol is not found in man's attempts to communicate, but in sex, religion, politics, or economics. Thus, while we "observe" religion (or any social institution) through its "symbolic manifestations," these have little to do with the latent and "real" nature of religion. Communication, it seems, must be explained by everything but communication. It must have, as we read so often, a "referent," and while this referent is social, the social, it turns out, has no "referent" in language. The communicator, like the ventriloquist's dummy, is simply the voice of interests, drives, or needs, none of which he originates or controls.

I do not accept this view. I argue in the following pages, as I have in all my work, that *how* we communicate determines *what* we communicate, just as others argue (and rightly so) that *what* we communicate determines *how* we communicate. Communication occurs in forms, and these forms are public as well as private, for if there are no common symbols there can be no common meanings, and hence no community. And since sociation in role enactment depends on public communication (just as the ego depends on "interior" communication among "inner" selves) a knowledge of communication is basic to an understanding of the structure of relationships within as without the self. All symbols are universals. No matter how "interiorized" symbols may be, or how particular our symbolic expression may become, it is impossible to say anything that is absolutely particular. Even in our wildest dreams, or our most haunting memories, the forms of phantasies and images, obscure and absurd though they may be, are yet drawn from symbols common to a given time and place. In his lecture on symbolism in dreams Freud asks how it is possible to understand dream symbols about which the dreamer himself can give us so little information. His answer indicates the need, in *any* theory of symbolic interpretation, of assuming a public content to private imagery.

His reply, that we learn from fairy tales, myths, buffoonery, jokes, popular manners, folklore, customs, sayings, and songs, as well as poetic and colloquial use of language, indicates the importance of the public content of symbols to Freud's thinking.[32] In Chapter VI of *The Interpretation of Dreams*, in his discussion on representation by symbols in dreams, Freud admits his failure to get at the meaning of dreams through free association. As he says: "The technique of interpreting according to the dreamer's free associations leaves us in the lurch when we come to the symbolic elements in the dream-content."[33] He decides that things "that are symbolically connected today were probably united in prehistoric times by conceptual and linguistic identity."[34] But, he warns, however great the interpreter's knowledge of symbols, the dreamer's associations must be analyzed carefully. Only a "combined technique," in which the analyst relates universal meanings to the associations (symbolic cluster) of the individual patient, can be used.

The great social revolution of the twentieth century has been in communication, the means whereby those in power create and control the images, or names, that will legitimize their power. Sociopolitical ideologies are *created;* their terrible power to goad men into wounding, torturing, and killing others, and even into destroying themselves in confessions of guilt, are not simply mechanical reaction to interests. They are symbolic forms, they are *names,* and whoever creates or controls these names.controls our lives. As any revolutionary handbook tells us, the first step in the seizure of power is the control of all symbols of power and means of communication. We may seize power through force, but it is the images used in daily communication that control us, and whoever controls the creation and communication of these controls society. Much has been said about how new kinds of media, such as television, are "determining" the public images that goad us to action. But media alone cannot determine images. The great communication revolution is rooted in new forms of relationships, not simply new media of communication. To understand them we must ask five basic questions: Under what conditions is communication taking place? What is being communicated? In what kinds of roles? By what means? For what kind of social integration?

The new relationships of our time are sociodramas which are mounted daily and hourly for mass audiences. As we increase the size and diversity of our audiences we must increase the range, diversity, and, above all, the intensity of our appeals. And we must do this in competition with others who seek to control the same audiences. As their appeals change so must ours. Today, permanence occurs *in* change. Leaders who think of permanence and/or change, and who confuse change with disorder, soon lose power. The "thousand-year Reich" of Hitler lasted but a few years. Force must be *legitimized,* the people must be persuaded that it is "right," even a "sacred duty" (as Hitler convinced his Germans), to wound, torture, and kill. We do not seek annihilation, but conversion, of the enemy. Broken and dead enemies do not make good customers, staunch allies, or willing workers.

Sociodramas move us through the intensity, as well as the diversity and range of their appeal. The great publics of our time must not be thought of as inert masses waiting to be "triggered" into action. As members of an audience we identify, as elements in a mass we cathect or polarize. Identification is a dramatic process. All legitimation of power rests, in the last analysis, on the acceptance of a style of life. We may usurp power through force, but we secure victory only when the vanquished admire, honor, and, finally, imitate our way of life. Movies, radio, television, the popular press, all forms of modern mass communication, reach their greatest power in their creation of socio dramas which, like art drama, are staged as struggles between good and bad principles of social order. The people do not want information about, but identification with, community life. In drama they *participate*.

The high moment in traditional sociodrama is the moment of victimage, the *personification* of evil powers which threaten community order. The torture and burning of heretics, the execution of traitors, like the hanging of criminals, were once public dramas of salvation. The suffering of the accused in torture and imprisonment were "necessary" to break his proud and evil will. In the confession and guilt of the victim the scapegoat was born. It was not his individual will which led him to heresy and crime, but "possession" by evil powers. If the community is to survive these evil powers must be driven out. Thus the punishment of victims becomes a sacramental act of purification in which the community is purged. Hitler's Germans killed Jews to prevent contamination of Aryan blood, the "racially innate element" which alone could preserve human culture and civilization. Stalin killed opponents after "purge trials" in which victims confessed their treason, and sacrificed themselves (even willingly!) in great public dramas of purification.

The effect on mass audiences of these German and Russian sociodramas of violence and killing is grim proof of the social power of victimage. The popularity of war news staged as brief sociodramas of the kill, our television Westerns with their "shoot-outs," man hunts, as well as the sadistic depiction of murder and vengeance in crime films, are witness enough to our terrible need for real and symbolic victimage. Modern mass audiences identify with their leaders, and with each other, through violence. In factories, offices, stores, and schools the individual is losing his sense of identity. In the filth of our ghettos and the mud holes of rural slums the poor have no sense of community with each other, or with their leaders in American society. But when the Negro turns against his oppressors and applies the lessons in victimage he has been taught so well by his white oppressors in the Ku

Klux Klan, he finds in riot and pillage what he cannot find in peace and work. Thus far his victimage has been symbolic. Cursing, looting, stone-throwing, random shooting, and burning stop short of the kill. But for how long?

8. SOCIOLOGICAL JARGON

There is nothing more ludicrous than obscurity in communicating about communication. "Sociologese" is one of the horrors of modern discourse, and I have no desire to add to it. It stems from the belief that when you talk in mechanical metaphors you are talking "science." Confusion of technique with science, as when we present our techniques of research as the sole justification of the problem whose solution is supposed to establish our research, is rampant in American sociology. This confusion of science with technique is really a kind of magical thought which hides behind the mask of science just as magic once hid behind the altars of religion. The least we should do as sociologists is to define what we are talking about (as well as to "refine" our instruments of research), for until we do we cannot avoid the dark suspicions of thoughtful men that ignorance, not profundity or originality, is at the root of sociological obscurity.

Making sounds like a hard scientist, twisting sociological terminology into a jargon modeled after physical science discourse, or confusing abstract nouns with theoretical concepts, is much the fashion in current sociological discourse. The deficiencies of sociologese have been duly noted in Fowler's *Dictionary of Modern Usage*. Students of society (Americans, alas!) who call an informal talk "a relatively unstructured conversational interaction" are not talking science; they are using jargon. They are also being pompous, and attempting to mystify us through the use of an abstract terminology which is difficult to understand, not because it is profound, but because it defies definition. When we say that we do not know why we are doing something but that we are doing it "properly," we have abandoned all pretence to rational inquiry. Method has a magic of its own. We are warned against the incantations of tribal magicians, but we are not so well armed against the magic of technology where *how* we do something is considered sufficient grounds for the legitimation of what we are doing.

Deification of means, as well as ends, leads to mystification. When *how* we do something determines what we do, we are in the realm of magic and mystery. Veneration of means is no different from any kind of veneration. The decline and fall of our great urban centers as fit habitations for human beings should be warning enough of what happens when technological means displace humane ends. The engineer's mystique of "efficiency" turns out to be a spatial mystique. The shortest distance between two points may be a straight road, but if this road destroys neighborhoods where social bonds have grown over the years, and these roads glut cities with traffic, the shortest distance in space becomes the longest in time. Means must be tested by ends, just as ends must be tested by means. When what we study in society is deemed scientific because we use the language and instruments of physical sciences we are defining through analogy, not observation. False analogies lead to jargon, the mystification of technique.

9. DEMOCRATIC BIAS OF THIS BOOK: EQUALITY AS A FORM OF SOCIAL ORDER

The social bias in this book is indicated by the inclusion of equality as a form of hierarchy similar to superiority and inferiority as a determinant of social order. In my view equality must be considered a form of *authority,* just as doubt must be considered *necessary* to social integration. I argue that equality as a sociopolitical factor in human relationships depends on rules which are possible only when the will of equals can manifest itself. Doubt, comedy, ambiguity, and all the phases of conduct we label "uncertain," I do *not* regard as aberrations or weakness, but as a source of strength in social relationships. Without them there would be few of the benign forms of social change which offer some hope for escaping the terrible kinds of victimage we have seen in our time. In relationships which depend on rules that can be changed at will, but that must be obeyed once agreed to by the majority of those who are to apply the rules, the test of a rule is a *rational* test. Rules are always open to discussion when those who created them, and subject themselves to them, find them to be unsatisfactory or unworkable. A rule, unlike tradition, law, or the dark mysteries of religion, never derives its power from appeals to a sacred or supernatural source.

Rules, like fashion, are ephemeral, but it would be a great mistake to confuse change under rules with disorder. Indeed it may be that the opposite holds true. Quick and frequent changes in human relationships may be signs of strength as well as weakness. Only when the *forms* (as well as the contents) of human relations can be changed swiftly and easily can there be a strong society. And if there is danger in too much change, there is equal danger in too much rigidity. It may be true, as Disraeli taught, that experiments mean revolutions, but it is no less true that dogma and sacred beliefs also lead to change by violence and discord. Rules are the realm of change and experiment in social relations. We change rules often, and in such change feel less threat than in change of law, tradition, or belief. The power of rules is derived from their form, the *ways* in which they determine action. Fair play is play according to rules which are the same for all. The superior is the guardian of an inferior's honor ("It is the nature of the many to be amenable to fear but not to the sense of honor." Aristotle: *The Nicomachean Ethics*, iv.), just as the inferior is a jealous witness to the honor of his superior (as when we say of a courtier that he is more royalist than the king). But equals are jealous guardians of rules, for it is only through rules that equals can reach agreements which bind them together in common action.

Nothing better illustrates the power of form in social relationships than rules. In play, games, manners, and all moments of pure sociability we are bound to each other by the form of the game. Such forms function as bounds and determinants of conduct. As Mead taught us, in games we play our positions in terms of assumptions about how other players will play theirs. But these assumptions, however internalized, are objectified in forms of play which must be followed if the game is to be played fairly. Once rules are made and codified so that all concerned may know them, we appoint an umpire to serve as guardian of the rules we ourselves have made or accepted. His power is derived from his knowledge of the rules and his ability to apply them quickly and surely in all moments of play. He "speaks from the book (of rules)" and can "throw the book at us," as we say in America. Like the judge in common law, the umpire must remember that he applies, but does not interpret or create, rules.

Reason in democratic society is born in discussion that depends on disputants who remain loyal to the rules of discussion. In a society based on discussion there are no "revealed truths," any more than there are "laws" (physical, biological, or historical) of social process which "determine" human conduct. Nor, for that matter, are there fixed logical canons of inquiry. What we do try to fix, and make binding on all, are *rules* for discussion. Opponents not only tolerate but honor and respect each other because in doing so they enhance their own chances of thinking better and reaching sound decisions. Opposition is necessary because it sharpens thought in action. We assume that argument, discussion, and talk, among free and informed people who subordinate themselves to rules of discussion, are the best ways to reach decisions of any kind, because it is only through such discussion that we reach agreement which binds us to a common cause. We assume also in democracy that the highest kind of human relationship is friendship, because friendship among people of very different ranks and capacities enlarges our understanding and thus strengthens the "will" of our social bonds. If we are to be equal, and if we believe discussions among equals is a way to truth, relationships among equals must find expression in many formal and informal institutions. Equals agree, inferiors obey, superiors command. Democracy lives in agreement, and it remains strong so long as there are many ways of reaching agreement.

To assume that whatever opens up difference is good assumes that differences can be overcome in some benign way. Unless we assume that communication is a random affair, or simply a "message track" for some reality beyond symbols, such as religion or politics, we must assume that it has formal qualities, and that these forms, like forms of any kind, are subject to inquiry. The paradox of contemporary social thought is that we have discovered, and continue to discover, regularities in physical and biological nature, and in economic, political, and tribal "structures" (just as theologians discovered regularities in supernatural realms), yet the medium through which all these vast systems are discovered, and in which our discoveries are reported and talked about, namely language, is not studied (at least, not in sociology) as a determinant of human relationships. How we have been able to study human relationships at all without using the observable data of relatedness—how we communicate—will be a question of great interest to future students of sociology.

As we shall discuss at some length, rules in our society stand beside law, religion, and tradition, as guarantors of social order. In the first section of his *Manual of Parliamentary Practise*, entitled "Adhering to Rules," Thomas Jefferson tells us that "the only weapons by which the minority can defend themselves [against] those in power are the forms and rules of proceeding which have been adopted . . . and become the law of the House." Although Jefferson spoke in a political context, he could do so only because there already existed in the American society of his time a belief in rules as a means to social order. For, as Jefferson said in his *Manual:* "It is much more material that there should be a rule to go by than what that rule is; that there may be a uniformity of proceeding in business not subject to the caprice of the Speaker or captiousness of the members." For Americans rules are a form of authority, and their study must not be limited to their application in play (important as this is) but to their general use in social action.

10. HOPES AND FEARS

I wish that as a lover of democracy I could end this introduction with a ringing note of confidence in the future of democratic man. But I cannot do so. Democracy was, and is still, the fairest hope of mankind. Will it survive? I do not think it will unless there are vast and profound changes in men and society, and certainly in the way we study society. Men enjoy war too much, and are honored too often for torturing and killing each other. Great and powerful actors now strut before the people of the earth as heroes and villains, rattling weapons that can destroy the world. And even these sounds, terrible as they are, do not drown out the cries of the victims of Hitler and Stalin. In the face of this, the faith of Mead and Dewey that "sharing" necessarily implies sharing only the good becomes incredible. Even those of us brought up in the benign society of the Middle West of America have learned that men share evil as well as good. Perhaps the best we can do is to give form to the evil of our time so that those who come after us—if any do—can use our records to confront, better than we have done, the horrible human need to torture and kill. At least those who come after us can learn from our example that we cannot become humane until we understand our need to visit suffering and death on others—and ourselves. We *need* to socialize in hate and death, as well as in joy and love. We do not know how to have friends without, at the same time, creating victims whom we must wound, torture, and kill. Our love rests on hate.

The sociology of our time must begin in anguished awareness that victimage is the means by which people purge themselves of fear and guilt in their relations with each other. These victims take many forms.

They range from the hapless scapegoat, such as the Jew in Hitler's torture and death camps, to symbolic scapegoats like the tattered sweating clown who is reviled, beaten and killed (symbolically) so that we can confront evils we are not permitted "officially" to confront at all. Popular art abounds in such victims; the villains of television dramas are beaten, shot, and killed daily in the only kind of community catharsis our art gives us. There are victims within us too, inner victims locked within the dark regions of the self. But they do not always stay locked up, and even at best, as we know from our fantasies, dreams, and bursts of hatred and rage, the victimized self waits impatiently for his moment to turn on the self who acts as his keeper. As we face the victims of our time, their anguished faces and terrible cries remind us that the philosophical foundations of American sociology supplied by Dewey and Mead were far too shallow. They offered us no vantage point from which to confront evil, or even to consider the social pathology of daily life. Fortunately for the vitality of American social thought, the work of Kenneth Burke corrects this error, and we now join De Sade, Pascal, La Rochefoucauld, Swift, and Freud in facing the terrible fact that men come together to enjoy inflicting pain, suffering, and death on their fellow creatures as they enjoy inflicting pain on themselves.

NOTES

1. Pitirim A. Sorokin, *Contemporary Sociological Theories* (New York: Harper and Row, Harper-Torchbooks, 1964), pp. 710-11. Originally published by Harper and Brothers in 1928.
2. Joyce O. Hertzler, *A Sociology of Language* (New York: Random House, 1965). Professor Hertzler, like Talcott Parsons, succumbs to mechanistic imagery. Thus in Chapter II, "The Basic Concepts Involved in a Sociology of Language: A Paradigmatic Treatment," we read: "men . . . exchange the meanings of their experiences. This they do by communication, that is, by the transmission of a "message" from originator ("sender") to destination or audience ("receiver"). Each combination of interacting individuals has its 'communication net' and a continuous 'flow' within the net." (p. 26).
3. Max Scheler, *Ressentiment,*, translated from the German by W. W. Holdheim; edited, with an introduction, by L. A. Coser (New York: The Free Press of Glencoe, 1961), p. 144.
4. Hertzler, *Sociology of Language,* p. 28.
5. Robert K. Merton, Leonard Bloom, and Leonard S. Cottrell, Jr., *Sociology Today: Problems and Prospects,* New York: Basic Books, Inc., 1959.

6. Robert E. Spiller, "Value and Method in American Studies," *Jahrbuch für Amerikastudien,* Band 4, 1959, p. 18.

7. Ibid. p. 22.

8. C. Wright Mills, *The Sociological Imagination* (New York: Oxford University Press, 1959), p. 18.

9. Published by the American Sociological Association (New York: New York University, 1962).

10. Ethel M. Albert and Clyde Kluckhohn, *A Selected Bibliography on Values, Ethics, and Esthetics in the Behavioral Sciences and Philosophy, 1920-1959* (Glencoe, Ill.: The Free Press, 1959).

11. This is quoted from my review in *The Sociological Quarterly,* Vol. II, No. 3 (1961), pp. 226-227.

12. *Images of Man: The Classic Tradition in Sociological Thinking,* selected and edited with an introduction by C. Wright Mills (New York: George Braziller, Inc., 1960).

13. Talcott Parsons, Introduction to Part Four, "Culture and Social Systems," *Theories of Society: Foundations of Modern Sociological Theory,* edited by Talcott Parsons, Edward Shils, Kaspar D. Naegele, and Jesse R. Pitts (2 vols.; Glencoe, Ill.: The Free Press, 1961), vol. II, p. 988.

14. Ibid. p. 977.

15. Kenneth Burke, *Permanence and Change: An Anatomy of Purpose* (Los Altos, Calif.: Hermes Publications, 1954). The first edition was published in 1935. The 1954 edition is now available in a Bobbs-Merrill Paperback with an introduction by Hugh Dalziel Duncan. See *Permanence and Change: An Anatomy of Purpose* (Indianapolis: The Bobbs-Merrill Co., Inc., 1965).

16. In 1935, Louis Wirth, Professor of Sociology at the University of Chicago, called the attention of sociologists to the significance of Burke's writing.

17. Talcott Parsons, et al. (eds.), *Theories of Society,* p. 971.

18. Kenneth Boulding, "Two Recent Studies of Modern Society," *Scientific American,* Vol. 203, No. 1, January 1963, 157-60. This review contains a discussion of the author's *Communication and Social Order.*

19. Talcott Parsons, et al. (eds.), *Theories of Society,* p. 971.

20. Ibid. p. 972.

21. Boulding, "Two Recent Studies of Modern Society," p. 159.

22. In *Language in Culture: Conference on the Interrelations of Language and Other Aspects of Culture,* edited by Harry Hoijer (Chicago: The University of Chicago Press, 1954), there is an informative article, "Concerning Inferences From Linguistic to Nonlinguistic Data" by Joseph H. Greenberg (See pp. 3-19) with a discussion, "Inferences from Linguistic to Nonlinguistic Data," (pp. 127-47). The discussions of the Whorf Hypothesis (pp. 216-79) are very enlightening.

23. C. K. Ogden and I. A. Richards, *The Meaning of Meaning: A Study of the Influence of Language upon Thought and of the Science of Symbolism* (New York: Harcourt, Brace and Co., 1945), p. 310.

24. See *Man and Culture: An Evaluation of the Work of Bronislaw Mal-*

inowski, edited by Raymond Firth (New York: Harper and Row, Harper-Torchbooks, 1964), pp. 93-118.

25. See *Alexander Bryan Johnson: A Treatise of Language,* edited by David Rynin (Berkeley and Los Angeles, Calif.: University of California Press, 1959). This edition contains the full text of the *Treatise.*

26. *From Max Weber: Essays in Sociology,* translated, edited, and with an introduction by H. H. Gerth and C. Wright Mills (New York: Oxford University Press, 1946), p. 181.

27. Ibid. p. 187.

28. Ibid. pp. 189-90.

29. Ibid. p. 190.

30. Henri Hubert and Marcel Mauss, *Sacrifice: Its Nature and Function,* translated by W. D. Halls (Chicago: University of Chicago Press, 1964), p. 97.

31. Ibid.

32. See "Symbolism in Dreams," lecture X of "Introductory Lectures on Psycho-Analysis" in *The Standard Edition of the Complete Psychological Works of Sigmund Freud,* translated from the German under the general editorship of James Strachey (London: The Hogarth Press, 1953-), Vol. XV, pp. 158-59. As the editors point out in discussion of this lecture (in footnote 1), it was not until the fourth edition of the *The Interpretation of Dreams* (1914) that a special section was devoted to dream-symbolism. This, Chapter VI, Section E, and the lecture cited here, are considered by the editors to be Freud's main discussion of symbolism. "The topic [of dream-symbolism] appears, of course, in many other places both in *The Interpretation of Dreams* and in other works throughout Freud's life. . . . It may be added, however, that the present lecture has claims to being regarded as the most important of all Freud's writings on symbolism." In *The Interpretation of Dreams* Freud argues that things that are symbolically connected today were probably united in prehistoric times by conceptual and linguistic identity. (*Standard Edition,* Vol. V., p. 352) He cautions against arbitrary use of "prehistoric" connections. "We are thus obliged, in dealing with those elements of the dream-content which must be recognized as symbolic, to adopt a combined technique, which on the one hand rests on the dreamer's associations and on the other fills the gaps from the interpreter's knowledge of symbols. . . . (Dream-symbols) frequently have more than one or several meanings, and, as with Christian script, the correct interpretation can only be arrived at on each occasion from the context." (*Standard Edition,* Vol. V, p. 353) Freud's genetic theories of symbolic interpretation should be compared with Mead's telic theory, in which images of the future, as well as the past, are used to organize action in a problem-solving present.

33. Freud, *The Interpretation of Dreams,* in *The Standard Edition of the Complete Psychological Works of Sigmund Freud,* Vol. V, p. 353.

34. Ibid. p. 352.

II

AXIOMATIC PROPOSITIONS

New sciences (and sociology, the science of man as a social being, is very new) are descriptive, for until a science matures we must describe what we cannot analyze. But description involves selection, and in sociology selection is, or ought to be, based on ideas about social order. And sociologists who want to talk *with*, and not *to*, their readers must clarify their assumptions about social order. We assume in this book that how we communicate determines how we socialize. The twelve axioms which follow are really assumptions. Without them it would be impossible to create the theoretical and methodological propositions which come later. Axioms cannot be tested, nor can they be demonstrated to be true or false. They are more like the rules of a game which we agree to so we can play together. And, like rules, they ought to be clear and stated openly. Too often axioms are left implicit, and the reader must ferret them out for himself. Propositions often repel us because of their dogmatic sound. The following propositions are to be read not as dogma but as points in conversation with others, or in the talk with inner selves we call thought. Good talk is always exploratory. The paths opened up in the theoretical and methodological propositions are indicated in the first twelve axioms so that the reader will know something about the journey he is asked to undertake. These axioms should be read, therefore, as a guide into discussion, not as a dogmatic report of "discovered" truths.

AXIOMATIC PROPOSITION 1

Society arises in, and continues to exist through, the communication of significant symbols.

(a) By "significant symbol" we mean a symbol which not only "signals" to or "stimulates" another, but also arouses in the self the same meaning it does in others. Like Mead, we say that the significant symbol, like all spoken symbols, is an expression experienced as a form of address to the self when it is addressed to another. Communication thus determines social relationships because language gives us the capacity to indicate to ourselves what other persons are going to do, and then to assume their attitudes on the basis of that indication.

(b) No theoretical social system can be constructed without *some* category of communication. Even Parsons, whose equilibrium model of sociation is mechanistic, says that his social system could not be constructed without taking language into account, and in his discussion of his action frame of reference he tells us that the elaboration of human action systems would be impossible without relatively stable symbolic systems. For without such systems the "situations" of two actors could never be identical, and if we could not abstract meanings from particular situations, communication would be impossible. The stability of a symbol system, in turn, extends between individuals and over time because it occurs in a communication process determined by the interaction of a plurality of actors. In saying this, Parsons expresses a traditional sociological view: that it is impossible to think about society without thinking about symbols.

Cooley stated that the psychosocial basis of all human association, as of all distinctively human traits in personality, is communication. Dewey argued that society continued to exist not only by transmission, by communication, but *in* communication. For Dewey there was more than a verbal tie between the words "common," "community," and "communication." Sapir held that language was the "collective art of expression." Malinowski found that the knowledge of a name, the correct use of a verb, the right application of a particle, has a mystical power which transcends the mere utilitarian convenience of such words in communication from man to man. Radcliffe-Brown held that the sentiments expressed in ritual and myth are essential to the existence of the society. Mead made communication his basic category of sociation. Communication involves participation in the other. This, in turn, requires the appearance of the other in the self, the identification of the other with the self, and the reaching of self-consciousness through the other. Dilthey stated that a study belongs to the human studies only if its object becomes accessible to us through the attitude which is founded on the relation between life, expression, and understanding. Warner agrees with Dilthey, as when he tells us that the reality which the individual learns is provided by the symbols of the culture he learns in various situation contexts.

(c) Although Freud does not make communication a constituent category in his theory of motivation, few modern thinkers have paid more attention to the power of words. In his *General Introduction to Psycho-Analysis*, he points out that psychoanalytic technique is dependent on symbolic analysis. In psychoanalytic treatment nothing happens but an exchange of words between the patient and the physician. The patient talks, tells of his past experiences and present impressions, complains, and expresses his wishes and his emotions. The physician listens, attempts to direct the patient's thought processes, reminds him, forces his attention in certain directions, gives him explanations, and observes the reactions of denial thus evoked. Freud believed that words and magic were in the beginning one and the same thing, and that even today words retain much of their magical power. In his writings he points out how words spoken by one to another cause the greatest happiness or bring about utter despair. This is because words evoke emotions and are universally the means by which we influence each other. Freud thought his use of the Oedipus legend was a great contribution to human understanding. As he said in Chapter VII of his *Outline of Psychoanalysis*, in which he sums up his work: "I venture to say that if psychoanalysis could boast of no other achievement than the discovery of the repressed Oedipus complex, that alone would give it a claim to be included among the precious new acquisitions of mankind."

(d) Obviously, then, if words have such power, some theory is necessary to explain how communication affects motivation, and if the analysis of motives is so dependent on the interpretation of symbols, the reduction of symbolic theory to some kind of methodology is crucial to a science of psychology. Consciousness can be explained only through communication; since the instincts must seek gratification in the outside world, there must be some kind of mediation between them and the world beyond the biological self. In Freud's view, a thing enters consciousness through becoming connected with the word presentations corresponding to it. What, precisely, are "word presentations"? They are "residues of memories," at one time perceptions, and like all "mnemonic residues" they can become conscious again. Anything arising from within the psyche (apart from somatic feelings) that seeks to become conscious must try to transform itself into external perceptions. Such perceptions become possible through "memory-traces."

(e) Now if symbols do what they are said to do by philosophers, anthropologists, sociologists, psychologists, artists, educators, and artists, then communication must be a constituent category of experience. And if we refuse to believe that symbols, like Jung's engrams or Freud's memory-traces, are "derived" from some kind of archaic heritage or archetypes which are passed on through the "collective unconscious," then we must show how symbols do affect social relationships. If we say that we cannot act toward objects and persons until they are named, and that the process of naming is a symbolic process, and, finally, that this process is subject to laws, we must state the grounds for this assertion. The search then for an understanding of how society and communication are related must *begin* with questions on *how* symbolic laws operate in social communication, not with statements, however elaborate, that there are such laws, or that because we use certain techniques to study communication, that this is the way communication "works" in social relationships.

○

AXIOMATIC PROPOSITION 2
Man creates the significant symbols he uses in communication.

(a) Machines signal through built-in message tracks, animals communicate through gesture and sound, but man, and man alone, *creates* the symbols he uses in communication. He is able not only to communicate, but to communicate about communication. No matter how "fixed" a meaning may be in ritual, magic, or tradition, it must always pass the test of relevance; that is, it must help men to deal with problems which arise as men act together. Action is always tested in the symbolic phase of the act by exploring in imagination of the past and future the ways in which ends and means can be related to action in the present. All symbolic phases of action are hypothetical. We act "as if" the way we are acting will reach an imagined end, and the end imagined determines the means we select to reach this end. Thus, while action may be fixed in tradition, it is fixed only so long as traditional forms of expression help us to organize activity in a present, just as utopian forms of expression are fixed as permanent goals only so long as they help to solve problems in the present. The present, in which man communicates with other men, is the locus of social interaction.

○

AXIOMATIC PROPOSITION 3
Emotions, as well as thought and will, are learned in communication.

(a) A feeling is a somatic charge, not an emotion. I feel hungry, but I satisfy my hunger through the conventions of eating proper to those with whom I eat. I feel sexual desire, but I can find a "proper" sexual partner only through observing the proprieties of courtship. We "need" a woman as a "sexual outlet" but we demand a certain kind of woman, not any woman. I want to rule others, but I must rule according to proper canons of ruling. Emotions thus depend on formal expression. There is no unexpressed emotion, for there can be no emotion until the feelings, which are the biological base of an emotion, are expressed. *How* an emotion is expressed, the *form* in which it is expressed, determines its effect just as thought in mathematics is determined by the kind of mathematical symbols available for use in such thought. Emotions arise *in* communication. At birth we do not know shame, envy, pride, disgust, remorse, and the thousand and one emotional nuances we "feel" as we act together. We learn these "social feelings" in communication with others whose response teaches us what our acts mean to them, and thus to ourselves, as we play our roles in the community.

○

Symbols affect social motives by determining the forms
in which the contents of relationships can be expressed.

(a) All social relations are born in appeals to others to respond to us
in ways which satisfy social, as well as physical, personal, supernatural,
and linguistic needs. The child cries and reaches for the breast of the
mother, men and women court each other to relate sexually and to
create families, superiors parade before inferiors to convince them
(and themselves) of their majesty and sublimity. *How* they express
needs, the *forms* of expression, determine satisfaction. Without form
there can be no content, just as without content form becomes meaningless in social experience. And in purely social relations, as Simmel
points out, we play society through social forms called manners, whose
meaning (in purely social moments, at least) can be explained only by
our pleasure in the formal play itself. Manners determine status, but
they also are forms of sociation which bind us together in moments of
pure sociability simply by their power *as* forms.

(b) Images, visions, and all imaginings of the future are symbolic
forms, for when the future becomes the present, and thus becomes
"real," new futures are created to guide our search for solutions to
problems in the present which emerge as we try to create order in our
relationships. Every act contains a past, present, and a future, but the
temporal structure and function of symbolic actions is determined by
our need to act in a present. We turn to the past, as well as to the future, to create forms in which we can act. The recapture of the past is
really a reconstruction, just as the vision of the future is not "real" as
action in a present where our relations are both "real" and "symbolic."
But even the simplest motor act can be directed to its end only through
the organization of attitudes that direct this act to an imagined goal.
Attitudes are formed in communication, because only in communication
can we envision the end we hope to reach in acting together. So, unless
we assume that action is "patterned" by some extrasymbolic "force," or
is "determined" by a past, or a future, or is simply a random activity,
we must assume that action is determined by the forms in which men
communicate as they act together, and that the creation of such forms
is, therefore, the creation of the ways in which we relate in society.

O

From a sociological view motives must be understood
as man's need for order in his social relationships.

(a) *Some* kind of structure must exist in social relationships if we are
to act at all. Such structures range from the loose informal ties of a
small group sauntering down a street, to the highly formal "sacred"
order of a religious body. Man in society, we are told by social theorists, is determined variously by nature, family, economics, politics, or
God. And so he is. All we can stress as sociologists is the irreducible
social element, the need for forms of relationships with others, which
is the basis of human society. These social elements cannot be explained sociologically by anything beyond social experience itself. But
to be more than a simple assertion, this statement must lead to analysis of the *forms* in which social action takes place. For, just as there is
no act which is not motivated by some interest, drive, instinct, or need,
neither can there be action without some kind of *form* whose expression is believed to create, sustain, or destroy social order.

(b) Social forms, the *ways* in which we satisfy needs, determine the
satisfaction of the needs. Needs are always satisfied in relationships;
relationships, in turn, are possible only because we understand what
people mean by the forms in which they play their roles. Role-playing
is the enactment of a part in some kind of social drama which, from
a purely sociological view, is a drama of order. Social drama is a
drama of legitimation, the attempt to legitimize authority by persuading those involved that such order is "necessary" to the survival of the
community. In personal relations, manners, customs, tradition, mores,
and style are used to legitimize our right to purely social status. It is
how we court, *how* we eat, *how* we rule and are ruled, *how* we
worship, and even *how* we die, in short, the forms in which we act,
that determine our feelings of propriety regarding our own actions and
the actions of others. For it is through such forms that we interpret
the meaning of actions performed by others, just as they interpret the
meaning of our performance. Such forms, then, *are* the relationships
between us. We do not have social relations and then seek forms to
express them, any more than, as individuals, we create every form we
use in social relations. Forms exist in *systems* such as economics, poli-

tics, art, science, and religion. Only in art do we experiment with symbolic forms as form.

O

AXIOMATIC PROPOSITION 6
Symbols are directly observable data of meaning in social relationships.

(a) All we know about the meaning of what happened, or is happening, in a social relationship is what someone says about its meaning. "Saying" involves many kinds of expression. A diplomat *participates* in foreign negotiations. Historians *describe* a battle. An Australian savage *dances* the history of his tribe. The Indian *paints* his myths of tribal origin in sand. Witnesses verify what "really happened" through creating expressive forms in which they depict the event. Ascriptions of meaning to forces, processes, energy, or cathexis, are based on analogies, not on direct observations of concrete human acts. Like all analogies, such ascriptions are interpretations, *not* observations. If we follow the canon of parsimony in science, we must, in our study of society, turn to the most directly observable of all social data, namely, the symbols we use in social relationships.

(b) Interpretations of forces "beyond" symbols must still be interpretations of symbols. Thus, even though we "know" the manifest content of the dream is not its "real" meaning, we must show how the "real" meaning can be reached through symbols which are "manifest" to us. Invoking "archaic heritages," "social equilibrium," "ritual," "social sanctions," or the "social bond" explains nothing unless we can show, in the symbolic material under consideration, how such "forces" or "energies" are doing the things we say they are doing. Until we do this, we do not have a methodology, but simply a series of assertions, fictions, or abstract nouns, which cannot be reduced to hypotheses. Every field of data has characteristics of its own; language and all expression in communications has a characteristic structure and function which is determined by the nature of symbols *as* symbols, as well as by the physical, biological, social, economic, political, and religious uses to which they are put.

(c) When we say that there is some reality in human relationships which lies "beyond" symbols, we are still bound by symbols in our "report" of the operations of the "extrasymbolic" phenomena we have observed. We are, therefore, forced into a paradox: we must report what lies "beyond symbols" through symbols. What we demonstrate about nonsymbolic phenomena in society, we demonstrate through symbols. Such symbolic expression, like all symbolic expression, takes place in forms which are determined as forms by rules, laws, conventions, and usages common to expressive forms of all kinds. Thus, the purely formal aspect of a symbol system (whether mathematical or linguistic) in which we "report" what we have observed about human relationships, will determine what we can "report" about what we have observed, just as it determines what we have observed, for it is only as we name things and events that we can relate to them as social beings.

O

AXIOMATIC PROPOSITION 7
Social order is expressed through hierarchies which differentiate men into ranks, classes, and status groups, and, at the same time, resolve differentiation through appeals to principles of order which transcend those upon which differentiation is based.

(a) Social order is always expressed in some kind of hierarchy. This differentiates men and women in ranks determined by age, sex, family lineage, skill, ownership, or authority, which are scaled in some kind of social ladder. Such differentiation is always resolved through appeals to some universal "higher" principle superior to local principles in which ultimate principles are "latent," or struggling to perfection. Men and women differ greatly in their masculinity and femininity, and make every attempt to express this difference in dress, manners, bearing, and behavior, but this difference must be subordinated to a "higher" social principle of marriage, love, or parenthood. Social classes and status groups struggle to differentiate from each other, but they can do so only because their differentiation is understood as a "way" to some kind of order which transcends their differences.

(b) Authorities seek to invest local symbols, the symbols of their institutions, class, or status groups, with universal symbols which are "above" local concern. This is done by persuading us that local symbols will guarantee social order because in using them we pass from a "lower" to a "higher" meaning. In language we move from the particular to the general, in religion from man to God, in science from description to analyses, in law from anarchy to order, in nature from the animal to the human. Sexual love is justified only because through such love we create a family, and through learning to love our family we learn to love our community, until finally we learn to love God. Thus, we justify each level as a step toward a higher level, and every level is invested with belief in some "final" or "universal" kind of order which justifies hierarchal differentiation because the immanence of a final end (the moment of transcendence) makes each a step toward the absolute where all steps end—as they begin.

○

AXIOMATIC PROPOSITION 8
Hierarchy is expressed through the symbolization of superiority, inferiority, and equality, and of passage from one to the other.

(a) In hierarchal relations we are superiors, inferiors, or equals, and we must be prepared to pass from one position to another as we are born, marry, age, and die. Positions of superiority, inferiority, and equality must be signified clearly, and we must be taught, as we must teach others, how to play roles as inferiors, superiors, and equals. This is true of all societies. Even the most powerful father must meet as an equal with other powerful fathers to decide issues which cannot be decided within the family alone. The proud aristocrat must meet with other aristocrats in courts of honor where all are equal in the honor of rank, if not in wealth, power, and skill. In times of war democratic communities give their war leaders absolute power.

(b) Positions of superiority, inferiority, and equality are fixed, but only through passage from one to the other. Fixed social positions can be opened to new members, and can be filled with those who possess skills required for community survival. There is a time, in intimate familial relations as in the community, to rule, but there is a time to be ruled, and, finally, there is a time to die. There is a time to wage war and a time to seek peace. If we are to live in peace, leadership of the community must pass from men of war to men of peace. Passage always involves desanctifying the old, providing bridges from the old to the new, and entering—or, more rarely, creating—a new role. These moments of passage are a constituent element in hierarchy and must never be subordinated in theory to "changeless" sacred moments of fixed positions of social order. A social order is an order *in*, as well as *beyond*, change. A social structure exists *in* passage from old to new, as well as in fixed principles of order.

○

AXIOMATIC PROPOSITION 9
Hierarchy functions through persuasion, which takes the form of courtship in social relationships.

(a) Superiors must *persuade* inferiors to accept their rule. This is done through the glorification of symbols of majesty and power as symbols of social order in many kinds of social dramas wherein the power and the glory of the ruler as a "representative" of some transcendent principle of social order is dramatized. Such dramatization is intended to create and uphold the dignity of the office as a representation of a principle of social order, not the man himself. Hitler did not rule as a man, but as a "savior" of the German people. His life was an allegory of every German life. His mandate, so he taught and so his followers believed, came from some supernatural "historic" source. He was an agent of a "higher power," whose mystery could be penetrated only by semidivine heroes who did what they "had to do" because they were moved by a divine historic will. Yet no one in modern times was more careful than Hitler to stage great community dramas in which the German people were persuaded to believe in laws of destiny which were immutable and "beyond" reason.

(b) Inferiors must persuade superiors to accept them as loyal followers, but in doing so they must subordinate themselves to principles of order, as well as to the personal will of their superiors. The ideal subordinate (from the superior as well as the inferior point of view) must believe in the "right" of his superior to rule because he rules in the name of a "sacred" principle of order. Max Weber calls such beliefs "legitimations," and distinguishes tradition, charisma, law, and usage as grounds for such rights. We ask inferiors to obey us because what we ask them to do has always been done in a certain way (as when we teach children table manners). Or we uphold honored tradition (as in marriage ceremonies). Or we obey the law because the law creates equitable relations among men. Or we follow the commands of a sacred leader because truth is revealed to him by some supernatural force (as when God speaks to the holy man, or the musical genius incarnates the spirit of art in human life in his music). We may also ground legitimations, rights, or whatever we call the integrative factors in community life, in nature (human or physical), a role (as when we believe that salvation will come from political, economic, aesthetic, or military leadership), means, ways, instruments, or agencies (as when how we do something determines the rightness of what we do), or, finally, we may ground our beliefs in great "transcendent" ultimates such as the nation, ideologies, ways of life, gods, or cosmologies.

(c) Inferior and superior alike keep a wary eye on each other to guard against threats to the glory of principles of social order whose radiance and purity must be kept alive through expression of this order's "mystery." Courtship, the rhetoric of hierarchy, fails when the glory of a principle of social order is tarnished or destroyed. "Affairs of honor" were once settled on the dueling ground, known as the "field of honor," according to a highly stylized art of dueling. It was not enough to be a good shot, and to be brave in the face of death. The code was a dance of death in which *how* one faced death or wounds determined honor. In the duel, honor was personalized, but this was possible only because the punctilio of the duel was observed strictly. But in America, if not in Germany, the duel became illegal, and, finally, ridiculous. Duels with weapons were replaced by forensic duels in courts of law. Even love affairs, once the sacred domain of personal honor, and the subject of so much art, were argued in court under the guise of "alienation of affection" suits. The lawyer, not the gentleman, became the arbiter of honor in America.

(d) Inferiors must learn to propitiate their superiors. This is done through various kinds of obeisances which indicate submission. Ges-

54

tures of deference are often very formal and contrived. We read of obeisances in classical China in which several degrees of humility were expressed. The Confucian indicated submission by bowing low with joined hands, bending the knee, kneeling, kneeling and striking the head on the ground, kneeling and thrice knocking the ground with the head, until, finally, in the presence of the Emperor he knelt and struck the ground nine times. We read in the Bible that Abraham fell upon his face before God when he covenanted with Him. Cowering, crouching, crawling, like bowing among us, are used, as are all forms of prostration or deference, to communicate submission in the courtship of superiors.

At first glance, the dramatization of inferiority in courtship offers no problem. The inferior submits to the will of his superior, just as a dog, afraid of being beaten, crawls and licks the hand of his master, or throws itself on its back with legs in the air. But biological explanations, like Spencer's evolutionary explanation of obeisances in his *Principles of Sociology,* do not help us to understand the ceremonial elaboration of gestures of deferences into what may be fairly called systems of courtship. As Weber, Spencer, Maine, Bagehot, and other social theorists point out, custom precedes law, just as status precedes contract. Spencer begins his discussion of ceremonial institutions (Part IV of his *Principles*) by saying:

> If, disregarding conduct that is entirely private, we consider only that species of conduct which involves direct relations with other persons; and if under the name government we include all control of such conduct, however arising; then we must say that the earliest kind of government which is ever spontaneously recommencing, is the government of ceremonial observance. More may be said. This kind of government, besides preceding other kinds, and besides having in all places and times approached nearer to universality of influence, has ever had, and continues to have, the largest share in regulating man's lives.

But what, precisely, is "ceremonial observance," and how are we to study it? Subordination is more than mere submission, it is a *drama* of courtship, an expression of reverence to gods, rulers, or elders. And while this reverence is shown to a person, it is to the role enacted by the person, not to the person himself, that we pay homage. The glory of a role must be kept alive. The majestic utterances of the king must be matched by the veneration and homage of his courtiers. The charm and beauty of a great lady must be matched by the fervent homage of her gentlemen. The dignity of elders is sustained by the obedience of the young. Inferior and superiors relate in dramas of courtship which are believed to create and sustain order among men. The forms of social courtship, in which superiors, inferiors, and equals place one another within the hierarchy of their group, has its own organization, just as political, military, and ecclesiastical institutions have theirs. In performing obeisances properly, we create and sustain the majesty of the roles played by our superiors in the social drama of life. The inferior, no less than his superior, regulate courtship in its purely social sense, just as the penitent kneeling in prayer regulates the worship of his God.

Courtship is often discussed as ritual, but we must not confuse the social forms of courtship with religious rites of worship. Religious and civic ceremonial are often very close, but they are not the same. Masters of protocol, banquet toastmasters, authorities on manners, and all masters of ceremonies may seem to direct the homage paid by inferiors to superiors in somewhat the same manner as the chief priest directs the worshippers of a god. And it is true enough that "keepers of the rites" may believe that status worship leads to divine worship. But even in ancient China where the Board of Rites regulated the etiquette to be observed at court, the dresses, carriages and riding accoutrements, the retinues and insignia of the courtiers, there was another and quite separate department to superintend the rites to be observed in the worship of deities and spirits of departed monarchs, sages, and great men. Liturgy may sustain courtship by linking it with supernatural power, but here on earth, courtship, the drama of hierarchy, sustains liturgy.

(e) Relationships between equals are completely "given." The aristocratic paradigm, or "ideal type" of equality, is friendship. As Confucius teaches in the *Analects,* we cannot have friends who are not equals. Both Cicero and Gracian define a friend as a second self. Only to a true friend can we impart griefs, joys, fears, hopes, suspicions, advice, and whatever lies heavy upon us. Relationships among friends (as Bacon reminds us) become a kind of "civil shrift or confession." With friends, we are completely open. We choose friends, just as we terminate friendships, at will. No one can force us to be friends, nor can law or custom be invoked to sustain friendship. Friendship, as our aristocratic aphorists hold, lives in honor. Honor, Weber argued, determined status because "above all else a specific *style of life* can be expected from all those who wish to belong to the circle." Style, in conduct, as in art, is essentially an aesthetic conception. In its purely social sense, style is an identification; we dress like others whose company we cherish, just as by not dressing like others we indicate our estrangement from them.

Democratic equality is not grounded so much in honor as in a style of life, expressed in rules. Equals court each other through agreement reached under rules, as we see in the many voluntary associations which are so characteristic of American and British life. These associations are formed to create free, open, and informed discussion and action. Rules of order are agreed upon, or simply adopted from standard handbooks of such rules (such as *Robert's Rules of Order*). Rules also are used in games and sports to insure fair play. So long as players bind themselves to rules they are equal. In one sense art is dominated by rules of form. In art, as in sports and war, and in many voluntary associations, members of American minority groups have found their greatest chance to rise in American society. An American white may refuse to eat with a Negro, but will play beside him on a team, accept him as comrade in arms, or work with him in the creation of art.

Honor, or at least the aristocratic conception of honor, is an exclusive concept. Only peers are honored, just as in feudal times only noblemen were considered capable of honor. In the plays of Racine and Corneille, as in Shakespeare, honor is pitted against passion, greed, family, ambition, lust. But only the great are considered capable of such struggle. The degenerate knight Falstaff abjures honor. In *The Art of Courtly Love,* Andreas Cappellanus, after saying much about the subtleties of sexual courtship among peers, advises his noblemen to rape peasant women if necessary. "Do not hesitate to take what you seek and to embrace [the peasant woman] by force." Under the code duello a commoner could not challenge a nobleman. But in relations governed by rules, distinctions of rank are not allowed. Even skill in playing under rules is equalized through the use of handicaps. For if equals must find many ways to reach agreement, they must also pit themselves against each other in competition, rivalry, and disagreement. So long as these are governed by rules, and these rules are guarded by umpires skilled in their application, contest among equals is used not to crush inferiors, but as a means for common enjoyment or for achievement of common goals.

(d) Hierarchal positions are given, not taken. We can seize power, buy our way to the threshold of high society, or force a woman into marriage, but until the other admits our "right" to the position, we really cannot occupy it. We must win the approval of our audience, for only through such approval do we "internalize" the social meaning of rank, position, or status.

(e) The greatest analogue for courtship (in contemporary discussion) is sexual courtship, but the forms of sexual courtship are really derived from historical forms of social courtship. We do not seek "sexual outlets," but "sexual partners," and in our society we seek partners in a drama of romantic love called courtship. In this "feudalization of love," it is the social, as well as the sexual, expression which determines success in erotic love. In our tradition of courtship, we must be humble, courteous (that is, be a "gentleman"), and convey the conviction (if only for a few months) that "love is all that matters." As lovers, we must be humble and abject in our devotion to our "beloved." We must obey our lady's slightest wish, indulge her whims, and acquiesce in her rebukes (however unjust). Love is a "service" (in our society a service of money), a vassalage of an inferior to a superior. But for the superior it is also a service in which he pays homage to the spirit of love. The beloved, too, is bound by the conventions of her court. She must be a "lady," which in our society means she must know how to spend money "graciously" (as we see in the "Christmas madonna," the giver of gifts money will buy).

(f) There is equality, as well as superiority and inferiority, in social relations, and if we are to live successfully in society (authoritarian and democratic alike) we must learn to live in agreement with peers, as well as to command inferiors and to obey superiors. Peer relationships are public in committee relationships, comradeship in arms, membership on a team, and in all forms of play; they are private in friendship. We learn to relate as equals by acting together under rules, for only through rules which are subject to change by those who made them (and thus represent the will of equals) is democratic community possible—just as only through open, free, and intimate talk is equality among individuals possible. We court friends because a friend is another self, the most important self to our development as an individual. In talk as friends we explore the meaning of social experience, our role playing, on a very personal basis. The burdens of rank fall away in all equal relationships; we know as equals that agreement under rules binds us together, and while we recognize the compelling nature of bonds forged under rules (as in concepts of honor), we know that we can change them through common agreement.

○

The expression of hierarchy is best conceived through forms of drama which are both comic and tragic.

(a) The social drama of hierarchy is both comic and tragic. Those in power present themselves as heroes struggling against villainous powers who seek to destroy sacred principles of social order. When we suffer deep guilt, or live in fear of defeat, we turn to tragedy, which is based on a principle of victimage. Tragic victims range from the public scapegoat on whom we project our evil to a guilty inner self whose punishment expiates our sin. In the eyes of authority, sin is simply disobedience, "the breaking of the commandments," and guilt is fear of being excommunicated by authorities with whom we must communicate if we are to have order in our relationships, and thus to be saved from the stress of disorder and the chaos of revolt.

(b) Since the social appeal of tragedy is based on guilt and fear, and offers us vicarious atonement through the suffering and death of the sacrificial victim, its power is very great. We cannot live long in fear, any more than we can long endure a heavy burden of guilt. Public punishment of others, like public and private punishment of the self, is a kind of purgation. As we revile, torture, and kill the villain, either on the stage or in the streets (as when we torture and kill a Negro, execute a criminal, or hunt down Jews to ship them off as victims for ritual cleansing of German blood in torture and death), we personify our fear and guilt. Because of such personification, we are able to act, as well as to feel, and to think, "about" our guilt. In social, political, and art dramas, we enact a drama of purgation, a drama in which dark fears are given forms, and thus brought into consciousness, so we can express attitudes and take part in actions necessary to the riddance of fear and guilt. Tragedy thrives on mystery; it makes its final appeal to ultimate and supernatural powers through invoking mysterious and dark powers with whom we seek to communicate even though we may believe that such powers are "beyond" communication.

(c) The social appeal of comedy is based on belief in reason in society. Comedy is sanctioned doubt, a permitted and honored way of expressing doubt over the majesty and wisdom of our superiors, the loyalty and devotion of our inferiors, and the trust of our friends. Comedy, like tragedy, punishes the "sin of pride," but of pride against men, not the gods. Comedy teaches us that only so long as reason can function openly in society can men confront and correct their evil as men, not as cowering slaves or as worshipers of gods who "reveal" but do not communicate their truths to men. Comedy teaches that whatever separates men from men, not from the gods as in tragedy, is evil. The ultimate good in comedy is a social good which can be reached only so long as men can communicate freely as men. Comedy is never simply an "escape valve" or a way of "blowing off steam," but a form in which we bring into consciousness the many incongruities between ends and the means employed to achieve them. Tyrannies and democracies alike use comedy for this purpose. *Krokodil*, which circulates widely through the Soviet Union, is the *official* Soviet humor magazine.

O

AXIOMATIC PROPOSITION 11
Social order is created and sustained in social dramas through intensive and frequent communal presentations of tragic and comic roles whose proper enactment is believed necessary to community survival.

(a) The community is kept alive only by intense and frequent re-enactments of the roles believed necessary to social order. Savages dancing before the evening fire, college students cheering and snake-dancing at a pre-game rally, political parties parading down main street, women thronging to a fashion show, salesmen gathering for a rally before the opening of the "Big Sale," are creating or recreating the meaning and purpose of their roles. In dancing, cheering, singing, talking, or marching together, we develop a deep sense of community because we are acting out in the presence of each other the roles we believe necessary to life in the community. Social euphoria, born of laughter, deepens our social bonds; simply being together in euphoric moments becomes a kind of communion. Comedy allows us to face problems in community life which we cannot face in any other way. To blaspheme against God brings swift and terrible punishment, but in jokes about gods, parents, and all authority, we are permitted to say things which do not threaten the majesty and mystery of our gods, even though their mystery is opened to doubt and inquiry.

(b) Social groups must stage themselves before audiences whose approval legitimizes their power. Audiences, in turn, must see the problems of the community acted out in some kind of dramatic presentation, for it is only through the forms created in such action that community problems become comprehensible as *actions*. We learn to act, not simply by preparing to act, or by thinking "about" action, but by playing roles in various kinds of dramas. These roles begin in simple play, then pass to games, festivals, and ceremonies, and the formal dramas of art, until finally we end in rites which fix community values. The artist struggles to achieve a "pure" form of art in his dramatic presentations, but whatever his intention, his community turns to him to learn how to stage dramas of community life, just as the individual turns to art to discover forms which he can use in playing his own role in society. The staging of roles in dramatic structures is, then, a staging, or presentation, of our selves to public and private audiences whose approval gives us a sense of identity or belonging.

○

AXIOMATIC PROPOSITION 12
Social order is always a resolution of acceptance, doubt, or rejection of the principles that are believed to guarantee such order.

(a) Order in society comes from resolving conflicting claims to power. There are three basic modes of adjustment to those who seek to legitimize their power over us in the name of some principle of social order.

We may accept their commandments as our duty; we may doubt their commandments, in the hope that in doubt and inquiry we can overcome incongruity; or we may reject them. Doubt is not simply the absence of belief, but a method of inquiry which society institutionalies as much as it does acceptance and rejection of principles of order in religion and politics. Our schools teach us to question how we know what we know, and thus institutionalizes critical intelligence; our comedy clarifies incongruities between ideals and practices; our parties in power (in democracies, at least) honor their "loyal" opposition; our businessmen use commercial magicians to make customers doubtful and discontented with what they have. Criticism (in its various social forms) exists when a lack of congruity between means and ends is recognized, and when there is hope that such incongruities, once recognized, can be overcome. In democratic society the expression of difference in debate, discussion, and argument is not a way to discord but to a superior truth, because opposition, in competition and in rivalry, makes us think harder about the rights of others and leads us to act in more humane ways. It is our *duty* to disagree, if only to *help* our opponent, as we in turn expect him to disagree with us, for in doing so he tests our thought. Thus, in our society, the ability to tolerate disagreement, and in turn, to develop skill in argument and disputation, is considered strength, not weakness.

III
THEORETICAL PROPOSITIONS

The following propositions are based on a sociodramatic model of human relationships. The structure, or form, of a model is determined by its function ("how it works"), just as the function is determined by the structure in which this function takes place. If we say that social relations can be interpreted by a dramatic model we must say why we selected one form of drama and not another as our basic form (as did Freud in his use of the Oedipus drama in the construction of his Oedipus Complex). And the function of this form, how it works in human relationships, must be described as a *social* function. The theoretical model proposed here is constructed as a tool for thinking about action and passion in human conduct. It is *not* constructed to analyze the function of thought (the cognitive aspects of relationships), but of action, in human relationships.

THEORETICAL PROPOSITION 1
Social order, and its expression through hierarchy, is a social drama in which actors struggle to uphold, destroy, or change principles of order which are believed "necessary" to social integration.

(a) A community is created and sustained in the enactment of roles. The structure of social action is, therefore, a dramatic structure, and it becomes the task of sociology to create a *dramatic model* of sociation (just as anthropologists have constructed a ritual model) which can be applied to individuals acting in concrete situations with other individuals. From a sociological view, the drama of community is a drama of authority, a struggle by those in power, or those seeking power, to control symbols that are already powerful, or to create new symbols that will make orderly relationships that cannot be made orderly through the use of traditional or sacred symbols. Thus a community is born, and continues to exist (from a sociological view), in struggle over beliefs about how to create order in human relationships. It can exist only so long as its gods, heroes, and rulers, who *personify* principles of social order in their enactment of their roles as rulers, continue to wage war (on a symbolic as well as real level) successfully against community enemies at home and abroad. For even gods have enemies whom they must conquer and destroy, and every community, no matter how powerful, contains principles of disorder as well as order. Every individual, no matter how strong, struggles to overcome passions which must be checked and disciplined. Thus order and disorder define each other. The form and content of such struggles is personified in heroes and villains, gods and devils, friends and enemies, whose actions in the great social dramas of community life serve as models for the roles played in society.

(b) A principle of social order must always be personified in some kind of dramatic action if it is to be comprehensible to all classes and conditions of men. People do not vote for democracy, but for candidates who embody (that is, who enact through role-playing) democratic principles. At election time we do not simply stage a discussion of the issues, but a drama in which each candidate styles himself as a hero struggling against villains who would destroy the community. Tyrants like Stalin and Hitler understood this well (too well!). Russia and Germany were at war against dangerous enemies at home and abroad. *Mein Kampf*, as the title suggests, is a story of struggle, a myth of origin in which Hitler's new Germany is born in struggle, continues in struggle, and deifies those who die in struggle. Stalin's Russia was born in war against enemies within and without the state. The struggle against enemies within continues (the traitor is a stock figure in Soviet literature). This struggle within the state, like the Roman struggle against the Christians, is a highly publicized and carefully staged drama of discovery, pursuit, and capture of an enemy of the state. He is tried (if at all) not only to determine his guilt, but to dramatize it, so the community will know the strength and cunning of enemies within and without. Such enemies can be vanquished only by leaders devoted to an "ultimate" principle of social order, and by the devotion of people who follow leaders through whom the ultimate principle "makes itself known."

(c) Order within the psyche of the individual, as well as without among roles in the external community, is also born in struggle. We "conquer" our instincts. The soul is a "battle" between good and evil. We (or at least the Puritans among us) "wrestle" with the devil. We punish a self we despise to placate another self we honor. Even Freud's early mechanistic model of the psyche becomes personified in the struggle between Eros and Thanatos, the Id, Ego, and Super-Ego, between the son and the father for the mother, or finally, between culture and instinct. In 1924 (in his essay "The Economic Problem of Masochism") Freud reduced Fechner's category of the "tendency towards stability" of energy to the *Nirvana* principle, which expresses the trend of the death instinct, while the pleasure principle represents the demands of the libido, and the modification of the libido represents the reality principle. None of these three principles (Freud tells us) is actually put out of action by another. They "tolerate" one another; conflicts arise from the differing aims that are "set" for each.

(d) Hierarchal struggle is resolved through purification of the crimes committed in the struggle to power. For the paradox of all authority is that it must uphold pure principles of hierarchy by impure means. In the struggle to attain and hold power we must kill or be killed, use magic (or, as we call it, propaganda) or have magic used against us, make pacts with those we hate or despise, or see our enemy make such pacts. And, most perplexing of all, we must explain how all powerful principles, as vested in gods, need to struggle at all; for when we struggle we admit our need to overcome an opponent who threatens our "absolute" power. But unless the principles of hierarchy are "pure," they cannot be "absolute," and, therefore, they cannot be invoked to resolve struggle. They must be in, and yet above, the battle. Thus, we torture, wound, and kill our enemies in the name of social order. We discipline and punish our children in the name of the family. We mortify the flesh through fasting and penance because such suffering "cleanses the spirit," and "opens our hearts" to God. Any kind of violence, torture, and killing is believed "necessary" so long as we believe that it wards off threats to social order, or "purifies" the soul of evil which weakens us in our struggle to create and uphold principles of social order. For, as we teach our young, our strength becomes as the strength of ten when our hearts are pure.

(e) Cleansing the community, as the self, of guilt is done by appeals to "higher" authority in the hierarchy under whose name we act. Thus, if we loot a neighboring state, it is to uphold the "honor" of our country, or to get "living space" for a superior race (ours); if we indulge in sharp practices in business, it is to protect our family; if we torture and burn a heretic, it is to uphold the faith; if we jail political enemies, it is to rid the community of "enemies within"; if we degrade women in prostitution, it is to preserve the family; if we reduce human beings to machines, we do so for the sake of "efficiency"; if we depict horrible crimes, we do so to uphold art for art's sake. Thus, every hierarchy has some ultimate into which the true believer makes a final leap, and which can be used to explain any crime. While these leaps are described best, and most frequently, in religious systems ("By grace are ye saved through faith; and that not of yourselves; it is a gift of God." Ephesians II:8), they are common to all. We must study therefore *all* appeals to supernaturals to discover clues to the operation of such basic assumptions in systems of hierarchy. And we must study how men communicate with their gods to legitimize various forms of social order. For the supernatural, like any other power in society, functions only in and through expressive symbols, and is, therefore, bound by their laws as social symbols.

○

THEORETICAL PROPOSITION 2
Social differences are resolved through appeals to
principles of social order believed to be ultimate and
transcendent sources of order.

(a) Every hierarchy of values, ranks, principles, or roles reaches an "ultimate" legitimation in some kind of "god-term." These ultimates are symbolized in many ways, but common to all is the capacity of such symbols to create the belief that social order is impossible without them. Their power lies in the manner in which they can invest each stage of action, the lowest as well as the highest, with profound belief that each step on the ladder of social hierarchy is but a step toward a perfect social order. Religious beliefs in supernatural ultimates differ in degree, but not in kind, from beliefs in abstract essences of being, or pure forms of knowing, as when we talk of laws of nature in science, realms of pure beauty in art, bravery in war, the honor of the lady or gentleman, the elegance of fashion in high society, or the power of wisdom in education. It is out of belief in such "transcendent" ultimates that social offices, as social roles, attain their power over us.

O

THEORETICAL PROPOSITION 3
The structure of social action involves five elements:
(1) the stage or situation in which the act takes place;
(2) the kind of act considered appropriate to upholding order in group life; (3) the social roles which embody social functions; (4) the means of expression used in the act; (5) the ends, goals, or values which are believed to create and sustain social order.

(a) In a theoretical system, "structure" must be the structure of a function that exists in the same field of experience as the structure. That is, if we "gear," "mesh," or "cathect," roles, we cannot talk about the symbolic *meaning* of roles, for how can we jump from mechanical structure in space to symbolic function in consciousness? A mechanical model of sociation that is "gearing" cannot be said to communicate through symbols, for how can gears communicate meaning? An integrative function that "meshes," or an interactive situation in which Alter and Ego have "sets of expectations" and "transact," is not a communicative function, and such a function cannot be likened to role-playing. In mechanical models of interaction, men signal, they do not communicate; gears do not interact, they interlock. Meanings that arise when we play our roles are not a "generalized set of patternings"; they are dramatic rehearsals in the imagination of how others will respond to us as we act together to achieve a social goal. Such dramatic rehearsals are possible only because we create symbols that have general, universal, and stable forms, as well as potentialities for new, emergent, and novel meanings. There are regularities of permanence and change in the use of symbolic forms, and the canons of scientific theory and methodology must be applied to the study of these regularities as they are to regularities in physical or biological nature.

(b) We must create a model of human interaction which can be applied to change as well as permanence in social relationships. Authority based on tradition, custom, and the sacred has been developed as a tool of analysis in the ritual concept used so effectively in anthropology. A model of change and emergence of the new must be constructed to stand beside this ritual model. For if there is custom there is also fashion. The radical stands beside the conservative, the prophet beside the bishop, just as youth challenges its elders. Old and new are like Roman masks of the drama, different faces of social order. Machines cannot invest the signals they use, nor can they discourse about discourse, and thus create new symbols. All explanations of motivation based on mechanistic-materialistic analogies such as "energy," "force," "process," patterning," "structuring," "homeostasis," or "equilibrium" can be used logically in models of social action only in so far as they reduce motives to motion, or to field in experience where choice has already been made. Wild leaps from quantity to quality, as in the work of Parsons, where a system of action functions through expressive symbolization but is "structured" mechanically, make it impossible to construct a model of symbolic action as meaningful action.

(c) Play, the game, and conversation have been proposed as models of the act by Mead, but Burke's "dramatistic" model is more comprehensive, and far less inferential, since it deals directly with the observable data of human interaction, namely, the symbols we use in communication as we act together. Burke distinguishes five elements in the dramatic structure of symbolic action. These are *scene*, or the conditions of the act (when and where it was done), *act* (what was done), *agent* (who did it), *agency* (how it was done), and *purpose* (why it was done). In more sociological terms we can distinguish (1) man's spatial and temporal relationships (as in ecology, demography, human geography, or social history); (2) the basic actions in group life (as in the study of social institutions); (3) the roles that are created and sustained in the community (as in the study of roles); (4) the means men use to uphold their roles (as in the study of communication as a sociolinguistic factor in social integration); and (5) the kinds of social order, and the legitimations of such order, used in the enaction of social roles (as in the study of value systems).

(d) The drama of social order is played before various audiences whose approval is necessary to authorities seeking to legitimize their symbols of power. Such audiences identify positively or negatively with those seeking to gain or sustain power over them. Authorities seek to create attitudes of obedience, loyalty, and devotion, in which the will of the superior becomes the duty of the inferior, and the will of the inferior reaches fulfillment in the leadership of the superior. There is authority among equals too, as when all agree on a leader to carry out a common resolution under the guidance of rules reached through agreement and subject to change by agreement. Inferiors identify with superiors only so long as the power and glory of the social order upheld by superiors instills deep belief in the capacity of this order to create and sustain social integration. Such integration is at best a hardwon resolution of contending views by those who seek to maximize the power of their symbols through appeals to larger audiences outside of the institution, through appeals to various audiences within the institution, as well as through appeals to conflicting audiences within the self.

(e) In struggles for control of traditional symbols that retain their power to move men to act in community, or for the creation of new symbols that will solve problems left unresolved by traditional symbols, old roles must be abandoned, new roles created, and passage from old to new roles must be established. Traditional roles are common in religious ritual, while symbols of passage and change are common to art, which (from the sociological view) is the realm of role experimentation. For if society must have fixed roles, it must also have roles in which search for new meaning can occur. Thus, if we must "sanctify" certain forms of social order by making sacred beliefs in "rights" to the allotment of community resources, we must also "desanctify" such beliefs whenever change is desired.

(f) Failure to provide sanctioned means of passage from one social condition to another leads to social disorder. If a boy's mother will not let him become a man, or a Negro cannot rise in society because of his race, or a Jew cannot find employment among gentiles, open revolt or secret rebellion will occur. When we stir up wants, and, at the same time, deny their satisfaction, as in the passage of sumptuary laws, or in honoring customs and traditions that require inferiors to know and to keep their place, we must expect disorder. A society based on discontent over money cannot function well unless yearnings for more money, and the right to spend it in ways glorified by our commercial magicians, are satisfied. Discontent over, and terror of, death, the great and fearful passage from life, must be faced. Until priests are supplanted by functionaries who can ease the terror of passage into death, religion will continue in power. When conflict among social roles cannot be resolved by passage to a "higher" role through sanctioned forms of debate, criticism, argument, and inquiry, then killing, as in war, or victimage, as in sacrifice, will occur.

O

THEORETICAL PROPOSITION 4
All explanations which ground social order in "conditions," "environments," "the body," "forces," or "equilibrium," are situational explanations.

(a) Purely "environmental" explanations of social order are like explanations of the action of a play by its stage setting, or of the playing of a game by the shape of the playing field. Nature may exist "outside of" human perception, or be subject to "immutable laws" which we can know but cannot change, but in so far as we *communicate* about nature, we do so through symbols which we do create, and do change. This is not to say that nature and symbols are the same. Having a baby is very different from reading or writing a poem about motherhood, or reading or writing a pamphlet on how to have a baby. Poems do not feed a hungry man (although they can lead men to hunger strikes). But as we symbolize nature we make it a scene or stage upon which we enact our drama of social order. Thus, the environment of man is a symbolic environment. He acts *in* and *through* symbolization of his physical and biological environment, and the environmental "laws" which affect him are symbolic as well as physical and biological, for when man communicates about his environment, he is acting in the realm of symbols, not only in "nature," "environment," or "force," and the "laws" he must seek to understand are the laws of symbols, as well as of nature.

(b) Man selects stimuli which will give him the responses he needs (or believes he needs) to achieve order in his relationships. We see our environment in certain ways because we want to do certain things in it. But the environment is not given form by perception alone. The perceptual object becomes an object because of the *organization* of the environment through symbolic forms. Thus we are not only stimulated through sex, hunger, and aggression, but are moved by attitudes toward our stimulations. In so far as perception arises in communication it occurs within an act which contains a stimulus, and an attitude toward this stimulus. Attitudes arise in the imagining of the result of responses. This imagery may be drawn from the past (as in memory, history, myths of origin), or the future (as in utopian visions of perfect communities, or the perfections of ends to serve as guides to action in the present), but this image is a consumatory image of the act as completed.

○

THEORETICAL PROPOSITION 5

Social institutions are the most directly observable units of action in society. Eleven such basic units may be distinguished: these are (1) the family, (2) government, (3) economic institutions, (4) defense, (5) education, (6) manners and etiquette (pure forms of sociability), (7) entertainment, (8) health and welfare, (9) religion, (10) art, (11) science and technology.

(a) Men seek mates; they learn to rule and to be ruled; to provide for food, clothing, and shelter; to defend themselves against enemies at home and abroad; to create and transmit ideals, purposes, values, and skills believed necessary to the preservation of their society; to associate in purely social ways; to entertain themselves in play, games, and parties; to cure themselves of social, emotional, physical, and spiritual maladies; and to create and sustain cultural values in art, science, and religion.

O

THEORETICAL PROPOSITION 6

In analyzing social roles we ask: what function is supposed to be performed in what role, and how is this role played before various audiences? what style of life is involved in role enactment, and how is this style used to legitimize beliefs in certain forms of social order?

(a) Role enactment is a performance whose social meaning is determined by its style as well as by its content. If we assume that content alone ("latent" or "manifest"), as described in drives, interests, or rights, determines the "meaning" of a role there is no way (or, indeed, no need) to explain the forms of sociation. But even when we assume this we must admit that the immediately observable manifestations of content are styles of expression. If we explain style by its content alone we still must base such explanation in forms, for these are all we can really observe. Content is inferred, form is observed. The "factuality" of a social relationship is its form, *not* its content.

O

THEORETICAL PROPOSITION 7

Symbolic means of expression, the media in which we express ourselves, must be analyzed for their effect on what we communicate.

(a) *How* we try to achieve social order, our means, instruments, or agencies of action, compose the fourth element in the structure of the symbolic act. Belief in the power of proper "ways" to achieve order in relationships range from beliefs in sacred liturgies to the assumed efficacy of correct utterance of magical spells, to the carefully coached and staged sociosexual dramas of masochists and sadists. In religion we do not simply pray, we pray in certain images of social order ("Our

72

Father which art in heaven . . ."). In magic there must be no deviation from tradition in the *way* the spell is uttered, the gestures made by the magician, the staging of the spell, or the responses of the audience. Manners are codified in books of etiquette which contain solemn warnings about the "right" way to act in social situations. Scientists tell us that it is how we know what we know which determines the scientific validity of a study, and much scientific discussion is, therefore, discussion of method and technique. Children hold to secret or magical words, signs, or gestures, which, like passwords, gain them admittance to the company of those with whom they seek to identify.

(b) In America, appeals are made constantly to the justice of a society based on laws, not men. *How* a decision is reached, not *who* reaches it, is decisive. Thus we read in the *Encyclopedia of the Social Sciences* that the method of appointing arbitrators or judges is less important "than the actual judicial process" which determines the issues, and one of our legal classics is entitled *The Nature of the Judicial Process*. Arbitration boards are staffed with lawyers because they are considered expert in judicial process. We think of the judge as an umpire who judges in terms of rules. He does not make law, but upholds rules of procedure. Belief in judicial process as a way to justice is so ingrained in our society that we find it difficult to recognize incongruities and mystifications in legal process—as when a jury of laymen decide on evidence submitted by experts whose testimony is far beyond their comprehension. We elect lawyers to rule us in the legislature and the courts because they know how to frame laws that will "stand up" in court and, above all, because they know how to create and sustain conditions suitable to argument among legislators elected by the people. But judicial process in our society is the process of rules. Our laws are not sacred revelations, hallowed voices of the past, statements of cosmologies, or utterances of inspired prophets, but "ways" of reaching agreement through rules that are created in discussion and that can be changed in further discussion.

○

Social action cannot be analyzed solely in terms of
situation, institution, role, means of expression, or
beliefs in certain principles of social order, but only in
a synthesis of all five elements.

(a) Situational images based on spatial constructs alone cannot be
used to explain meaning in conduct. Too great stress on interests,
needs, drives, or wants, blinds us to social form, or what Weber calls
the "style of life." Roles must be related to problem-solving as well
as to solutions of past problems (as in ritual, custom, tradition, and all
forms of "eternal" order). The media of communication do not in
themselves explain the message. The study of the means of expression
tell us how messages are conveyed, not what is conveyed, or why one
message, and not another, was sent. Beliefs in certain principles of
social order cannot be abstracted as "essences" or "ideas" in which
conduct originates, or as goals whose attainment is "sought."

(b) Social principles of order are legitimized in communication in
which who is trying to legitimize what value, under what conditions, by
what means, and in what role, must be taken into account. Situation, act,
role, medium, or goal are not in themselves alone enough to explain
action in society. The day of monistic explanations of conduct has
passed. The medium is *not* the message, any more than is sexual cathexis, or class "rights," or tribal taboos, or human "nature," the sole
explanation of social motivation. At best these are but partial explanations of conduct which must be synthesized into a universal proposition which transcends, as it includes, such monistic views. For if social
action takes place in space, it also occurs in time which involves a past
and a future, just as it occurs in entities called acts which are formed
in social roles, which, in turn, are expressed in certain ways to attain
certain goals.

○

Superiors, inferiors, and equals must expect disobedience, indifference, and disloyalty, and while those who
control social order must teach us to feel guilt over the
commission of such hierarchal "sins," they must also
provide us with ways of ridding ourselves of fear and
guilt, so that we can act with confidence in the efficacy
of the principles of social order under whose name we
act.

(a) Principles of social order are always expressed in terms of "thou
shalt" and "thou shalt not." The framers of a constitution pass laws,
and at the same time they decree punishments for infractions of the
laws they have just passed. Indeed, quite often more time is spent on
describing how to punish those who break the law than on describing
the blessings of those who obey. In a democratic society rules and laws
are powerful because we believe that all will obey rules which represent the "consent" of the community. The covenant as well as the "consent" between the lawmaker and his people is made in the name of a
sociopolitical ultimate, as in our society when we invoke the principle
of the "greatest good for the greatest number" to justify the administration of a law.

(b) Authoritarian rulers rule by consent derived from some form of
supernatural power. The right of kings is a divine right, for as Thomas
Hobbes and Joseph de Maistre tell us, the covenant between a king and
his people is made between God and the ruler, or as Stalin and Hitler
taught, the covenant between them and the people of Russia and Germany was a covenant with "historical destiny." When the charismatic
leader speaks, God speaks. An authoritative parent or teacher, like the
charismatic leader, rules by divine fiat. When the father speaks, the
child hears a great voice whose power over him is absolute. The child
has complete faith in his parents' power and authority; for him the
words of his parents are commandments which have little to do with
his consent. Obedience creates order, disobedience creates disorder,
within the psyche of the child, as well as in the child's relationships
with people and things. The word of the parent defines the situation in
which the child acts, not through discussion, agreement, or argument,
but through decree. The child yearns to be told what to do by his

parental gods. And since the child is father to the man, yearning for such absolute authority remains. In moments of anxiety, dread, and guilt, we return to this childhood longing for authority "beyond question" because in such authority we knew order in our social relationships.

(c) To lawmakers, as to those dependent on laws for order in their lives, law is a covenant between those who consider themselves too weak to protect themselves and the strong who can protect themselves and others. But such protection passes from usurpation to social order only when superiors are "bound" by principles which are believed to create and sustain order in human relationships. Inferiors are obedient to the commandments of their superiors because of their belief that superiors uphold sacred principles of social order. Disobedience, in the mind of inferior and superior alike, is a sin because it destroys the power of the leader and thus threatens the safety of the inferior. Since the power of the leader depends on the sacredness of the covenant between him and his followers, whoever breaks the covenant undermines the sacred foundations of social order. In such a view, agreements between ruler and the ruled do not represent the will of the ruler, or the consent of the people, but the will of some supernatural principle of order, such as God, the spiritual origins of the state, the course of destiny, the future of humanity, or the spirit of equality. The relationship between the ruler and the ruled here is like that between an agency, or instrument, and the agent, or actor, who, in turn, is but an instrument of a supernatural power which manifests itself "through" the actor.

(d) Punishment is believed to be a sign of grace when it is accepted as a sign of concern on the part of gods desirous of keeping us "on the right track." The greatest suffering our parents can impose upon us is not punishment, but indifference. For it is only through communication with the parent that the child develops any sense of himself as a self in the family, just as later it is only through communicating with equals that the child develops a sense of roles which exist outside of the family. Only the parent can heal the fear and anxiety he has caused in the child, for the child has perfect trust in the power of the parent to make all things right. Childhood anxiety, embarrassment, worry, and guilt do not originate in doubt over the majesty and power of household gods, but in concern with how to communicate with those gods. Our deepest fear as children is not punishment, but indifference, for this marks the disappearance of our gods. When our gods do not attend to us we are lost. We have no sense of identity, and until our parents renew communication with us we are nothing. If the child is father to the man, the sociopathology of everyday adult life has its roots deep within the trauma of noncommunication.

(e) Those who believe in the supernatural power of gods fear their indifference as much as the child fears the indifference of the father. When conscience is guided by belief in some great principle of social order we suffer if we do not live in commitment to that principle. Conscience is born and sustained in acting together in love and hate. Before there can be communion there must be communication; before communication can take place there must be someone to address. Our gods must attend to us, for until they do we cannot be sure that we are being heard, and if we are not being heard how can we have communion with the powers which give us being? Yet how can a lowly inferior be sure he is communicating with high and powerful gods? In sacrifice we make offerings to our gods to tell them we desire communication, and humbly beseech them to allow us to communicate with them. We do not ask, demand, argue with, or persuade our gods, but beg, supplicate, beseech, propitiate, or petition them to hear our prayers.

Only when symbolization has proceeded so far that a distinction between a seen and an unseen world is clearly accepted can we speak of communication with powers who create and sustain social order by divine fiat. Sacred communication is necessary to redemption, for communion with the dieties is the only means by which we can be delivered from evil, sin, and guilt. Our gods' silence, not their anger, our inability to reach them, not the pain of punishment, are the great fears of those who seek communion with supernatural powers. Thus Luther tells us: "There is no greater anguish than when God is silent, and talks not with us, but suffers us to go on in our sinful works. . . . God often, as it were, hides himself, and will not hear; yea will not suffer himself to be found. Then we must seek him; that is, we must continue in prayer. . . . In such sort must we persist in praying, and waken God up." For nothing is more terrible than silence. "Ah, God, punish, we pray thee, with pestilence and famine, and with what evil and sickness may be else on earth; but be not silent, Lord, towards us." (*Table Talk*, LXXXIII).

○

THEORETICAL PROPOSITION 10
All hierarchies function through a "perfection" of their principles in final moments of social mystification which are reached by mountings from lower to higher principles of social order.

(a) Authorities turn to their artists and their priests to dignify and spiritualize their symbols of power, just as priests and artists turn to symbols of authority to add weight and resonance to their symbols. Certain symbols are used only to describe the celestial order. Others are used to depict the worldly social order, or to bridge sacred and secular realms. Symbols explicitly social may be implicitly celestial. Celestial symbols often gain their power and glory from social symbols of rank and office. In all such depictions there is movement, a progression from one level to another, the unfolding of hierarchy in symbolic action.

(b) In America, popular artists, and especially commercial artists, make use of a symbol—money—which has been heavily invested with glory. Like the Holy Grail, money has become radiant, mysterious, remote, and awesome. We *believe* that money brings success in courtship, dignity in citizenship, and majesty in social relations. We are encouraged to spend as individuals, as well as to enjoy vicariously money spent on public projects. We have few sumptuary laws over money; we often discuss human rights as the right to spend, and freedom itself as a free market. We are goaded into spending *before* we earn. In youth, as in adulthood, we are encouraged to impersonate plutocrats. We can be punished for impersonating military and police officers, priests, or the sex opposite to our own, but we are esteemed for impersonating a plutocrat. "Putting on the dog," as we say in America, is a sign of ambition, not arrogance or blasphemy. We rent plutocratic clothes, equipage, cars, or a house in which we can stage a great entertainment organized by a caterer who supplies goods, service, and even guests.

(c) We learn from the use of money in our society that the power of celestial symbols does not lie in their remoteness, incomprehensibility, or exclusiveness, but in their communication of a promise to attain a "higher life." Thus, while money makes us all equal under the sign of money, and individual spending is transformed into spending for the public good (as in our slogan, "spending for prosperity"), it is the promise of an ever-increasing standard of living which gives money its radiance and power. At the moment I spend I am as good as the next man, and at the same time I am superior to those who do not spend as much. In each stage of spending there is immanence of a higher life, an ever-increasing standard of living which ends in visions of an orgiastic future where, as we say, "the sky is the limit." This upward way of money in America does not end in a state of financial and material bliss where all will have "enough," but in a state where everybody will have the promise of more. Where money has been spiritualized, as in our American capitalistic paradise, discontent over money is truly divine.

(d) Businessmen, scholars, priests, soldiers, lawyers, artists, politicians alike attempt to maximize the mystery of the symbols used to express the power of rank and office. Even the scholar, devoted to inquiry and reason, and by his vocation specifically against priestly mystification, retains awesome feudal ceremonials to infuse education with awe, wonder, and mystery. Gothic architecture, majestic ceremonial music, stately processionals, feudal academic gowns, evoke images of a sublime ruling class. At commencement the voice of the academic orator rings in solemn prophecy. Flanked by the flag and the cross, symbols of country and god, the orator's rising periods evoke the wisdom of academia as savior of the world. As we walk to the Gothic throne where the majestic Chancellor stands to offer us our diploma, ancient processional music fills the nave of the cathedral. At such moments the scholar is moved by his great Passion, the Passion of wisdom. The persecution and execution of Socrates, the sufferings of More and Erasmus, the struggle of Faust, the Promethean myths and legends of the heroes of wisdom who suffered and died to bring wisdom to men, fill our souls. As we identify with these heroes and sacrificial gods of the humanist, a deep sense of community is born. Deans, chancellors, trustees, professors, and students now play their parts in a mystery drama of wisdom.

(e) All hierarchy, even the most "rational" hierarchy, rests on progression from a lower to a higher stage in which any improvement of status is a kind of transcendance. The power of those who control the "mystery" does not reside in the power of each rank to dominate an inferior rank, but in the acceptance by each rank of the principle of order which governs all. For when we move into the realm of principle, we are not "of the world" but "of God," as Christians say. Here, the principle of hierarchy is "perfected." Its levels, developments, unfoldings, progression, the drama of struggling upward, is not enough to uphold the mystery. The principle of social order on which the hierarchy rests is not dependent on development at all. It is "prior" to any development in time, for it existed before the hierarchy began, and will exist after the hierarchy ends. As we read in Chinese lore: "The spirit has no form; yet that which moves and transforms the form is the spirit." The spirit of a hierarchy cannot be achieved only in struggle, or by the selection of a certain means to power, for how can an end be determined solely by its means?

(f) As good secularists we have been taught to keep a weather eye on the supernatural mystifications of religion, but as we now begin to live in a world which can end at any minute, not by divine but by scientific fiat, other mystifications begin to weigh heavily upon us. When we are asked to subsidize "pure" science, even though such science promises an end to our world, or we are asked to believe that societies "move toward an equilibrium," we are in the realm of mystification of method. Now the scientist joins hands with Roman jurists who said: "Let justice be done, even though the heavens fall!" The only way we can protect ourselves—if we can at all—from such mystifications is to develop a methodology that will expose the workings of *all* hierarchies of ideas and spirit. When we are told that technology will bring us plenty, and thus rid the world of want, we should immediately assume the opposite and make those who uphold the glory of science and technology prove their assertion. For the power of all great ultimates lies in the power they give authorities to make us believe that the kind of facts recognized by authority have a direct connection with ideal ends, purposes, and values, which, like all supernatural ends, are beyond reason even though they determine it.

(g) In mystical thought the god incarnate lurks in every simple commonplace. When we begin to discover "immutable laws of nature," and "tendencies toward rationalization," or "social forces trending toward equilibrium," we are linking purely material environmental images with some abstract principle or idea. Incarnation, the visit of the spirit to the earth, whether the spirit is a person who "embodies" God's laws, a law of nature, a sacred act of creation, or a scientific method, is a *mystification* and should be submitted to rational inquiry. Such inquiry must ask: What *is* the relationship of the incarnate God, the law of nature or society, or the "structure of the mind" as expressed in language, to decent order in human relationships? Ignorance may prevent us from answering this well, but only the trauma of mystification leads to the conclusion that the question need not be asked at all, or that asking it is an act of blasphemy.

○

THEORETICAL PROPOSITION 11
Five types of audiences are addressed in social courtship: these are, first, general publics ("They"); second, community guardians ("We"); third, others significant to us as friends and confidants with whom we talk intimately ("Thou"); fourth, the selves we address inwardly in soliloquy (the "I" talking to its "Me"); and fifth, ideal audiences whom we address as ultimate sources of social order ("It").

(a) In the construction of our dramatistic model of address we distinguish five types of appeal to audiences. First there is the general public (the "They" of "what will 'they' say"); second, there are community guardians ("We"); third, others significant to us as friends and confidants with whom we talk intimately ("Thou," which internalized becomes "Me"); fourth, the self we address privately in soliloquy (the "I" talking to its "Me"); and fifth, ideal audiences whom we address as ultimate sources of social order ("It"). Drama, and especially comic drama, supplies us with many examples of these types of audiences. So too does the courtroom, and the staging of political speeches in American life. An American court trial is conducted before a general public (either in the courtroom, in the newspaper, or on television). Each speaker addresses a jury whose members are appealed to as responsible citizens; lawyers argue with each other before a judge who personifies a transcendent principle of justice. In his summation each lawyer weighs his case before the community guardians (the jury), as well as before the general public in the courtroom and members of the press, radio, and television, who act as delegates for general and special publics.

(b) Comedy offers many clues to our model of address, because in community use of comedy, various audiences are exposed to each other. The comic hero addresses the general audience, the chorus, or whoever represents the "responsible men of the community," other actors, himself (as when he soliloquizes over his conflicts in making sense out of conflicts in social roles, or between individual and social roles), and, finally, he invokes some principle of social order. He begins by exposing the vices of one audience to another. He discusses openly, and at length, the vices of each faction in the cast. There is always an air of conspiracy about the address of the comic hero, as if the audience addressed is above the strife of the actors, and is not taken in as are other audiences. The comic hero assures his immediate audience in dialogue, as he assures the general audience who "overhears" such dialogue, that these mortals here below are like children, whose attempts to deceive others, and themselves, are obvious to all.

We see the same types of appeal in stage revues led by a master of ceremonies. As he strides on the stage, the "MC" greets the general audience, exhorts them to applause, and keeps up a line of "happy talk." He addressed the musicians on the stage or in the pit as the guardians of art (the "knowing" ones). He assumes they know how to perform well, how to judge good performances, and talks with them in a confidential way about performance. He singles out other performers for dialogue. Occasionally he turns aside in soliloquy to talk to himself as others listen. Finally, he invokes the spirit of art in the "wonderful show," in this "great town," and as he finishes may even invoke the flag or (like Red Skelton) wish God's blessing upon us. These audiences are addressed very differently. The members of the orchestra are never addressed in the same manner as the audience beyond the footlights. Sly comments to one audience are "allowed" to be overheard by others.

(c) We learn early in life that there are different kinds of audiences which we must learn to address in different ways. We cannot address

82

community guardians as we do friends, and we cannot talk to ourselves as we do to general publics. We must learn to address various audiences, and we must be given opportunities to exercise our skill. When a hierarchy becomes so stratified that inferiors cannot talk to superiors, or must talk to them only through cold and distant intermediaries, the inferiors will soon turn (as they did in Russia and Germany) to other superiors. Our gods must ascend to their remote and mysterious heavens, but they must also descend and dwell among men, so that they can communicate in ways comprehensible to the mortal powers of men. No matter how rich, powerful, beautiful, holy, or wise we may be in our social roles as banker, general, Miss America, priest, or educator, our power is determined by successful address of publics necessary to our success.

(d) We learn too that we must address one audience in the presence of another. The child says things to his mother that are heard in the presence of father, brothers, and sisters. As he addresses one in the presence of the other, he knows that what he says to one may not be pleasing to the other. He soon learns that how he addresses one affects others. He can make his brother or sister jealous, irritate one parent by dawdling with the other, or fasten attention upon himself by violent disagreement or refusal to obey. He learns too that if he is too obsequious, or if he makes a great effort to communicate with his superiors, his equals may accuse him of toadying or "showing off." If he is too stern with his superiors, or too protective of his inferiors, he is accused of being arrogant, or of not letting his inferiors "be themselves." If he is too familiar with his equals he may be accused of being common, vulgar, or lacking in pride. Thus even the small, intimate audience of the family, our first "society" and our first group audience, is differentiated. What we say to one is conditioned by the presence of others.

Communicating with one audience in the presence of another is always difficult. When we please one we risk betrayal of another. We watch, sometimes furtively, sometimes openly, to see how we are affecting those significant to us in various ways. A father wants his son to be a manly little fellow when he talks, his mother wants him to be polite and charming; his younger brothers and sisters do not want him to talk too much, while his older brother or sister may hear him out with amused tolerance or marked disdain. We are conscious too of the differences between the demands of inner and outer audiences. The beautiful lady I address so politely may be addressed in quite other ways by a lustful self who yearns to be heard but must be kept in check. The boss or the dean I address so carefully becomes the object of a sudden rush of hostility. Patience and control in addressing restive students can easily give way as we imagine all sorts of dire punishments for churlish inferiors who do not attend to our brilliance and wisdom.

(e) Sometimes we think of these inner conflicts as the result of conflict between "natural" impulses and "social" or "cultural" needs. In this view origins for "natural" impulses are discovered in a distant past. Ages ago we were eating (or at least trying to eat) each other; or as members of a primal horde, we were banding together as brothers to kill our father because he controlled the available supply of women. We hear, too, that the content of the unconscious is the result of the repression of instinctual drives. But much of what is called repression is the result, not of conflict between sexual and cultural needs, but of difficulties in communication which originate in role conflict. It may be that the basis for uneasiness and embarrassment in adolescence is the conflict between the desire for sex and the desire for status (that is, having "proper" sexual relations with the type of partner approved by the group whose rules of courtship seem important to us). The enactment of a role which must satisfy both sexual needs and status needs is difficult because there are so many unresolved problems in the enactment of social and sexual roles in our society.

(f) We learn in childhood to resolve conflict through turning to parents who can tell us what is right or wrong. Yet even in these years of innocent faith in authority, there are moments when the commandments of our family simply do not make sense or, if they do make sense, are difficult to obey. Our parents may be our first, but they are not our only authorities. Parents are members of a group, the family, and it is in the family that we learn for the first time how to communicate as inferiors, superiors, and equals. A mother may want her son to stay clean and to be a "little gentleman" in his stool habits, table manners, and the observance of the proprieties about making noises with either end of his alimentary tract; but his playmates, a cruder and more boisterous lot, may have quite opposite requirements for identification with them. In place of eating quietly, he is supposed to eat with gusto, instead of repressing a belch, he finds himself in contest to see who can belch the loudest, instead of quiet and discreet "passing of wind," he finds the roaring fart of a companion greeted with cheers and congratulations.

Household gods themselves are not always at one in their pronouncements. If a boy is too well groomed, or too dainty with his hands, his father exhorts him to roll up his sleeves and get his hands in the dirt like a real man. The differences among audiences whose approval or disapproval tell him the social meaning of his acts are very confusing. This confusion begins very early in life. As we walk into a bank a slogan on the wall exhorts us to borrow "wisely," as well as to save "carefully." One bank office extols the virtues of regular savings, another, of "putting money to work" through "judicious" borrowing. If we kill a thousand men in battle we are heroes, yet if we so much as strike a man in civilian life we are subject to arrest. The girl we treat as a lady or a madonna becomes impatient, even angry, if we do not know when to stop such treatment. We learn very early that parents do not always match words and deeds. Finally, we come to realize that conflict over social roles must be harmonized by the self. For, whatever the conflicting appeals made to us, we must, as individuals, make choices or "transcend" conflicting roles, if we are to act at all.

(g) Role conflict arises in communicating with different audiences necessary to our sense of identity. We have classified such audiences as "They," "We," "Thou," "Me," and "It." We experience discord and conflict among these audiences as soon as we begin to communicate. We are taught very early that the family is very different from the world outside the family. We learn that we must not relate to our parents as we do to our brothers and sisters. When we go beyond the family we discover that playmates differ from brothers, sisters, and parents. As we grow older, and seek friends and mates of our own, we discover that we must relate to strange and alien others, very different from those we know within the family. We learn also that to communicate well in one set of relationships we must reject another.

(h) As children we are told that it is proper to act in certain ways because other families, far less admirable than our own, do *not* do things in our way. The girl who would attract us holds our attention by telling us that she takes great pride in *not* being like other girls.

Negatives in conduct are not simply a lack of some positive quality; they are actions in their own right. As we communicate with others (as with ourselves) we tell them that we are very busy not doing certain things. As we accept one audience, we reject another, and our rejection is as much a part of the other's awareness of us as it is of our consciousness of ourselves.

(i) In relations with peers, as in friendship, we learn a new kind of relationship. This is equality, which is as necessary to social order as superiority and inferiority. Among equals the child learns to express doubt over the commandments of parents, teachers, and other adults in power over him. We are taught that a parent's command is a judgment derived from an "absolute" standard of right and wrong. Thus, while our obedience is to the person of the parent, we feel (and parents often remind us) that we are not obeying them as persons but as bearers of principles of order (the family) which must be upheld. A father punishes his son not because he enjoys asserting authority, or out of anger, but because he must "make a man out of him." He reminds him that this parental duty is not a pleasant one, and may even go so far as to say that the punishment he inflicts hurts him more than it does his son. A child is seldom told that his only reason for being clean is that it will please mother or father. What he is told is that "nice" boys and girls keep clean. Screaming and fighting at the table is not simply displeasing to his parents; it is just not done in "good" families. Or (among "enlightened" parents) that while there is nothing really "wrong" about dirtying himself, in doing so he behaves like a "slob," i.e. a lower class child. He is told to stop what he is doing because "proper" people do not act like those whose speech, manners, skin color, nose shape, etc., differ from his. Because of this the child learns to think of a difference as a negation, or even a "sin," and the avoidance of such negations as an end in itself.

(j) With peers, as later with friends, we do not follow commands, but agreements reached through discussion. In play we discover that we must make rules before we can play at all. In the creation of these rules we have our first and most profound experience of equality. Next to family ties, friendship, in which the "I" speaks to its "Thou," is the most profound of all relationships. A friend is a second self, an other self, in whom we find our self as we enter into free and open talk with an other to whom we can say things we have said only in fantasy, or repressed in shame and guilt. A friend does not judge; he does not hold the decisions of guardians over us, nor hold court like an angry god. With friends we learn the most characteristic of all human acts. This is talk, conversation, in which we learn to relate to significant others as equals. Only with a friend can we "open up" about our problems with superiors and inferiors. Our masks of majesty and loyalty drop, as we talk of our hopes and fears. Friends serve as intimate audiences to each other, a kind of mutual confessional in which we unburden ourselves on the problems of dealing with superiors and inferiors, and of creating some order out of the pressing claims of the Id, Ego, and Superego. A friend may not judge like a parent or a teacher, but he helps us to become the self we want to become as we experiment with new attitudes and roles, struggle to follow the commandments of our leaders, and live within the traditions and laws of our community.

(k) Friendship, the most profound of freely given social relationships, is possible only among equals, as Confucius ("Have no friends not equal to yourself.") and Aristotle remind us. It cannot be taken, forced, demanded, bought, or sold, but must be given, and given by equals. Social theorists who use models of domination and submission (like psychological theories of the authoritarian personality) often substantiate such views through illustrations taken from feudal and aristocratic society. But no society prized friendship, the relationship of equals, more than aristocrats. "Life is nothing without friendship:" "When men are friends there is no need of justice between them, but though they be just they still need friendship": "Friendship is the marriage of the soul. . . ." These utterances on friendship, from Cicero, Aristotle, and Voltaire, are small samples of the aristocratic literature on friendship. For in aristocracies, where rank was expressed in courtly dramas of domination and submission, much time and effort were put into friendship. Bacon summed up the aristocratic view when he said: "A man cannot speak to his son but as a father, to his wife but as a husband, to his enemy but upon terms; whereas a friend may speak as the case requires, and not as it sorteth with the person." As superiors and inferiors we speak in terms of rank or status, with friends we speak as equals. In Bacon's view, friendship, like superiority and inferiority, was necessary to aristocratic life.

(1) Children squabbling over rules are learning to play roles which are not determined by the authority of the parent, but by the players themselves. In aristocracies as in democracies, with brothers and sisters as with playmates, there must be equality as well as superiority and inferiority. If we do not learn to be equal, we do not learn to govern ourselves through rules, and we must surrender our will to an authority who is beyond reason because he is beyond discussion. Among free people the gods themselves must hold parliament; among slaves and despots gods command in divine right and their followers know only one principle of social order—absolute submission to authority whose decisions can be changed only by "revelations" from "on high," not by discussion among men here below.

(m) We choose friends, and in their company we learn what it means to be free and equal. The bonds of friendship are self-imposed, and they can be broken at will. Unlike the public opinion of the people, the opinion of friends originates in intimate face-to-face relationships (what Cooley called "primary" relationships). Much has been said about the weight of mass public opinion. But the public opinion of friends is very powerful too. For in the judgment of friends there is trust and confidence. These create very deep roots for social integration. We love friends, and in this love we discover our love of equals. Democracy and aristocracy alike extol friendship; it is not the *content* of friendship, its meaning and use in social relations, but its *range* over which there is disagreement. Whitman, the democrat, calls all men brothers and comrades. Cicero, the aristocrat, calls only the chosen few of Rome his comrades. A slave society honors friendship, but only among the "few."

(n) Our various audiences of "They," "Thou," "Me," and "It" are often reached through delegates. The master of ceremonies, the keeper of protocol, the private secretary to the queen, the social secretary of the parvenu, the board of lady managers arranging the presentation of social luminaries in a civic pageant, the umpire at a baseball game, all are delegates of audiences where response is believed to determine order in society. Protocol determines the social structure of social drama. The actors in this drama may believe their rank to be grounded in nature, the sacred traditions of family, society, political power, God, or the elegance of hierarchal forms (as in high society), but they still must act out their rank through proper address of their superiors, inferiors, and equals. The skilled diplomat must know how to be respectful to superiors, majestic to inferiors, and familiar with equals.

(o) Much of the glamour of hierarchy derives from strangeness or mystery, but this mystery must be communicable. Men covet honor, as women do glamour, yet few can really define these terms. And those who do often tell us far more about dishonor than honor. Superiors rule us through guilt, as peers do through fear of dishonor. The American businessman invokes "sweet mystery" of love and status to peddle billions of dollars of cosmetics and clothes, just as the *Junkers* used the dueling code to sustain their myth of courage and duty. Social dramas of authority must bedazzle us, yet we must not be so completely overcome that we cannot communicate with those who would rule us. The structure, as well as the contents, of relationships must be clearly communicated. This can be done by personification of the will and authority of the group. Whoever is given power to resolve contending claims serves as a kind of personification of the rules, traditions, laws, or customs which bind the groups together. For if there is to be dramatic enactment of principles of social order these principles must be personified. But whoever personifies the hierarchal rules which determine the structure of the social bond must not be *too* personal. He must be in and yet above the social drama, for while he plays a part in the drama he must play it as a delegate of his society. He is a guardian of social order because he dramatizes a sacred principle of order. Through his actions we know the social meaning of a role.

(p) In the egalitarian society of America, where conflict and rivalry is contained by rules as well as by honor, we seem to lack the strong authority of rank, caste, or tradition. But we give great power to another guardian of social order. This is the functionary whose power is derived from our belief in what Jefferson called "umpirage." The power of the American umpire (like the second in the aristocratic duel) is derived from his knowledge of, and skill in, the application of rules. As we say, "he knows the book," and can "throw the book" at us if we get "too far out of line." But as much as we bow to rules, and as careful as we are to codify the will of equals in "rules of order" in everything from baseball to parliamentary procedure, we know that a book of rules at best is a codification of rules which worked in past situations.

(q) Present problems often cannot be solved by rules of the past. Because we must act under rules within a present we endow the office of umpire, who personifies rules, with majesty and solemnity. As children we select referees to resolve disputes so the game can be played. We usually seek someone in authority—a teacher, a parent, an adult, an older boy—who will apply accepted rules. But when we cannot find such authority, we turn to anyone who will agree to apply the rules which we have made or accepted. We may even instruct him in the rules, and as the game goes along coach him on how to make decisions. For the honor of the game is not only in winning, but in winning according to rules, and under the judgments of an umpire who is an appointed guardian of the rules we have made or accepted. In the figure of the referee we experience the authority of rules. We learn to submit to a new principle of social order. Unlike the commandments of our gods, the "processes" of natural law or historical destiny, the drives of human nature, or the edicts of supernatural power, rules have no mystery beyond the will of those bound by them. It is not a sin to challenge rules. Rules bind us as equals; achieving success under rules is the glory of life in a democratic society.

In baseball and football, our national games, great care is taken to uphold the majesty of the umpire. In American baseball he dresses in black, walks to his position slowly, takes a dignified stance, and delivers his judgments in a solemn and judicious manner. He stalks the field like a remote god; he cannot joke with the players, and must turn a deaf ear to the jeers and cheers of the crowd. Players and their managers may argue over his decision, but argument must not go too far. The "jawing" of the disputants must return to a conversational tone, the umpire must not be shoved or pushed by those disputing his judgment. An attack on the dignity of the umpire is an attack on the dignity of the game, and of the society whose national game it is. When the dignity of his office is threatened the umpire must know how to raise his arm majestically and banish the player from the game.

Like the judge in democratic courts of law, the umpire is not supposed to make rules; he is supposed to make decisions according to existing rules. In their final transcendence as a principle of order in democratic society, rules are, therefore, both personal and impersonal. They are personified in the office of the umpire, referee, or arbitrator, an office whose majesty and mystery must be upheld. For whenever the mystery of the umpire, referee, arbitrator, or judge—all those who uphold the realm of order determined by rules and law—vanishes, the rule of law vanishes with it. Then we must turn to voices who speak as the voice of God, or of the big battalions. In the struggles between the gods of war there are no umpires, because there are no rules which depend on the will of men as reached in agreement and expressed in communication of such agreement.

(r) Weber argues that the ultimate power of law rests on force—actual and implied. This is not true of rules. The umpire may punish us for infraction of the rules, but the game cannot be kept going unless the contestants agree to the justice of the punishment. The purpose of "umpirage" is to create consent based on agreement among contestants. If, as Lincoln said, no man is good enough to govern another man without his consent, or, as Thoreau said, the authority of democratic government can have no right over a person or his property but what the person concedes to it, then social integration must be based on consent. Weber states that status begins in usurpation through force, guile, or cunning, but, however gained, status continues in rights, or, as Weber calls it, legitimations of power.

(s) Rules, as well as law, tradition, and charisma (Weber's forms of legitimation), are a form of legitimation. Their transcendence, or mystique, lies in what we call fair play, which has been carried far beyond the game, to mean equitable, impartial treatment. Such treatment, among us, is just treatment. And, thus, as we see, playing "fair and square" under rules becomes a cardinal principle of order in American society. Jefferson said in his *Manual of Parliamentary Practice:* "It is much more material that there should be a rule to go by than what that rule is; that there may be a uniformity of proceedings in business not subject to the caprice of the speaker or captiousness of the members." The mystique of the rule lies in agreement. It introduces a third element, the impartial third, whose mystery resides in his power to bring us to agreement on how to act under rules whose mystery moves us so deeply.

(t) Rules, like all social forms, are external to the players, yet it is in and through their purely formal quality that players can relate in honorable competition and rivalry. The powerful teams pitted against each other in American football, like the teams of salesmen competing against each other, glorify competition. As Americans we are taught to believe, after Henry Clay, that of "all human powers operating on the affairs of mankind, none is greater than that of competition." We compete in business ("competition is the life of trade") as we do politics, because we believe that competition creates and sustains energy. Rules increase social energy because they make it possible for us to pit ourselves against one another in honorable ways. Rules, unlike law, do not exist in the shadow of force, but in agreements among men who have given their word to follow rules.

(u) The basic sociological question in the analysis of any social drama is: How is the principle of social order represented? Or, in more dramatic terms: Who is the hero, and who is the villain, of social order, and in the name of what principles do they act? The sociological clue here lies in the name of what principles of social order the various voices within the audience are harmonized, or, in more modern usage, "integrated." The political orator knows he must appeal successfully to many kinds of audiences. As we say in America, a candidate wears many hats during a campaign. Even during a single speech, the political orator must recognize several audiences within his great audience, and hope to appeal successfully to each. The American politician begins by greeting the "good people" of the town (his general audience); he then turns to the distinguished guests beside him on the platform. During his speech he breaks off into soliloquy where he identifies with the past and future glories of his audience, as when he says: "When I was a mill-worker in a town like yours (or a student, a soldier, or whatever role will identify him with his audience), I said to myself. . . ." He then closes with an invocation to a great principle of democratic social order. American political speeches are staged as great community dramas in which opponents struggle as heroes and villains (to each other and to the community) for the soul of America. Seasoned politicians do everything they can to create a campaign "issue," for if they do not, people will not attend their rallies. The people of America want to see their political leaders *contend* with each other, not act as messengers bringing truths revealed to them by God or destiny. We believe it safer to assume that politics—and certainly politicians—are made on earth, not in heaven.

○

The general public ("They") is a symbolization of the whole community.

(a) The general public is not a mass, a mob, or a "receptor," but an audience. It is not "patterned," or "geared," or "triggered," nor is it moved like a magnetic field by "forces." It is moved to attitudes which are aroused as incipient stages of action, and pass into action through specific forms of communication in which the public identifies with various actors who accept, reject, and doubt the social principles they personify. Speech is the most important means for doing this, and speech, like any public communication, takes place on a stage and is carried on by actors who mount a drama of a certain kind, for certain ends. The social meaning of address to general publics arises in various forms of expression used in role-taking. Role enactment before general publics can be understood by analysis of the kind of act it is (the social themes and plots of the performance), the social roles involved in the act, the kinds of actors selected to perform these roles, the means used in public appeal, and, finally, the principles of social order invoked to justify what is done.

(b) The social drama mounted for general publics by one institution is seldom without competition from another institution for the attention of the same public. Even an autocratic state, or institutions like the church, army, court, and city within the state, compete for control over communication to general publics. The people are always courted, and they must be courted well, for if they are not, taxes will dwindle, armies will not be up to strength, and work will slacken. Leaders who know how to court the people, and take the trouble to do so, soon rise to power. Indeed, future historians may mark it as one of the great ironies of democratic society that we have paid *less* attention to cultural communication than did Stalin and Hitler, who were very careful to stage great political and cultural dramas for their people. This is not to say that we have neglected business communication. As we approach our greatest holiday, Christmas, the drama of American public life becomes a drama of buying and selling (what we call shopping). Enormous sums of money and time are spent in creating and sustaining a drama of shopping that will appeal to general publics. Art and religion alike are subordinated to money.

(c) The staging of appeals to general publics is usually done on such a large scale, and with such simple and direct means, that there is little difficulty in interpreting the kind of social hierarchy involved. In political rallies, sports events, festivals, holidays, ceremonies, and all great community gatherings, the community dramatizes itself before its people. How people travel to these ceremonies, how they are admitted, where they are seated, how they are addressed, by whom they are controlled during the event, how they relate to each other, how they communicate with the actors, what people are presented to them, what community symbols are invoked, and how they leave, tell us much about the power of the general public in relation to social order. Since architecture creates the stages for social dramas in the community, the theories of architects on what space does to people (how architecture affects human relationships in space) is as important to the sociology of life in the present as to the archaeology of life in the past. As the American architect Sullivan reminded us, a building is an act, a staging of life.

(d) The people must have heroes and villains whose struggle to uphold or destroy the principles of social order is depicted in easily understood dramas of community life. This is not because the people cannot "reason," or are swayed only by passion, but because there is no way to understand what an action means in human relationships unless it *is* depicted as a dramatic action. There is no way to learn how to act except by watching the actions of others in social drama, by playing roles as children do when they play "grown-up," and, finally, by playing actual roles in community drama. People who are hungry, resentful, living on charity, bored, ill, or fearful want to act, not simply think about their condition. In this the people are no different from any other class in society. The administrator who tells me in great detail why the budget will not "permit" my raise in salary, may talk brilliantly on how to think about budgetary problems, but he is of no help to me. Demogogues and dictators understand well how to mount social dramas which inspire us to act—even though such action often ends in suffering and death. We do not unburden ourselves of guilt by thinking about guilt, but by acting as a self with other selves in social dramas through which guilt is purged.

(e) Such phrases as "the revolt of the masses," "the century of the masses," "the Americanization of Europe," and "the rise of the common man" have become commonplace in social discussion. Americans taught the world how to mount great public dramas of community life based on politics and business. Stalin, Hitler, and Ghandi developed other forms of mass communication. Now the world is locked in struggle between two "peoples' societies" in which the power of leaders rest in the last analysis on skill in staging great social dramas which give the people an active role in the creation and protection of social order as determined by political order (as the church did once in the enactment of religious order as a drama of social order). The American businessmen and politicians, the leaders of the Nazi party in Germany and of the Communist party in Soviet Russia, have been careful to create and sustain social dramas in which great numbers of people can take part. American universities are just beginning to develop this art. University struggles between administration and students are now "news items." We are becoming comprehensible to the people, not because we pursue wisdom (if we do), but because our struggle can be dramatized for the people as a struggle between generations.

(f) If there is any art of rhetoric characteristic of our time in tyrannies and democracies alike it is the art of what we call "mass appeal." In American business we call it salesmanship, advertising, and public relations, or in more refined expression, "consumer education." In Russia and Germany it is called "democratic education of the people." But whatever it is called, and however it is done, successful appeals to the people are now recognized as the basis for all power in modern society. *How* to appeal to the general public, not *whether* we should appeal, is the modern problem in communication. Elites who reach decisions of their own, and then tell the people how to carry them out, are now obsolete. In their place we now have elites who are masters in the art of communicating to general publics through mounting frequent and intense dramas of social order.

O

THEORETICAL PROPOSITION 13
The community guardians ("We") symbolize the conscience of the community.

(a) The second type of audience can be likened to the chorus in art drama; or to the community elites who are given places of honor at community ceremonies; or to those selected to staff arbitration boards, adjudicate affairs of honor, or hold council of war—in short, those who are selected as the "best people" to meet an institutional or community crisis. Such community leaders present themselves as guardians of the community at all ceremonial occasions when the community stages social dramas to exalt the social principles on which order in the community is based. These guardians respond as a group to the appeals of individuals. Like the members of a jury, the guardians may differ among themselves as individuals, but they agree on certain principles of social order. Their spokesman upholds a group view, for he thinks of group, not individual, survival. A college president, a bishop, an army general, is expected to relate action to the "sacred principles" of learning, religion, or defense, not to question such principles, to offer original views about them, or to open institutional ends, values, and purposes to doubt and inquiry.

(b) The voice of the guardians is antithetical to soliloquy where the beliefs of the guardians and the convictions of individual actors are turned over in doubt and question. The guardians express the ideals of the community. In art drama, celestial choric groups of angels, spirits, or gods are solemn, majestic, and sublime. In community celebrations the guardians embody the dignity and honor of community ideals. The soldiers who parade before the community compose an "honor guard," a group trained and drilled to perfect the image of the soldier's ideal of discipline, obedience, and military spirit. Often, indeed, this symbolic function is the sole function of such a guard. When community guardians address individuals struggling to make sense out of conflicting loyalties, they speak with deep conviction and power, because they speak as the conscience of the community.

(c) Whenever the community or an institution parades itself before audiences within or without their own group, the guardians are singled out and placed in some kind of "reviewing stand." At a family party, elders are given places of honor and every guest is presented to them. At parties given to celebrate an event of importance, there is a receiving line of dignitaries. At the awarding of degrees, there is a solemn group of learned scholars, majestic administrators, rich and powerful board members, and proud parents, before whom the graduating seniors must pass in review. In formal parades, the marchers straighten up and salute the guardians of the community, who return in solemn and cadenced measure the salutes given them. These community dignitaries are the personification in social office of principles which we believe determine order and continuity in the community. We salute them as our conscience, the best and strongest among us; for if we are to survive, we can do so only as brave soldiers, holy priests, wise teachers, businessmen devoted to the common good, great artists, and loving parents who create and sustain life. Guardians who struggle to uphold these values must create loyal followers who subordinate themselves to principles of social order, as well as to the person or power of authority, because such principles must be upheld by guardians and people alike if order is to be preserved.

(d) In comic drama (in art as in society) the guardians of the community often raise their voices against individuals who violate traditions and beliefs. In comedy these beliefs are not treated as sacred, but as "common" sense. This is done on the stage, and especially the comic stage, through various kinds of chorus groups (or figures such as the silent mimes who comment in song, gesture, language, and dance, from their point of view, as the choric delegates of the community guardians). I have described (in *Communication and Social Order*) the choric response of good British tars, the crew of *H.M.S. Pinafore*, to their captain's fatuous lies and empty postures as a great British sea dog. The crew does not object to a little bragging, and are resigned to pompous admirals and captains, for that seems to be the way of British naval authority, but when the captain is so carried away by his own greatness that he boasts he is never, never sick at sea, his crew revolts. The captain may put on all the airs he likes, but it simply violates the common sense of a hardy British tar to act superior to the common vicissitudes of life at sea. The chorus of tars challenge him at once: "What, never?" The captain tries to maintain his stand: "No, never!" But the crew persists: "What, *never?*" And the captain knows that he has offended common sense: "Hardly ever!" His return to common sense is a great relief to his crew, who greet his sudden burst of honesty with cheers and song.

(e) In the social dramas which institutions mount to display themselves before the community, institutional guardians are expected to extol the virtues of their group, yet even at these solemn moments a comic chorus is often used to hold this pontification in check. In

American Legion and Shriner's conventions, as in their street appearances and parades, comedy and solemnity are intermingled. As the portly, aging Shriners swing down the boulevard dressed in the costly formal American dress of American plutocrats, or in the costume of oriental potentates, there is no doubt that we are witnessing a parade of successful businessmen, "the boys," as we say in American parlance, "who have made it." But it is not long until clowns appear to mock the majesty of these portly guardians of plutocracy. Seedy clowns, whose dress caricatures plutocratic elegance, march in mock-solemnity behind and beside their solemn brothers. Other clowns range through the crowds watching the parade, turning loose rubber snakes, exploding firecrackers, engaging in fake fights, flirting outrageously with pretty girls, teasing children, and taking copious swigs from bottles of fake (and perhaps real) whiskey. They even invade the reviewing stand where the dignitaries are gathered, and mock their solemn charade. The wife of a rich merchant may find a splayfooted clown sitting in her lap, gazing longingly in her eyes; a gentleman attendant to the president of the Order may find that his top hat has suddenly been appropriated by a red-wigged clown, who goes to the forward rail of the reviewing stand and accepts the salutes of the marchers by doffing the hat and bowing.

(f) Both tragic and comic actors speak for the group and attempt to keep individual actors and the general public loyal to virtues which the guardians believe will insure community survival. If individuals in soliloquy and dialogue are allowed to comment on the arrogance or stupidity of the community guardians, the guardians, in their choric role, express their views, in turn, on the conduct of the individual actors and the general public. The most common form of such address occurs when the guardians speak as protectors of the great principles of social order which sustain the community. In this guise the guardians are the voice of tradition and custom, or of the utopias which lie ahead for all those who do their duty. In solemn and majestic speech, gesture, dress, and bearing, the guardians warn individual actors, and the general public, of the doom that awaits those who violate the sacred principles of social order which uphold their community. And since community elites regard themselves (and are regarded by their followers) as sacred guardians of these principles, their warnings become the "official" warnings of angered gods. In their seats of honor in community celebration the guardians present themselves as upholders of customs, usages, and traditions to which the individual must submit if the community is to survive.

But the clown too is a guardian of social order, and if the majestic guardian arouses awe and wonder, the people's fool arouses equally profound reflection over autocratic threats to social order. Community clowns are critics, and while they are treated familiarly and even with disdain by other actors, there is a curious air of complicity and familiarity in their address, as there is in the replies given them. Unlike tragic guardians, comic guardians are allowed to enter into dialogue with anyone they please. Even during the action of a staged play, or the high moments of social drama in community festivals and ceremonies, comic actors may turn from one audience to another. Clowns may even take over the stage and mock the solemn antics of other actors. The most powerful social function of the clown is his exposure of the incongruities between the values cherished by the community and the means taken by individuals and groups to achieve these values. In this the comic guardian is just as conservative as the solemn community guardians who prophesy awful punishment to those who disobey the gods. In comic eyes disobedience is failure to understand that pride, arrogance, envy, sloth, and hate are deadly sins because they destroy social bonds among men as well as with the men we make into heroes and gods.

The comic guardian admonishes us to keep a weather eye on the solemn and tragic guardians who act as messengers of the gods to visit doom on those who disobey their commandments. Juvenal, a comic guardian of Rome, reminds us that someone must guard the guardians. The comic guardian, like his tragic counterpart, struggles to ward off threats to the community. For men cannot live in love and reason so long as they live in fear. The comic guardian seeks, therefore, to open the mystifications and the awesome rites of community priests to reason through laughter. For if the "old Adam" in man must be disciplined by priests, so too must the priests of harsh and avenging gods be held in check by the reason of man. If men must fast, they must also feast; if they must fear their gods, they must find joy in them too. If pious platitudes, drooling sentiment, or threadbare slogans are offered the public by the solemn guardians, then comic guardians must expose such stupidity by holding priestly utterances up to the light of reason.

○

The significant other ("Thou") is symbolized through dialogue in which the self is created and sustained.

(a) The individual or private self, in contrast to the social or public self, is born in dialogue with individual others. We exhort, command, or mystify general audiences; we plead our case before the community guardians; we beseech men of power and authority to approve our purposes, and give us what we need to achieve them. But the others we address in soliloquy are not real; they are fantastic selves we address because we cannot address real others, or because we do not know how to communicate with them. We invoke, beseech, and pray to gods who embody the great principles of social order which we believe necessary to survival. But in address to individual others we enter into dialogue; the "I" speaks to a "Thou" whose response is necessary to the "I" because in it the "I" discovers his unique meaning and significance as an "I," just as "Thou" discovers his in the response of the "I."

(b) No social self exists, or exists in knowledge of itself, save in the response of an other (real, fictive, or fantastic, as the case may be). The forms of address which arise in dialogue are fundamental realities, because it is what happens between man and man, his relatedness in and through the communication of significant symbols, which constitute human personality. We discover ourselves in others, as they discover themselves in us, because in the commitment to the other we find a freedom which we do not have in our communication with the general public, the guardians of the community, or whatever ideal (however personified) we worship as the guarantor of the principles of social order. This freedom is the right to experiment, to search, to express doubt and hate as well as love and reverence. We are not selves *before*, but *after* we communicate with other selves. "Individuals" and "society" are not waiting to be sparked into becoming "forces" which "stream" from one pole to the other and form fields or patterns. In the address of one being to another each discovers himself through the responses of the other, and longs for the profound social moment when communication becomes communion. In such moments of perfect communication, a profound sense of community is born because we are, as we say, "one."

(c) Address to real others is always a moment of commitment. For if the self is born in the response of other selves, the power over us of the other is very great. And since the responses of others must be won through social courtship, we are dependent on whatever symbols are available for such communication, our skill in using them, and the presence of others who are willing to communicate with us. Each moment of significant communication is a moment of deep anxiety. Like the stricken actor trembling with stage fright, we go before significant audiences in fear and anxiety. Significant audiences make us miserable or happy because we accept their definition of us as our definition of ourselves. Like the parvenu waiting to be announced at his first admission to a party attended by the high and mighty of the social world he so admires, we stand in awe before the power and glory of those whose glamour overwhelms our lives. We wait in anxiety because our social identity will be determined by their acceptance, rejection, or indifference.

(d) All through our lives we search in reality, as well as in the fantasies of the day and the night, for ideal others with whom we can "really" communicate. Like the child playing "make-believe" we stage ourselves before an audience which listens patiently and lovingly to our search within for the self we long to become. As we look back on our moments of friendship or love, we think of them as moments in which a cherished other heard us out, and, as we say, "understood" us. But we look back, too, on moments of hate and indifference, for we know that hate as well as love rules our lives. We *need* to satisfy hate as well as love. We need to communicate about ourselves, indeed, we often talk ill of ourselves rather than say nothing at all. And when we try to give social definition to what we observe of love between men and women, it is easy to believe (with La Rochefoucauld) that the bond between lovers is the bond of speaker and audience, for love is a "talkative passion" in which lovers never tire of their favorite subjects—themselves. And while it is true that communication needs are not the only needs satisfied in love, it is also true that as a social emotion love is an ideal, perhaps indeed *the* ideal, moment of communication. The social pleasure of love, as of all intimacy, is the discovery of the self. Lovers, friends, parents, teachers, are (in their benign moments, at least) perfect audiences. And when we pray in deep communion with our gods, we address the greatest audience of all, the one with complete power to define us to ourselves.

(e) Individual disorganization originates in the indifference of those whose responses are necessary to our definition of our self. Hate, as much as love, organizes our social energies. Nothing keeps love or friendship alive more than a common enemy. Political bonds, too, are often forged in hatred of a common enemy; liberals may hate conservatives more than they love democratic principles of social order. War arouses the community to great effort, just as hate increases individual energy and power. But when love and hate cannot be expressed, they cannot be shared with real others, and must be turned inward against the self. These inner dramas lack clear forms by which we can confront our love and hate to discover what they are, and in what they exist. When indifference of those we love continues we must hate them if only to keep our selfhood intact.

(f) When I cannot have the audience I need I cannot find my social being. The desired but indifferent other prevents the birth of the self. We have not only a "father-longing," as Freud taught us, but a "society-longing," too. It may be that our need for the other is but a need to use him as a reflection of our self-love. In our struggle to create and preserve our selfhood we are often like a queen of high society who struts and preens before audiences who despise her, audiences whose sole concern is how to destroy her majesty so one of them can become queen. And in our wars, our terrible wars, where we wound and kill millions of our fellow beings as we risk our own mutilation and death, we seek each other in deadly hate. Even at the risk of suffering and death we seek out each other, for men are primarily *social* beings who must exist in terms of each other, even in destruction and death.

(g) A friend is an equal. Our "covenant" with a friend is not like that between God and man, lord and serf, or father and son. We do not want to dominate a friend, for when we do the friendship does not exist. This "otherness" of the friend, our willingness to allow him to exist on his own terms, is granted because we know that he in turn grants it to us. We are bound, not because we are alike, but because we are different, and know that in the resolution of such difference we discover a greater self. For it is in sharing differences that we develop, just as it is in coming together as male and female that we transcend the solitariness of being male *or* female. And this is the burden, and the source, of hate as well as love in friendship. It is not that my friend "knows" me in that he knows my secrets, but that he *defines* me as I define him in the mutual give and take of our relationship. He is the "court of last appeal," the other in a drama of absolute psychological intimacy. Friendship thus becomes a mutual confessional in which each gives audience to the other, so we can confront ourselves in all the range of our being.

(h) In the definition of friendship individuality is born. Before other audiences I play roles already fixed by tradition or by glowing visions of a future. But action in the present is never simply determined by the past or the future; the present is always a problem, a time of struggle and conflict in which action at best is hypothetical. I can express few problems before superiors and inferiors. For if my superiors are truly strong and great, how can I have any problems? And if my inferiors must find me strong and great, how can I express fear and anxiety before them? It is not until I discuss problems, and express the conflicts raging within me, that I become a self. Such discussion is never a solitary dramatic rehearsal within the self, any more than another human being is simply a mirror for the self. We do not resolve problems within the self and *then* communicate with others, but through dramatic dialogue which is thinking and acting *in* relationship, *in* the give and take of address. As we speak in dialogue we must stand our ground and wait for the significant other to speak. In such difference, the real difference of the other in dialogue, and, indeed, in all the oppositions of the other, lies the meaning of conversation as a social event. As we speak together with equals we enter into a mutual agreement not to silence or to deny our differences, but to *define* them.

(i) Words become names, and, in doing so, fix social meanings. In the meeting and response of conversation, relationships emerge which endure only so long as the self and the other continue in dialogue. A named thing or person exists both for the other and for me. Until it is named it has no social existence because it cannot be addressed (it has no "reference"). We are not solitary selves who "decide" what to say, and then find meaning in this decision. Nor are we determined selves wholly formed by forces in nature and society. The reality in which we live is the reality of the named relations between the things of the world and man, as well as between man and man. In friendship, the family, all the deeply intimate relationships—the "I" and the "You" become "I" and "Thou." So long as the self and the other, the "I" and "You," struggle, like the hero and the villain of a drama, to reach community through the resolution of difference, they are not only an "I" and a "You," but a relationship of "I" and "You" which makes up a "We." No matter how subjective I become, or how much I try to use another person as a thing, I discover my social existence in relationships with others. Because of this, indifference to others cannot be endured long, for in indifference there is no relationship, and hence no social being.

(j) We fear indifference more than hate, because we cannot address those who are indifferent to us, and we cannot be sure that if we do address them they will respond. Those who hate us *attend* to us, as we attend to them. We cannot endure being treated as things because this reduces us to quantities, and makes human relationship impossible. Objects cannot address each other, and, therefore, cannot enter into any kind of social relationship. And since objects, or men treated as objects, cannot be determined by how we communicate with them, they cannot become an audience of the kind we require for social being—the audience which responds and thus makes relationship in talk possible. Men create symbols in dialogue, not to measure space, but to name things, events, and relationships so they can act together. And since all such action, as social action, is dramatic, the life of dialogue is dramatic life. We address each other to find out what we are. We commit ourselves to each other, and this commitment becomes our social covenant, for as we address the other and he responds to us, we discover that we exist in terms of each other. So long as we are bound, we exist. When the bond is broken, when we no longer look the other in the eye, and yearn to hear his voice, when we stop trying to speak carefully so we will be "really" understood, we are no longer individuals, but "members of a collective," which is not a society of individuals but a "set" of role relationships in which we act out mechanically the "official roles" demanded by those in power over us.

○

THEORETICAL PROPOSITION 15
Soliloquy, like inner dialogue between the "I" and the "Me," is the symbolization of role conflict in society.

(a) Audiences are both private and public. I speak to external audiences only through my capacity to internalize them, just as I learn to address inner selves through learning how to address others. Not only must I learn to communicate with each actor in his own terms, but I must resolve within myself the different, and contending, voices of superiors, inferiors, and equals. Some times we are like actors in a play, at others we are like orators appealing to a jury. When I want a promotion I rehearse how I will act toward the dean in terms of how I think he will act toward me. I become my own audience through imagining myself as an audience to an other. Often there is great difficulty in reconciling the competing claims of superiors, inferiors, and equals. Status enactment also involves passing from one position to another. We must leave the old as we press on to the new. Sanctioned ways of obliterating the past, as well as embracing a future, must be provided.

(b) Private and public audiences are mixtures of superiors, inferiors, and equals, whom we love, hate, fear, or disdain. We often hate those we "must" love. As we accept the nomination of one political party, we reject another. Institutions within the same society compete for our loyalty. Often indeed, the same institution makes contradictory appeals. One professor urges us to study books, another to study people. We cannot do both, and while we do one, we are never quite sure that we should not have done the other. The individual must endure incongruities which do not exist for the institution which creates them. The bank profits from lending me money as well as from lending my savings to others.

(c) The turmoil of conflicting social roles is matched (and often surpassed) by the conflicts which rage within us. We love and hate friends and enemies alike. In dreams and wishes, we rape, murder, and torture at will. The suffering and disgrace of majestic superiors, the ridicule and abasement of loyal inferiors, the exposure of the pretensions and hypocrisies of peers, all delight us. But even in the dream there is an audience, sometimes many audiences, within the self.

(d) Freud stresses the father as the primal audience who must be placated before we can relate to others without guilt or anxiety. But superiors of all kinds—even fathers—often bewilder us. Authorities are often puzzling and capricious. They do not keep their own commandments, and worse, they themselves are often in conflict. The child has *two* parents, and these parents do not always agree. The younger child of a large family has several superiors who love and hate each other, and who visit their love and hate upon their inferiors. Sometimes they use the child against each other. The child is praised before the father for qualities which the father does not have, while father praises the charm of a daughter whom the mother is trying to discipline. Gods who fight and quarrel before their inferiors cannot remain remote and mysterious, and when they ask us for help to subdue another god their mystery soon vanishes. For the child, as for the adult, these quarrels can be tragic or comic. When they are tragic the child suffers deeply.

(e) Parents (fortunately) are comic as well as tragic. When differences among our family gods are expressed openly and in a comic vein, when parents are not despots but presidents of a wrangling parliament, we learn to relate to authority as equals as well as inferiors. Our first experience of rules, which are made by superior and inferior alike and yet are obeyed by all, is our first experience of democratic authority. To our delight and wonder we discover that gods who make rules can be bound by them. At this discovery no one becomes a better guardian of rules than the small child, and no one takes more delight in catching his gods in violation of rules they have agreed to uphold. Children learn, too (if they are permitted to do so), that there is power among equals so long as equals can join in love and hate against an authority whose commandments weigh heavily upon them. We discover all the joys of banding together against authority, but we learn, too, that if we are to continue as equals our relationship must be based on more than a common dislike or hatred of our superiors. We must learn to relate as equals, where love is not given to some remote and terrible god, or to an obsequious or fawning inferior, but to a friend and comrade. We learn, for the first time, what it really is to share, as well as to obey and command, in a human relationship.

(f) Sharing, like commanding and obeying, occurs in communication. When our masters refuse to communicate with us, either consciously, as when they will not recognize us (in all the variants of excommunication ranging from being sent into Coventry, being "cut dead" or snubbed, to being avoided), or unconsciously when they think so little of us that they give no sign of our existence, and treat us as a thing instead of a person, we cannot develop a sense of identity. Without the experience of communication as equals, as well as superiors and inferiors, our sense of social being cannot develop. Even punishment from superiors is better than nothingness, for in pain inflicted by another we are sure at least of a relationship, and thus of our social reality, however painful it may be.

(g) Sarcasm and ridicule also make communication difficult, as we see in the sarcastic parent who sneers at his child, the teacher who accompanies his assignments with expressions of heavy doubt over his students' ability to do the work, or the officer who commands in open despair at the ability of his men to follow simple orders. When a distant and majestic superior communicates only to remind us of our unworthiness, and when there is no other authority to whom we can turn, anxiety deepens. When such anxiety cannot be expressed, it cannot be endured. The child creates fantastic others with whom he can communicate, for he must communicate to rid himself of anxiety. He plays before his parents, brings things to them, entices them to play hide and seek. He seeks to attract and hold the attention of the audience which gives him a sense of being. Until he learns how to enact other status roles, and especially roles with equals, the child will relate only to superiors and inferiors, as he learned to relate to his parents. He may appeal to audiences only as superiors who must be placated, or inferiors who must be terrorized into obedience as he has been. Where communication is monopolized (as in authoritarian states or institutions), or very difficult because of great differences in understanding (as between generations in immigrant families), or impossible because of lack of common language, we cannot expect discussion, debate, and argument. Only equals can discuss and argue. Much of our rage and hysteria derives from poor opportunities and bad training in communication. If our social experience has precluded open discussion of difference with equals, we cannot be expected to welcome or even tolerate criticism.

(h) Whatever increases hierarchal strangeness and mystery increases glamour and thus adds to the majesty and sublimity of rank and social office, but it also adds new burdens to open and free communication.

In mockery we attempt to laugh away insupportable barriers between the self and others we need. The child playing grown-up parodies her elders, the chorus boys dressed as girls with bulging hips and stuffed bosoms debunk sexual glamour. We tell obscene stories about women whose ethereal, intellectual, or glamorous pretentions place them beyond approach and thus threaten the essential bond between men and women. Hostility is social as well as sexual. Differences in sexual roles are mocked in festivals such as Purim and farces like *Charley's Aunt*. The male feasts and riots in women's clothes and in doing so throws off the burden of pious rational masculinity. College students burdened with the mystifications of status glamour cannot work easily beside girls who must be regarded as equals and colleagues. In laughing at the sweet mystery of love and the power of rank, men and women laugh down barriers which increase strangeness and mystery of communication to the point where relationships become difficult or impossible.

(i) If we learn to face gaps and breakdowns in communication, and to express hate in symbolic ways, we may not need to fight. Perhaps we should encourage, not discourage, diplomats to become highly skilled in cursing. The press might be taught not to deplore international cursing, but to regard it as the critic does a play. Diplomats might be trained to dramatize, not to mask, differences. As we learn to express hostility short of war, our chances of survival might increase. Communal life is made possible by love, and Christians are enjoined to love one another, but no religion has given its followers so many opportunities to hunt down, torture, and kill its heretics and stamp out heresy—either outside the group, as among infidels, or within the self, as in mortification of the senses. Inequalities in themselves do not create social disorder and war, nor do specific conditions of ownership, such as private property. Every institution seeks to maximize its power; struggle over possession of symbols of hierarchy, whether of the church, army, state, school, or profession, is a condition of all social experience. It is only when inequalities cannot be faced in common expression that they become insupportable.

(j) Soliloquy is not simply a dramatic "device," but a characteristic of all social life. We talk to ourselves, hear others talk to themselves, and hold inner conversations of all kinds. These inner conversations are never buried very deep. Children talk to themselves, as do old people. Drunkards become audiences to themselves. All of us use animals, or things, as projections of a self whom we address in play. In humor and playful banter we comment on ourselves. In private (as well as public) acts it is impossible to narrow our address to one person alone; we must appeal to superiors, inferiors, and equals in the presence of each other. Our appeal to any one audience is conditioned by our need to create harmony in our relations with others. A subject loyal to his superiors must not be found servile by his equals. A man who is successful with his inferiors must not be too obsequious to his superiors. Equals must not risk their dignity in too great familiarity.

(k) The self alone is not the source of role conflict. Family, school, church, and other institutions within the community struggle for the soul of each individual. The individual struggles to develop an ego strong enough to resolve these conflicts. The ego must become a lord of counterpositions, not simply a go-between among institutional and social roles. Soliloquy is often an expression of conflict among "outer" roles, an individual struggle to confront, and, hopefully, to resolve contradictions and incongruities. Such struggles offer many clues to social problems. In Huck Finn's attempt to balance the conflicting claims of the inferior but loved Negro, and the superior yet inhuman aristocrat, the inner conflict of America over racial equality is revealed. In the years after the Civil War racial problems could be discussed safely only in fun, and the burdens of traditional racial attitudes exposed only in the guise of comic soliloquy addressed seemingly to no one yet "overheard" by all. In soliloquy the self can speak to the general public, and to the community guardians—the heroes and villains who importunately demand us to choose between them. The final audience whose response is necessary to our sense of order drives us to say in the anguished cries of soliloquy what we cannot say in open dialogue. As the individual states his dilemmas in soliloquy, he asks his community to face disrelationships as he himself must face them.

○

THEORETICAL PROPOSITION 16

Principles of social order are grounded in ultimate principles of order which serve as the final audience in social address.

(a) While it is common to think of religious appeals alone as appeals "above" reason to faith, deep belief in any ultimate functions in much the same way as supernatural belief functions in religious communication. The value, purpose, end, or goal of any act is "beyond" reason in the sense that no one before he acts can really "prove" that a specific end will follow from certain means. No one has returned from any of the heavens and hells, described in such detail by the devout of many faiths, to tell us whether or not we are "right." But lack of proof has little effect on belief, for we use our belief in the end or purpose of an act to organize action in a present.

(b) We legitimize social hierarchies on many grounds, just as we analyze social relations on the basis of various theories of knowledge about society. Thus we say that hierarchy is nothing but a "pecking order," and invoke biological "nature" as our explanation. Or we say that a social system depends on "the extent to which it can keep the equilibrium of the personality systems from varying beyond certain limits . . ." since the social system's own equilibrium is itself made up of many sub-equilibriums which "enter into a huge moving equilibrium . . ."; thus we discover the causes of social relations in physical nature.* Or we find our causes in "forms of sociation" or the "class struggle." Or we find our ultimate in a supernatural or a god. Or, finally, we say that social relations depend on "good" or "effective" communication, and we deify language as the final "cause" of social integration.

(c) Belief in any kind of social legitimation leads easily to supernatural invocation of these ends. Thus we hear of the "sweet mystery of love," of social systems which "maintain themselves," of "pure science," "art for art's sake," "things in themselves," "tendencies to stability," and the "wisdom of the body," or, as befits good democrats, that

---

* See p. 226 of *Toward a General Theory of Action*, ed. by Talcott Parsons and Edward A. Shils (Cambridge: Harvard University Press, 1952), where Parsons and Shils discuss the "Motivation and the Dynamics of Social Order."

the voice of the people is "the voice of God." We say, too, that "history teaches us," or that it is our "historic destiny" to plunder a neighboring country. In Freud and Jung we read of an "archaic heritage," a "collective unconscious," "primary hordes," or "the primal act." The Soviets assure their people that the most stratified society in the world is but a way to a classless society.

(d) When the Church Father Origen tells us that God must not be thought of as physical being, or as having any kind of body, but as pure mind and spirit, or when we read in the Bible that God exists outside of time and space, we are reading an *explicit* statement of supernatural values, ends, and purpose in social order. Other systems make the same use of great transcendent ends, but are far less explicit about them. The difference between partial and fully developed statements of transcendent ends in social order is one of degree, not of kind. When we appeal to reason as a way to social order, we *assume* that men are capable of reason, and that men will follow reason if and when they "understand" it. But those who love reason must admit that grounds for this belief are no more demonstrable than those on which all supernatural beliefs rest. For, as George Bernard Shaw reminds us, as scarce as reason may be, the supply still exceeds the demand. We trudge to our laboratories, lecture halls, and classrooms under the spell of reason.

(e) Explicit and implicit appeals to supernatural powers believed to be beyond reason (and not determined by communication alone) take many forms. If we believe in physical causality, we talk about a nature which determines action through "immutable" forces or laws of space, time, or motion. If we believe in personal charisma, we turn to divine, semi-divine, or heroic actors whose personal qualities alone determine social order. If we believe in method, as in magic, where how we do something determines its effect in conduct, we turn to techniques and operations as the "way" to order. If we believe in ends, goals, or values, we turn to ideals, heavens, and utopias, which are "known" to all true believers (even though they have never been reached). And, finally, if we believe that symbols constitute social order because they are "signs" given by some supernatural being, it is only natural for us to decide that language as the "Holy Word" can become a "final cause." For as we read in the Bible: "In the beginning was the Word, and the

Word was with God, and the Word was God." (John 1:1). Language itself develops generalizations atop generalizations, until we come to some "final" use of language which is both the cause and effect of meaning. For unless we believe in some kind of "perfect" communication, and consider a given literary style or genre of literary expression in terms of some "perfected" model of its kind, aesthetic criticism is impossible.

(f) In our roles as scientists, priests, soldiers, statesmen, artists, educators, or philosophers, we must act in, as well as think about, the world. Values in action are used to infuse the beginning, the middle, and the end of our act with social meaning. Belief in values gives us confidence to act in a present because it resolves difference, doubt, and ambiguity. Belief in ends, goals, or purpose, as expressed in ideals, ideologies, heavens, and utopias which are "known" to all true believers, even though they have not yet been reached, inspire us to act with vigor and force. So, too, do beliefs in traditions, as when we turn to Edenic myths of origin, a paradise from which men "fell" or "strayed," but to which we can return through supernatural grace. In science we invoke "scientific method" as a cure for the evils which beset our community.

(g) In our time we have shifted our belief from acts of creation by divine gods or inspired heroes, to social and physical "forces" whose natural "laws" we "discover" and "obey." Yet even in our philosophies of materialism there are several natures, as once there were many gods. Highest of all is a moment of "nature's perfection." In neo-behaviorism, nature's mystical moment is its "tendency to self-maintenance" where equilibrium "determines" order. Once a social system "maintains itself" by equilibrating processes (latent, as in "adaptiveness," or actual, as in "integration") such processes become both cause and effect. Suddenly motion becomes, like the celestial mechanics of the deistic heaven, a "higher" level of explanation. As we enter this level of final causes, we are in the realm of transcendence, where values are both cause and effect.

(h) Forensic appeals based on the transcendence of law are used everywhere in American life to determine justice and truth. We submit the acts of our executive and legislative branches of government to the courts. Arbitration boards are staffed with lawyers because they are considered expert in the rules of judicial process. We send lawyers to our legislatures because they know how to frame laws—that is, how to bargain with other lawyers to get laws passed. We think of the judge as an umpire who decides on rules of procedure, not on the quality of the law itself. Belief in judicial process as a way to truth is so ingrained that we find it difficult to recognize incongruities and mystifications in legal process—as when a jury of laymen decide a case on evidence submitted by experts whose testimony is far beyond their comprehension.

(i) Absolutely unmodified utterance of traditional spells determines the efficacy of magic. The slightest alteration from the original pattern is fatal, since the principle of order involved is upheld by fixed, standardized procedures. Our science, by its claims wholly against mystification, is peculiarly subject to this type of mystification. Few people in our society have as much power as scientists, who express themselves in symbols far beyond the comprehension of those whose lives are yet determined by what they cannot understand. Even those of us able to make competent judgments in one field must rely on authority in another. Like the faithful swallowing the bread and wine consecrated by their priests, we munch digests, abstracts, and résumés. We believe what we read, not because we really know how to test it, but because the technique used is "correct," or the expression is "scientific," or simply because a recognized authority speaks in a "professional" journal.

(j) All goals, ends, purposes, heavens, hells—any ideal future whose immanence invests action to such a degree that what is happening *now* can only be understood by what will happen *then*—offer peculiar temptations to mystification. Christian eschatology, Marxian classless heavens, Wagnerian erotic immolations, are but a few of these imaginary, yet powerful, futures. Millions of men have been doomed to starvation, slavery, and death by these promises of things to come, the "last things," as the Bible calls them. Once the promise is symbolized and these symbols become sacred, they are no longer subject to critical discussion. No one has returned from heaven (Christian or Marxian) to tell us about it, yet the true believer "knows" it exists, and is often capable of torturing and killing those who do not share his vision.

He "knows" because he believes, and thus is superior to rational beings who believe because they know.

(k) Those in power always legitimize authority in their assumed roles as guardians of sacred principles of social order. Following Max Weber, we can think of four types of legitimation. We can base decisions on knowledge of means-ends relationships. Or rational action can be determined by orientation to an absolute value. Or we can act in terms of affectual orientation, as when the emotions of the actor determine what is done. Or we can act in the name of tradition, as we do when we say we are doing something because that is "the way things have always been done." In his study of religious authority, Joachim Wach (following Weber) proposes that we use Weber's theory of leadership as a basis for a typology of religious roles, as in the Founder of Religion, the Reformer, the Prophet, the Seer, the Magician, the Diviner, the Saint, the Priest, the *Religiosus,* and the Audience.

(e) Burke bases his description of social order on the relationship between language and the supernatural. In his scheme there are four realms of order to which words refer: (1) there are words for the natural, which is defined as the things, conditions, or motions there would be in the universe even if all ability to use symbols were eliminated from existence; (2) there are symbols for sociopolitical order, or what we in sociology call "social relations"; (3) there are words about words and symbols of all kinds, the realm of dictionaries, grammar, rhetoric, poetics, dialectics, what Burke calls "logology"; and (4) there are symbols for the supernatural. The first three orders of language—the natural, sociopolitical, and symbolic (symbol systems in art, science, etc.)—are concerned with everyday experience, and belong to the empirical realm for which words are pre-eminently suited.

(m) But the supernatural is also a part of everyday experience in communication. For even those who do not believe in a specific religious supernatural will recognize that, so far as the purely observable facts of language are concerned, languages do have words and symbols for the supernatural. If all words for the supernatural or the "ineffable" are borrowed from our words for the natural, the social, and the symbolic, empirical study of the supernatural can be undertaken in terms of how the supernatural is communicated. Burke distinguishes six analogies between words as commonly used for words, and words as used for the divine. In theological usage, words are referred to as an agent of creation, as Spirit to Matter, as a principle of negativity, (as when we define God in terms of what he is not); as a form of entitlement which rises to higher and higher orders of generalization until it reaches the Divine; as a statement about time and eternity in which "time" is to "eternity" as "the particulars in the unfolding of a sentence are the sentence's unitary meaning"; and, finally, as relation between the name and thing named, as the relations of the persons in the Trinity. We can, therefore, demonstrate in the use of symbols how to get from the secular to the sacred, and from the sacred to the secular.

(n) Ultimates are addressed as final courts of appeal in the determination of social order. We can distinguish five types of such ultimates. There are ultimates of the person, as when the personal authority of parents, prophets, or gods is invoked; of laws and codes, as when we say that "laws, not men, uphold social order"; of nature and environment, as when we ascribe causes of order to "tendencies," "processes," or "laws" in nature; of means, as when we turn to methods, techniques, instruments, or magic; and, finally, of the perfected end or ideal of social order whose immanence infuses social relationships with meaning. Every institution seeks to maximize its power by universalizing local names, slogans, and principles which are believed to sustain order within the institution. Thus when we say, "Let justice be done, though the heavens fall," or we hear God say, "I am Alpha and Omega, the beginning and the end, the first and the last" (Revelations XXII), or when we read, in Parsons and Shils, that social systems maintain themselves by equilibrating processes, or read "It is written, but I say unto you," or that art exists only for "art's sake," we are in the realm of immanence where what is happening *now* can only be understood by what will happen *then* under the name of a deeply believed principle which is "beyond" the finite (that is, social) mind of man, and yet is communicated to him. The social power of these ultimates is not so much that they are ends which we arrive at finally, but that they infuse every phase of the act—the beginning as well as the end—with their radiance and glory.

○

Social order is legitimized through symbols grounded
in nature, man, society, language, or God.

(a) We explain the existence, within any hierarchy, of superiority,
inferiority, and equality by grounding hierarchy in our biological nature, (as in the example of the "pecking order" among chickens), or
in physical nature, as when Parsons tells us that the "tendency" to
maintain equilibrium in the interaction process is the "first law" of
social process. Or we say that hierarchy is characteristic of human
nature, as in Freud's Oedipus complex. Or we ground hierarchy in
sociopolitical experience, as when we say that "class-struggle," "circulation of elites," "legitimation of authority," or "the nature of the
social bond" determines the structure and function of a hierarchal
system. Or we say that social order is based on language, and all the
ways we express ourselves, and that since it is only through such forms
that we communicate, knowledge of the laws of communication will
give us knowledge of society. Or we ascribe social order to some kind
of supernatural agency, whose ultimate principles can only be "discovered," "heard," or "communicated through," but never created by,
man.

(b) Whatever we assert to be the grounds for social order, we are
bound by the kind of language we select, and this, in turn, is determined to a large degree by the language available to us. Thus we
quantify in sociology because quantification is the "language of science." It is possible to create purely symbolic systems, as we do in
pure mathematics, theories of musical harmony, or in any kind of
fully developed symbolic grammar, but in sociopolitical experience,
the realm of what we call the "social," symbols must be bound to a
specific content, the content of *human* relationships. They may be
"about" nature, human nature, the supernatural, or even about language itself (as in the study of grammar and rhetoric), but for the
purposes of creating a sociological model of human relationships based
on communication, symbols must be thought of in terms of social
interaction.

(c) Images of social order "derived" from nature, man, society, language, or God, seldom stand alone, but are frequently linked to each

other, and, indeed, powerful and radiant symbols of authority usually base their majesty and glory in all five grounds of order. Thus we hear that God created nature, man, the family, and language, out of his "Being." Or we hear that man evolved out of nature to produce the family which "guarantees'" the "continuance of the species." Nature's "laws" cannot be created but only "discovered" through experiments in which symbols are but "instruments" of discovery. Or we hear of sociopolitical laws such as the "class-struggle," which is to end in a "classless society"; this is the "trend" of history, and this trend determines the ways men relate to each other in their allocation of rights and duties in obtaining and holding property.

(d) While recognizing that man is determined by the ways in which he symbolizes the integrative power of physical nature, his "human" nature, God, and symbols themselves, sociologists must create a symbolic model of sociation. In doing so we must keep alert to the nature of symbols as factors in communication in general, as well as to their use in sociopolitical relationships in particular. Thus, of the five orders commonly used as grounds for systematic explanations of human relationships (man, nature, society, language, and God) we will select two, society and language, as basic to our system. We will hold to language, and all forms of symbolic expression, as our data, and try to develop methodological tools for analysis of such data. We do not deny the significance of nature, human nature, and God in determining man's social motives, but we argue that since all orders of explanation are based on man communicating in society, communication and society must be our key terms. It is only as we perfect our model of social action as a communicative act that we can apply it to action in society, and, conversely, it is only as we perfect our dramatistic model of communication as social drama that we can apply it to communication in society.

(e) There is one element in social integration which cannot be explained by bonds whose "nature" is derived from extra-social bonds. This is what Simmel designated as "pure forms" of sociation, the ways in which we relate in purely social ways. We call this bond etiquette, manners, "good form," or breeding. We come together to satisfy sexual, economic, political, religious, and aesthetic needs, but none of these can be satisfied wholly unless they are expressed in forms considered "appropriate" to the occasion. There is nothing "subjective" about these standards; on the contrary, they are highly public, as we know from the codes of manners published in books of etiquette and the many daily articles in the press on how to behave in love, business, school, marriage, and almost every social situation. These codes are codes of forms, the *right way* to do something, what Weber (among others) called a "style of life."

(f) Thus, while the social bond has many strands, and human motives are determined by many things, the social bond also derives its power from purely social forms—those we see in play, games, parties, talk, fashion, style, and all the purely formal arts we use to stage ourselves as we play our many roles in society. The forms of manners are created to achieve certain effects. We see this clearly in dress and adornment. Dress is always practical, but as we attempt to define what we mean by "practical," we soon discover that the "practicality" of dress ranges all the way from protection of our bodies, work clothes, to the expression of the most fanciful kind of play, sports clothes. In well-established traditional institutions, such as the army, the "practicality" of dress lies in its ability to communicate rank. Through military dress we make it known that we are of a certain rank in a certain regiment, that our regiment belongs to a certain division of the army, and that our army belongs to the armies of the United States of America. (And in great public ceremonies, our priests assure us all that our army belongs to God.)

(g) Before battle, officers of Napoleon's army bathed, shaved, dressed carefully, pomaded their hair and beards, and powdered and perfumed their bodies. Their uniforms were cleaned, brushed, and pressed, brass and gold trimming was shined, boots were polished to a glassy perfection, while the horses of the officers were groomed meticulously. And these men, who were about to hurl themselves into cavalry charges, where freedom of movement and small concern for elegance would have increased their efficiency as soldiers, wore clothes that fit so tightly that freedom of their arms and bodies were greatly restricted.

(h) What bravery is to the soldier, holiness is to the priest, and wisdom is to the teacher, tact is to social life. The tactful person is the hero of the evening because in exercising tact he places social values above every other value. Tact may be defined as an acute or nice discernment of what is appropriate to do or to say in dealing with others. Tact is never prized when it is used to satisfy individual needs, or to further ambitions which are extrinsic to the purely social elements in a social situation. A "smooth operator" in America, like the courtier of old, is adroit enough socially, but his social skill is used for something beyond socializing. Like the salesman, he is a "live wire" with a "good line." But he is cunning as well as tactful.

Tact emerges in social drama where we struggle to achieve "good form." Whenever people meet, a struggle begins between individual or group interests which are extrinsic to the gathering, and purely social demands which are intrinsic to the moment. At faculty gatherings we meet as deans, professors, students, administrators, parents, or as men and women who are rich or poor, beautiful or ugly, stupid or wise. But soon we begin to relate within the purely social forms of the occasion. A tea is staged in a certain way, by certain kinds of actors, by certain means, and for a purely social purpose. Power, wealth, beauty, sex, wisdom, are all subordinated to the unfolding social drama of the moment. Ranks may be completely reversed. The lowly student who sits behind the silver in a handsome carved chair becomes a queen. Deans, professors, great scholars, even the majestic president of the University, approach her with deference, and each does his utmost to be charming and amiable. For at this moment the roles of dean, professor, scholar, and president undergo a subtle transformation. A new role comes into being, a purely social role whose power subordinates all others to its demands.

Any sudden or strong imposition of wealth, power, beauty, age, rank, erudition, shatters the purely social tone of a gathering as a rock shatters glass. At such intrusion the power of the social stage, the arrangement of the room in which we are gathered, the ways we meet, greet, and talk, the care we have given our dress, the playfulness and gaiety of our conversational sallies, the social euphoria we experience in being together, vanishes. As the learned scholar holds forth in tedious monologue on his latest research, or the dean discusses in great detail a new admissions policy, or an eager student queries his professor on how his field of study ought to be covered, or a boy and girl in love stand mute before each other, the purely social form of the gathering is destroyed. We are no longer striving to play roles determined by the form of the gathering as a *social* event, but are using the event as a stage to play our own individual roles in our *individual* event. We cannot, or will not, subordinate ourselves to the social demands of the moment. Soon it is obvious that there really is nothing "social" about the gathering; it is simply a gathering of individuals who, in failing to surrender themselves to the social forms of the moment, fail to play their parts in a purely social drama of sociation. As each seeks his own audience, social integration, the delight of being together, is destroyed. The party dies in boredom, and we take our leave.

(i) We reach social communion through skill in creating and sustaining social euphoria, the simple but profound joy in being together which originates in a deep sense of identification in each other. As laughter and gaiety mount, our spirits rise and we know deep joy. We are identifying with each other in the most profound kind of play man knows. This is the play of purely social forms, a golden moment when we soar into another kind of life. We are no longer animals who long to be gods. We are haunted no more by the long, slow, painful humiliation of aging and dying. Our unsatisfied yearnings to identify with strange and terrible others we love and need, even though we know they are indifferent to us and, indeed, often hate us, are now fulfilled. In the warmth and pleasure of the evening we experience a deep sense of joy in each other. We are in communion because we are finding ourself in another, as he is finding himself in us. We are "lost in each other," we "hang on each other's words." In such communication, the moment of communion, a deep sense of community is born.

(j) At the beginning of any purely social party or gathering we begin to play our parts in different roles, but soon we are subordinated to the social spirit of the occasion. We are guests, and if we want the gathering to be a social success must do all we can to be amiable, charming, and gay. We must *play* society, just as we play any game, or enact any dramatic role. Our mask is the mask of sociability, of seeking to maximize and intensify the feeling of being together in a kind of interaction which has no meaning beyond itself. Now we are no longer deans, professors, or students, we are members of a gathering whose success will be determined by our capacity to interact with others present. We are now players in what we call the "social game," a game which we can enter only if we are willing to give up the power and majesty of other roles and subordinate ourselves to the rules of a game of socializing. For only as far as we are willing to relinquish our power in other roles, that is, to *risk* relating to others on a purely social footing, do we really commit ourselves to the occasion.

(k) In any play-form of sociation there will be differences of skill, energy, effort, and will. Some will play harder than others, some will have positions which the rules themselves make more important than others. But this is not the same as differences in wealth, fame, social position, beauty, or erudition, which have been established by factors extrinsic to purely social roles, and which must be subordinated to the rules if the game is to continue. What remains purely personal, or reflects moods of depression, despondency, or exhilaration, militates against playing the social game. Intrusion of purely personal elements is tactless, we feel, not because we are insensitive to the sufferings and joys of the individual, but because in so far as we are playing roles in a group bound by rules, subjective personal expression spoils the game. This is one reason we use humor so much in play. Laughter breaks down the distance subjective concern creates between individuals. Gaiety takes us out of ourselves into a moment of pure sociation, because in gaiety we submit to others.

(l) The power of symbolic forms as social forms is nowhere better illustrated than in erotic play, where the most outrageous flirting is permitted, so long as it is done in fun. The woman desired as partner in such play is not the most beautiful, or even the one who stirs our lust, but the most skilled player of the erotic game. The laughter and gaiety she arouses eliminate all intimacy from sex. We do not need to consider this woman as an individual who must be courted and won. The mind is free, the mystery and estrangement of sexual difference, the heavy burden of lust, is now subordinated to social and intellectual needs. Sex is now expressed as a social form of expression, as well as an intimate form of expression between couples. Between couples, flirting may serve as a prelude to the sexual act; but within the group, erotic desire is transformed from pursuit, consent, or refusal, into play.

(m) Manners can become rites, just as prayers can become liturgy, but they are, in essence, play. Manners are play even when solemn and serious, as in the hunt. In ritual we seek to *fix* manners; as we seek to fix rules in law. But if we seek to fix manners in rigid codes, we also try to keep conduct open to change. For, what we cannot change we must destroy. Revolutionaries do not have opponents, they have enemies. Social integration (in a free society at least) requires the maintenance of sacred codes of conduct, but it also requires sanctioned ways of revising such codes when their integrative power fails. Societies which cannot combine reverence of their sacred symbols with equal reverence for freedom to change them when necessary can change only in hatred and violence.

(n) In purely social moments it is not edicts, laws, rites, or commandments which determine how we will interact with one another; but our formal skill in dressing, greeting, meeting, talking, and leaving. Manners have great power because they order the purely social elements of our relationships. They are a social identification, not simply an embellishment. There are many moments when manners are equated with morals, as when we believe that proper conduct will determine the moral order of the world, or even the course of nature itself. In the teachings of ancient China, good manners toward parents and elders was the foundation of domestic and civil morality. Social obligations were derived from family obligations. If the prince deserved to be beloved and obeyed it was because the people recognized in him a father. The father who taught his son manners taught him how to uphold social order and thus the cosmic order itself. The father's rights were "natural" innate rights because their proper exercise sustained order in society and nature. The laws of the family were, as Confucians said, "natural" laws.

(o) Change, like tradition, has its own institutional forms, as we see in the realm of fashion, style, art, play, and manners. A style of dress, a form of greeting, a way of entertaining, may be ephemeral, but such expression should not be considered unimportant, any more than growth should be considered unimportant, or ways of passing from one rank to another be considered less important than the rank itself. The individual must be subordinated to his community through identification with community symbols of order, but the community must in turn be subordinated to the individual, for individuals act, even though they act in community roles to uphold the established order of community life. Individuals must resolve conflicts and incongruities among and between community and institutionalized roles through experimentation and change.

(p) Through style we tell others that we want to be accepted by them, as they tell us of their desire for identification with us. But style is more than acceptance or rejection of group norms; it is an expression of the self, an attempt to dramatize the individuality and uniqueness we cherish in ourselves. In this sense manners are often ironic, comic, and playful. As we bow to our hostess, who stages herself in the elegance that only the resources of the great world can supply, and whom we know realizes that we are but simple burghers (as she realizes our similar understanding of her), our masks barely hide the irony we all feel in our sophisticated roles as drawing-room knights.

(q) Manners subordinate us to rules of our own creation. Those who believe in spontaneity in manners believe that bonds created in the free will of equals are stronger because they are more flexible. Social life requires change if for no other reason than that as we mature, age, and face death, we must pass properly from one stage to another. Change is never easy, and, as we see in revolutions, often occurs only in open revolt. Much political history is the record of what has happened during periods of change. Those fearful of passage try to reduce change by sanctifying the virtues of the past; those who regard change as a time for rational reassessment of the relationship between means and ends in society welcome it. But whether or not we believe in change, the "right" to change must be sanctioned and institutionalized in a tradition of change if we are to solve our problems in human relationships. For, obviously, if tradition worked, there would be no need for change. We must change, just as we must follow tradition, to survive.

○

THEORETICAL PROPOSITION 18
Social order, and its expression through hierarchy, is enacted in social dramas in which actors attempt to uphold, destroy, or change the principles of that social order.

(a) There are three basic roles, and three basic forms of community drama, in which social order is expressed. The first is called ritual, the realm of the sacred. Here tradition is sacred; we do things the "way they always have been done" because this is the way the gods or the founders of our community or institution acted, and what was good enough for them must be good enough for us. But the values of tradition are goals, ends, or purposes that must be recreated in social action. The power of tradition exists in the present (what has been imperfectly achieved in the past will soon be achieved in the present). The glory and mystery of the past can be reached again in the future, because it was reached ("in principle") once before. Men knew paradise and righteousness, but fell from grace through disobedience. Now they must repent "straying from the path" and strive to attain again the paradise they once knew. Thus tradition too is a promise, but a "real" promise of what is to come, for, unlike the future utopia or heaven, it *has* "happened," and as a known and understood paradise, it can be regained. The paradox of how a "perfect" past could produce an imperfect social order in the present is resolved by making man an "imperfect" actor who *chooses* between good and evil principles of social order, and sometimes chooses incorrectly because his finite mind cannot function adequately unless the infinite mind of God wills it so.

(b) The second role is also found in ritual, but a ritual based on a belief in a firmly fixed future. Faith in a future is the "substance of things hoped for, the evidence of things not seen." A fully developed rite has both a past and a future. God creates a perfect world, man falls from grace through disobedience of God's commandments, but strives to cleanse himself of sin in the promise of eternal life after death. Man can be perfect because he was created perfect before his fall, and he can return again to a state of perfection in a life after death which transcends the world and its sin. The characteristic of ends in ritual acts dominated by such belief is that they are fixed, dependent on faith "beyond reason," and can be known only to those who "open" their hearts and minds to some supernatural power which "gives" them knowledge of the end. History "teaches" the communist that the "dictatorship of the proletariat" will end in a "classless society" where men will live in peace. Those who do not share this vision must be "re-educated;" those who cannot believe in the communist future must be "liquidated." Thus, war and preparation for war against enemies without, and torturing and killing enemies within by purges, are only ways of "cleansing" the community.

(c) The third role we play in the enactment of social order, we play in art. Art, and particularly narrative and dramatic art, brings problems into consciousness by creating forms through which we can confront our problems in human relationships as problems in role enactment. Until we have such forms, tensions and conflict within as well as without cannot be controlled because they cannot be expressed. But, unlike religious ritual, art opens ends, purposes, and values to inquiry. Art is the realm of change, ambiguity, argument, and doubt. In art we institutionalize doubt, not only through logical analysis, as in the school, or through experiment, as in science, but through the dramatic depiction of action as a struggle to create and sustain order. In various dramas of social order—ceremonies, festivals, rites, parades, processions, and all occasions when the community enacts its "myth of origin"—doubt, change, and ambiguity are not expressed. In art which is functioning as art, and not as a channel for official messages, the capacity to doubt and to endure ambiguity, and even to revolt against the sacred principles of social order, is not considered weak or treasonable, but heroic. We seek to *open* ends to reason (i.e. discussion in dialogue) in action. The "inquiry" of art is an inquiry over how to enact roles, not one "about" the reduction of roles to environmental factors, as in physical science, or over how to stifle doubt through faith, as in religion. The "argument" of art is a dramatic argument, and its persuasiveness lies in how it gives symbolic form to human relationships. Art does not teach us how to "think about" relationships, or how to "argue about" them, but how to form roles so we can enact them in the social drama of community life. In the purely formal play of art drama, we experiment with attitudes. In the staging of social drama in rites, ceremony, and all community presentations, we learn to play our roles in the great social dramas in which the sense and purpose of community is created and sustained.

(d) In the social drama of rites, festivals, ceremonies, and all occasions in which a society dramatizes its principles of social order, tragic and comic victims alike are used to expiate guilt and to reduce fear so we can act together. The villain in art drama, the devil in religious ritual, the criminal awaiting execution, the "enemy within" and the "enemy without," are all symbolic figures created to form attitudes necessary to carry us into action, and to sustain our courage and confidence once we are committed to a certain kind of action.

Fear, anxiety, guilt, and dread must be brought into consciousness if we are to deal with them in public. This can be done only through some kind of symbolization, and such symbolization can arise only in communication directed toward action with others in the community. Symbolization must take forms which can become community or social dramas. Ritual is but one form of social drama, just as tragedy is but one form of art. We use comedy, as we use tragedy, to give form to social dilemmas, for until we have such forms we cannot communicate with ourselves, or with others, as actors in a drama of social order.

(e) Tragic ritual drama depicts victims who must suffer and die because they have disobeyed gods that embody the principles of social order which are believed to sustain the community; comic ritual drama depicts victims who must be laughed "out of court" because they have rejected a reasonable way of living together in the community. The final appeal of tragedy is expressed in a great leap into a supernatural. God, fate, destiny, country, ideology, or some such supernatural power is invoked to explain the suffering and death of the victim who symbolizes the evil that threatens the community. This supernatural power has been disobeyed, and since it can be communicated with only by authorities and such communication can be purified only by holy delegates of the community such as priests, the power of the gods and the power of those who control social order are easily linked. Where the family is a powerful institution, we hear the heavenly powers themselves spoken of as the Father, Son, and Holy Ghost. Where nobles and kings rule, we hear God spoken of as the Lord, and the devil called the Prince of Darkness. Disobedience of such great powers is punished by suffering and death. Even questioning the edicts of rulers who rule by "divine" right (religious, historical, traditional, or utopian, as the case may be) threatens social order, for how can we question "history," "manifest destiny," "the course of empire," the "faith of our fathers," God, or a "Holy Ghost," who is outside of time and space and who creates but is never created?

(f) Comic victims suffer, but not under the awful dominion of supernatural power, or the crushing weight of "natural laws of society." Comic correction of a victim of laughter is intended to bring him back into the group once he has learned the error of his ways. His sin is an offense against reason *in* society, not against faith in gods beyond reason (and thus *beyond* society). When the comic hero Don Quixote dies, his suffering and death transform him into the bearer of the values that really sustain social order as a human order. Such comedy gives men a sanctioned way to think about their problems; they raise their voices in laughter over their own foibles. Comedy censures those who separate men from each other; tragedy destroys those who separate men from the gods. Comedy opens incongruity between means and ends to inquiry and doubt. Tragedy opens the mind to the sacred, a supernatural above and beyond reason which often destroys reason in society. The comic hero is allowed, indeed encouraged, to confront us with our sins. In laughing at him, we learn to laugh at ourselves. Such laughter is sanctioned by the community in the figure of the clown and the fool, once the fool of god, later of the court, and now, in mass communication, the fool of the people.

O

THEORETICAL PROPOSITION 19
Hierarchal communication is a form of address (courtship) among superiors, inferiors, and equals.

(a) Address among superiors, inferiors, and equals is a form of courtship, and courtship is a form of persuasion, a presentation of the self before others who give us our place in society. In the rhetoric of hierarchy, we plead with superiors, inferiors, and equals as a speaker pleads with his audience. In such courtship the response of the audience is given, never taken. In forms of courtship familiar to us—the courtship of superiors and inferiors in feudal society and the patriarchal family, the courtship of God in worship and prayer, and the courtship of woman in romantic love—we treat parents, the supernatural powers we worship, and the women we court, as audiences whom we must "bend" to our desires. Like all rhetoricians, we believe that how we make our appeals to such audiences will determine the success or failure of these appeals.

(b) Such skill requires a knowledge of what to say, when and where to say it, by what means, and before what audiences. When we address parents, gods, colleagues, and inferiors, we know what we want, but we know also that we cannot get it without their response. The rhetoric of social life is always an exhortation to relate in certain ways. When we beseech our beloved to be "reasonable," we mean that we want her to be reasonable *in action*. When we pray to our gods to ward off evil, we want a sign of their *action*. When we plead with parents, we do not want a judgment over the propriety of our request, or the logic of our appeal, but a response that will allow us *to act* in one way or another.

(c) No individual is permanently a member of one public. The worker I boss in the plant bosses me in his role as village official. The child makes me an audience to the play or game he plays with his friends. Student leaders tell me what to do in their decisions on student government. Those who watch one sport take vigorous part at another. We change roles as performer and audience. We become audiences to ourselves, as when we exhort, coach, or beseech ourselves to do something we ought to do. When I pause to read what I have just written, I criticize it from the view of several audiences. My forms must create the order I alone need at the moment I write, but when I sit back to read what I have written I also act as a delegate of other audiences I am anxious to reach. These may be other writers, superiors whose help I need, or general readers. The "I" talking to its "Me" is an internalization of the "I" talking to its "You"—the public other we address as we do the private other internalized within the self. Thus we are not bound to an audience simply because of "traits" of class, caste, age, or sex. As members of an audience we are performers in social dramas, and the parts we play are determined by the nature of the drama as a social drama. The self originates and continues to exist, therefore, in a drama of address. Our various selves become audiences to each other just as they become actors, because only in such address can they move each other to the kind of action believed necessary to order in our relationships.

(d) Audiences may be real, as in a court before which we present ourselves for judgment by our peers, or imagined, as in a day of judgment when we will be judged by our gods. They may exist only in make-believe, as in our day or night dreams, or in memory, where we revive audiences before whom we still plead our case. The long-buried past revives suddenly and sharply when it becomes part of a drama in the present where emotions arise in expression and thus become communicable to ourselves and others. The aged parent is not simply reminiscing about his past to enjoy a tableau of "dear dead days beyond recall"; he is struggling to communicate in a present. As death nears we try to make sense of our lives, to give them form so that, as a member of a family, a nation, a church, or a community, we can pass on to those we love something of life's meaning. We exhort ourselves, as we exhort others, to conform to community and institutional norms. We talk to ourselves in hopes of persuading ourselves to be what society wants us to be. Sometimes we cannot tell ourselves what the various kinds of rhetoric in our society have tried to tell us. At such moments we are not yet persuaded. Only when voices from without speak in the language of voices within is persuasion complete.

(e) Hierarchical address tells us much about the distribution of authority. Speakers may be coy, majestic, arrogant, sly, cunning, sincere, and candid; they may speak of problems we must face in common discussion, not as favored stewards of the Lord to whom truth has been revealed; or they may speak as pundits who know the "laws" of nature, human nature, society, or God. The speaker may address his public as a general public, a public of his peers, or as a self struggling to make order out of conflicting roles. The censor of the dream, the image of the hated and loved authority watching the masochist inflict pain upon himself, the breathren of the early Christian community gathered to witness martyrdom, are great exemplars of "necessary" audiences. Their acceptance, rejection, or indifference determines the actor's judgment of himself, because their response is the experience of a "sacred" principle of social order.

(f) Self-address in art differs from address in the night or day dream because it is given public forms which are communicable to others as well as to the self. In the act of creation the artist addresses himself, but his self-address becomes public once he gives his address form. In dramatic soliloquy, even as in the soliloquy of daily life, we plead our cause with those whom we select to "overhear" us. We address various aspects of the self, not to repress or hide the self from others, but to communicate. All soliloquy is a sanctioned way of expressing problems which we cannot solve and yet must solve if we are to act.

It is a sanctioned way of making public the dilemmas which the private self cannot resolve.

○

THEORETICAL PROPOSITION 20
Disorder in society originates in disorder in communication.

(a) When people cannot communicate they cannot relate. Disrelationships are not *reflected* in communication; they *originate* in communication. If we cannot create forms for communication over new problems, or adjust traditional forms to new conditions of community life, there can be no consensus, and thus no common action. When differences become so great that symbols no longer possess a common meaning, people turn to leaders who do create new symbols of community. It is not differences of station, rank, sex, age, class, or condition that create pathological states in society (as well as in individuals), but a lack of symbols we might use to express differences yet subordinate them to some great social principle of order. The study of the breakdown of symbolic integration (when by integration we mean a resolution, not an obliteration, of differences) constitutes, therefore, the sociopathology of everyday life.

(b) The sociopathology of daily life begins in role conflict among the many public roles which constitute community life. Just as the Ego must make peace among the various demands of the Id and the Superego, so must the public self, the "person" we play in our characteristic social roles, resolve role conflicts. Roles, as well as individuals, are in deep conflict. The priest exhorts us not to kill, yet blesses us as we ready ourselves to wound and kill our enemies in battle; one official of a bank urges us to save, another, to spend; our philosophers tell us to live according to the dictates of reason, yet they also tell us (after Pascal and Hume) that the heart has its reasons which reason cannot know. Even proverbs, the small change of daily conversation, are contradictory, we hear that while a rolling stone gathers no moss, it does gain a beautiful shine.

(c) Social order cannot exist without integrative symbols. Relationships between men depend on names whose meanings are the same for both actor and audience. When symbols of love and brotherhood wane and die, symbols of hate and enmity take their place. Men share evil as well as good; our social relations are integrated through war as well as peace. Hatred, as well as love and doubt, creates social bonds. Only rarely does hatred or love suffice alone. Order, disorder, and counter-order (as in open revolt), define each other, for, as we say: "Laws make crimes." Comradeship in arms is born of fear and hatred of an enemy. His evil is our good, just as our good is his evil. If our good is a sacred principle of social order, his good must be "desanctified." This is done usually by declaring his guilt to be a categorical or "cosmic" guilt, like original sin in Christianity. Thus we are integrated as much through our hatred as through love, and what is deviant or evil for one is normal or good for another. Integrative symbols are born in love of brothers and, at the same time, hatred of enemies.

(d) When we cannot reach others believed necessary to our social being we create fantastic others to give us in make-believe what we cannot have in reality. Fantasy in night and day dreams, like memory of the past, and visions of the future, are used to organize action in a present. We recall and reconstruct pasts "useful" to the creation of legitimations for action in a present, just as we envision futures as goals we "must" reach. In public acts of commemoration of a sacred past or future we forge the great integrative names which bind us together in communication. But when our superiors mount these great dramas for us, and yet remain indifferent to our attempts to share in them, they drive us into fantasy. The American Negro, the poor white, the impecunious adolescent, are urged daily and hourly, by some of the most persuasive magicians known to history, to want everything that money can buy, yet because they are black, unskilled, or too young, they cannot satisfy these exhortations. The young are told they must repress desires created by their businessmen and stirred up constantly by the commercial magicians of the business world.

(e) Businessman, priest, warrior, teacher, gentleman, each in turn struggles to perfect his role and its underlying principle of order. The businessman idealizes trading, the priest holiness, the warrior bravery, the teacher wisdom, the gentleman tactfulness. Each, in turn, seeks to universalize his symbols. In doing so, each throws his role into rivalry and conflict with others. Unless there is some way to resolve conflict among local roles, order cannot be achieved. Such conflict can be achieved only through the use of symbols that transcend the symbols of the contesting parties. Symbols of transcendence in hierarchal systems must become an "upward way" (with a corresponding "downward way" for those upholding alien symbols of transcendence) in which the ambiguities and conflicts of heroes and villains (the personification of contesting principles of social order) can be resolved.

(f) When there are no upward ways to transcendence, conflict can be solved only in violence. Since nations have no international court of appeal to deal with threats of war, conflict must be resolved in battle, just as threats to honor were settled once in the duel. But force itself yields to other principles of order. Russian tanks decorated with doves of peace rolled into Hungary, just as American Marines landed in South American republics to uphold law and order. Through the magic of symbolic transcendence, war becomes a kind of peace.

(g) Modern communication increases symbolic rivalry, competition, and conflict, and greatly weakens the integrative power of local symbols. Even illiterates can watch and hear national and international political leaders on television. People know their national leaders only as "images" staged for them by image makers, just as actors are staged and presented by dramatists and producers. Modern politics thus becomes highly symbolic. We no longer deal with our leaders in person, or, indeed, as persons, but as actors (and, in keeping with this, two actors, Murphy and Reagan of California—the movie capitol of the world—have been elected to high public office) who present themselves to their audiences as protagonists in a struggle to uphold principles of social order.

(h) Although the transcendent ultimates which are believed to uphold principles of social order are reached by upward steps, the final step is reached in a great leap into belief. True believers do not reach an ultimate which is not already there. Few people can sustain trial and error methods of reaching solutions in social life, just as few can endure continual problem-solving as a way of life. Belief in method (of whatever kind) is still belief, and no different from belief in "laws of

132

nature," the "essence" of acts, the "basic drives" of human nature, the efficacy of ideologies, the perfection of language, or the glory of gods. There are technological, as well as religious, mystics.

(i) Tyrannies, as well as democracies, cannot survive wide gaps in communication. For if gods ascend to the heavens, they must also descend to the earth. Their priests must preserve their mystery, but the gods cannot become so remote and terrible that only priests may utter their names in worship, or only those separated from common men through election, training, mortification, and consecration, enter into communication with them. The power of the priests (and their gods) over common men depends not only on their ability to mystify, but on their ability to communicate this mystification in ways they can control. Members of a priestly caste may become so remote from the common people that any kind of contact with them is a defilement which must be cleansed by ritual. Parents may become so strange that children know their commands only through a nurse, or through weird fantasies in which they communicate with surrogate parents. Bureaucratic officials may become so concerned with the majesty of their command, and so insistent on "going through channels" in communication, that they finally disappear as persons and we come to think of bureaucratic consensus as an impersonal process dependent upon regulations (which somehow breed themselves), not upon the will of human beings.

(j) Gaps in communication are also caused by traditions (or myths of origin) and utopias becoming irrelevant to problems that must be solved if we are to sustain order in our relationships. In our time there is a shift in government away from businessmen to intellectuals (or "eggheads" in the vernacular), professors (the "professariat"), professional managers, and men and women recruited from the professions. It cannot be said that businessmen, who have highly skilled commercial magicians in advertising, and who control large areas of communication, have failed to communicate with the people. As any Sunday newspaper shows, business communication (the "Big Sale") is far greater in range, intensity, and scope than that of any other institution. Even at Christmas, our great holy day, it is business, not the church, whose message is communicated widely and intensively. The disquiet we feel about business control of communication is certainly not born of neglect, the remoteness of our business gods, or the strangeness of their language, but of concern over the relevance of money to social order. We are not so sure as we once were that we can spend our way to heaven.

(k) Another cause of failure in communication arises from confusing *all* communication with the kind of communication common to ritual, or what the anthropologists term the "sacred." Sacred communication reveals a paradoxical world. A worshiper does not believe that he creates the sacred beings he seeks in prayer. The child does not think he is creating his parents as he names them and communicates with them. The lover addressing his beloved does not feel that her charm and beauty exist only in his naming of them. And certainly Hitler's followers did not believe that his power and glory came from the way he communicated with them, or the way they, his people, communicated with him. Communication in ritual is communication of a truth which is believed to be "beyond" communication. In religion, the holy power creates communication but is not dependent on communication. As St. Paul said: "I live, yet not I, but Christ liveth in me." The word of God who speaks through men whose tongues differ in disputation is not to be confused with God's word. For, as we know from the Tower of Babel (Genesis 11), men speak in different tongues because God punished them for making a tower which would reach into the heavens.

(l) The paradox in all ritual is that the mystery which is beyond communication can be kept alive only in communication. When we cease to communicate with our gods, they cease to exist. The sacred world of gods, principles, or ideologies, on which social order is based, is sacred only so long as its numinous qualities are kept alive in the daily lives of men. The sacred must be kept alive in change as well as in permanence, just as, on a secular level of being, protocol, etiquette, and manners must be adaptable to new, as well as to old, situations. We must have order in our relationships, and this order must be founded on great principles personified in social dramas in which we play our parts. We must have order based on solving problems, not avoiding them, and we must not punish those who draw our attention to them, or teach us to use doubt as a means of inquiry into how we may meet our problems. Struggle for order must be based on the belief that relationships are created by symbols of change as well as by symbols of permanence. For no two experiences are alike, hence names derived from one act never quite fit another. There must be sanctioned and sacred ways of passing from one condition of life to another, and of changing names when we do so.

○

THEORETICAL PROPOSITION 21
Social disorder and counter-order arise in guilt which originates in disobedience of those whose commandments are believed necessary to social order.

(a) Although principles of social order are personified in the enactment of hierarchy among superiors, inferiors, and equals, "pure" principles of hierarchy do not depend on the personal charisma of gods or heroes. Superior and inferior alike feel themselves subordinate to some great principle in whose name each acts. The private who trudges along in the mud does not hate the general who rides by in a staff car so long as he feels they are both serving their country, defending their homes, or struggling to sustain an ideology which is the foundation of moral and social order. Great and small alike "serve" an ideal in whose name each acts. Disobedience is not simply refusal to obey the commands of a leader, or the voice of duty from within, but an active threat to the social order that makes common action possible. So long as a group is significant to us, disobedience threatens the group. This is as true (in a social sense) of a game played by rules, whose power comes from common agreement among players, as it is of sacred rites which establish communion with dark and mysterious gods who punish disobedience with eternal damnation.

(b) While guilt arises out of offences against divine powers, and these powers must be personified in social drama in which repentance and regeneration takes place, all such powers are themselves subject finally to the power of "principles," and "laws" based on such principles. In all fully developed systems of social order, gods and men alike are subject to law. In such cosmologies social order is a reign of law in which every act is a detail in an unending chain of cause and effect.

Every wrong deed or word, every evil intention and thought, must work out its result in society quite independent of any power beyond the power of social order itself. Faith and reason meet in belief in such laws, for belief in the rationality of the laws of society can be "demonstrated" to uphold social order. Thus, in classical China disobedience of parents created a "disturbance of the celestial routine." In our daily lives this is reflected in the shame and embarrassment we feel in the violation of decorum. Bad manners are violations of a "law," the law of etiquette. Such laws hold our world together, and it is in their name that we communicate with significant others who give us our sense of social being. The naughty child who disobeys his parents is made to feel that he threatens the existence of the family, and since the family is the child's world, his disobedience not only affects his parents as individuals by making them uphappy, but angers a remote and terrible diety who must be placated if there is to be order in the child's world.

(c) Whether we "obey" the "laws" of nature, man, society, god, or language, we do so through symbols in communication. And since communication depends on the use of symbols within some kind of social drama in which identification between superiors, inferiors, and equals must become a consensually validated bond, our capacity (and opportunity) to play a part in such dramas determines our feelings of failure or success in dealing with guilt. Embarrassment over doing "the wrong thing" at the dinner table, shame over betrayal of a friend's confidence, and deep guilt over sin originate in a sense of being judged by those we have wronged but with whom we wish to identify. These judgments range from the judgments of parents (or the whole family) to the solitary judgments we pass on ourselves for breaking a law of honor we believed to be a law of our social world. When we no longer identify with our judges their power dies. Even force must rest on belief. The victim must believe in his guilt, and in the right of his executioners to punish him. When such belief wanes, victimage passes into revolt. The revolutionary is an enemy, not a victim.

(d) In social experience, frustration, anxiety, and guilt are not the same. Frustration arises from not being able to communicate; anxiety from concern over whether we can, or have, communicated with others whose judgment determines our self-esteem; guilt from the judgment of authorities whom we accept as guardians of social order. Frustration turns us back into ourselves because we cannot communicate with real others who might absolve us of embarrassment, shame, or guilt. The burden of guilt originates and is sustained through communication with others (real or imagined) whose judgment weighs heavily upon us. It is not only the communication of judgment, but the redemption and atonement following judgment which makes guilt so powerful a factor in social order. The criminal is not frustrated, nor is he suffering from his disobedience. He has *organized* his disobedience. He has, so to say, made social order out of disorder. In his eyes, the law-abiding citizen is the "cause" of his criminal actions. Who would be a gambler if men did not gamble, a prostitute if men did not "cheat" on their wives, and, in the far reaches of such a question, how can there be evil in a society ruled by a wise, powerful, and good ruler, unless he permits it? Why do we execute a man who murders one man, and reward another who murders millions in the name of his country?

(e) The criminal is not necessarily "disorganized" or "guilt-laden." Indeed, he may suffer far less from social and psychological disorganization than those who cannot resolve the incongruities of a social order in which a good ruler uses bad means to keep order. We are not guilty in our social relations so long as we can ascribe the responsibility for what we do to something outside the social and moral order which binds us to each other. We may say that evil is a power in nature, a "law of nature" which is "outside" of man and beyond his control. Or we say that evil originates in human nature, and talk of "Old Adam," or the Id. Or we say the opposite: we teach that man is born innocent but is corrupted by society. Or, like the Manichaeans, and later Luther, we argue that evil comes not from God, who, as Luther tells us, is good, and wishes us well, but from the devil, "who is the author of plagues, fevers, etc." (*Table Talk*, DXCVIII). Or, finally, we may say that evil comes from the bad use of language, as when Milton warns us that when language in common use in any country becomes irregular and depraved, ruin and degradation in society soon follows. Thus, whether we ground our principles of social order in nature, human nature, God, or language and art, we can always explain disorder by some principle "outside of," and hostile to, our principle of order, and thus symbolize our guilt in some evil being whose destruction alone can save us.

(f) When the principle of disorder is embodied in a "perfect enemy," that is, an enemy like the "Prince of Darkness," as the devil was called, we do not feel guilt when we punish, torture, and kill him. For in doing this we destroy, not only another human being, but a *principle* of disorder whose continued existence and power threaten the life of our society. To be "just" to Jews in Hitler's Germany was *not* a sign of goodness (that is, to Hitler's Germans), but of criminal weakness. Even in a benign democracy we warn citizens that ignorance of the law does not excuse the crime. And do we not hear too about "sins" of omission? Germans under Hitler did not feel guilty about their treatment of the Jew, for the Jew had been declared (first by Streicher) to be "beyond" the pale of humanity, and then returned to humanity by Hitler as the embodiment of the evil principle which had caused Germany's woes. Hitler said that, while Streicher was reproached for his degradation of the Jew (in his *Stürmer*), the truth was that "he *idealized* the Jew. The Jew is baser, fiercer, more diabolical than Streicher depicted him." Punishment of heretics under the Inquisition was really a "merciful act," for if they were not forced to confess their heresy they would suffer the endless agony of eternal damnation, and "contaminate" Christian principles of order.

(g) Guilt feelings lead to a search for communication with those who can absolve us of our guilt. The first step in this is the symbolization of guilt in some form which makes possible confrontation of our guilt. Until such form is supplied there can be no public communication over guilt. The great suffering in guilt comes from not knowing in what our guilt consists, because we have not been able to communicate with anyone about our guilt or to communicate directly with those who make us feel guilty. When parents make a child feel guilty without telling him why he is guilty, or tyrants hold a prisoner incommunicado, or priests tell us we are born in sin, conceived in sin, live in sin, and must therefore face eternal punishment, they do not stop our search for ways to rid ourselves of guilt, but only force us to communicate with others who promise us release from our suffering. In dreams, day-dreams, and all kinds of make-believe, we create dim and fantastic others whose meanings still elude analysis, yet even the shadowy figures of the dream, like the horrible grotesques of the nightmare, are symbolic constructions whose meanings are born in attempts at communication, however hidden and secret. If only the shadowy other could understand us, we would be saved. But who is this other?

(h) As the principles of social order become more abstract and subject to laws based on reason, the need for personification of such abstract principles increases. For even when man is "determined" by social laws he can know but cannot create, he must act out these laws in some kind of social drama. When authorities make laws and constitutions, or plan utopias based in Edenic pasts or futures, they define social order as they define disorder. Authorities not only expect obedience and disobedience, they name them and thus create them. In the Christian drama of authority, legitimation of social authority is achieved through a mediator, Christ, who leaves the perfect realm of order to enter the realm of disorder, which is the realm of action. Christ, the mediator, is a sacrificial victim whose suffering and death restores communication between the perfect principle of social order, God, and the imperfect principle of disorder, the world of men.

(i) When there is no community drama of social order, with a struggle between a hero and a villain who personify good and bad principles of order, then chaos, not disorder, results. The emotional counterpart in the individual of chaos in society is the kind of deep anxiety which passes into "formless dread." Punishment in itself does not cause anxiety; indeed, the child may yearn to be punished by parents who pay little attention to him. So long as the parents punish and reward there is order in the world of the child. When the parents withdraw, and the child cannot communicate with his gods, there is no order in his life and he is miserable. As anxiety increases, the child's agony becomes so great that he will do anything, even commit crimes, to attract the attention of his gods. It is only as the child learns a new kind of authority, the authority of rules, and subjects himself to a new will, the will of equals, that he learns to live in community without being ruled by supernatural powers beyond reason. But even the most fortunate child never forgets the pain and agony of chaos, the formless dread of not being able to communicate with those who alone could bring order into his life.

(j) The basic social reason for guilt is the belief that we have been cut off from powers who uphold the principle of social order on which our society rests. Belief in the absolute power of authority is born in communication. Our sense of reality in social relations comes from the response of others, just as the sense of reality of the other comes from our responses to him. Many others respond to us, but it is the significant others—parents, friends, teachers, loved ones, children, wives, priests—whose response shapes and forms the self. Competition, rivalry, conflict, and hate, as well as communion, brotherhood, and love, are common to every attempt to communicate with those who can help us to become the self that we want to become. The problem, or at least the social problem of the self in a democratic society, is how to reconcile the conflicting claims of those whose response is significant to us and yet must be allowed, indeed *encouraged*, to differ with us. The problem in authoritarian relationships is how to communicate with authorities who admit of no competition, and yet become so remote in their majesty and power that we are never sure of how well we are communicating, or if we are communicating at all.

O

THEORETICAL PROPOSITION 22
Society must provide us with means to expiate guilt arising from sins of disobedience.

(a) Expiatory rites purge the individual of guilt over disobedience as they purge his society of the principle of evil which "caused" the disobedience. From an authoritarian social view man disobeys his superiors because of malign and evil powers which lead men to break the commandments of their lords; from the egalitarian view men disobey just laws because they are ignorant of the good life which obedience to such laws will bring. But whether authoritarian or democratic, a society rids itself of guilt and anxiety through the performance of various kinds of social dramas which make fear, anxiety, and guilt manageable. In ritual drama, we destroy guilt symbolically, but even in warfare, a highly motor phase of action, the defeat and death of an enemy is symbolized as a defeat and death of the evil principle which threatened our social order. We Americans have nothing against the Russian people, but we must destroy them to destroy the principles of communism which threaten our democracy. The Russians, in turn, are champions of democracy, "peoples' democracy," yet they discuss an "ideal" nuclear weapon as one which will not destroy the materials but only the people of the "capitalistic democracies."

(b) Expiation is not achieved through argument or preaching, but through taking part in some kind of social drama in which we banish, punish, kill, or destroy something or somebody which personifies, and thus objectifies (in a dramatic sense), the principle that threatens social order. Even in its most benign moments democratic society is not held together by political argument but by a drama of debate, disputation, bickering, in short, by an agonistic struggle for political power through public and private victimage. Expiation is a purgation because it is an enactment. The principle of disorder is destroyed so that the principle of order may live. Expiatory killings range from the killing of real victims to the symbolic degradation and killing of a comic or grotesque figure whose death is greeted with laughter. Hitler's Germans killed Jews to "purify Aryan blood." The "bad guy" is killed nightly on TV to make us enjoy as well as believe in the triumph of good principles of social order. The slapstick clown is chased, beaten, shot, and thrown away like a rag to assure us that such fellows need not be tolerated by decent people like ourselves who struggle to uphold the proprieties. But in every case, the victim, whether "real" or "fictive," is symbolic of some evil we seek to extirpate from our society.

(c) Expiatory acts are both inner and outer, local and universal, individual and social, institutional and communal. But for inner, local, individual, and institutional expiation to be effective there must be final or ultimate expiatory acts which purge the social order itself. No individual can purge himself of guilt; at least he cannot do so without risking severe repression and dissociation. Expiation is a social act, a drama played before audiences (real and imaginary) who represent the various groups and institutions in the community with whom we seek to identify. Such dramas have a beginning, a middle, and an end. The end is reached in presentation before the greatest audience of all: beings (corporeal or incorporeal) who are the court of final appeal before which we uphold our principles of social order. Society provides us with many such audiences, but whether the audience is a priest, psychoanalyst, counselor, judge, jury, or a larger audience of sectarians or friends, the power of such audiences to expiate our sins derives from their symbolization of a higher power, the power of social order itself.

(d) Basic to all expiation is belief in vicarious atonement, as well as belief in vicarious sin or disobedience. Christians are taught that in his suffering, Christ expiated our sins. Lincoln, a political leader, suffered the burdens of democracy. "Honest" Abe, the laughing god of the Frontier, is now a suffering demigod (and perhaps even a god) of American democracy, as the laughing hero of Athens, Socrates, became a god of Athenian democracy. Hamlet, an aesthetic hero, becomes the "modern man" who suffers and dies for our right to doubt and question. Huck Finn takes to the river and the woods to live with a tribal outcast, the Negro, to keep alive in the wilderness the principles of American brotherhood which he could not keep alive in the Mississippi valley towns of 1850. Others sin, and also atone for us: Adam sinned for all men. In democratic society the individual is responsible for all the crimes of his society, for the suffering and sin of one is the suffering and sin of all.

(e) The "symbolic other," and the use of things as substitutes for persons, have been described in a context far different from religious experience in the substitution of fantasy for reality in sexual fetishism. Krafft-Ebing describes how the whole sexual life of an individual may be absorbed by a fetish. Sexual interest may become so concentrated on some particular article of female attire, such as the shoe, that the lustful idea of this object can become completely separated from the idea of woman, and thus attain an independent value as a symbol. In all forms of fully developed dress-fetishism the article of clothing alone is used for the excitation and satisfaction of the sexual instinct. As the power of the fetish increases, the sight and manipulation of a shoe or a hankerchief affords more satisfaction than coitus. Restif de la Bretonne, from whose autobiographical account of his shoe-fetishism we have fashioned our model of sexual fetishism, describes vividly the power of the shoe as a symbol, as when he tells us how the sight of women's shoes arranged in a row made him tremble with pleasure as he blushed and lowered his eyes as if in the presence of the women themselves.

In case 113 of his *Psychopathia Sexualis*, Krafft-Ebing describes the development of the shoe-fetishism of Mr. v.P. "At the age of seventeen he had been seduced by a French governess, but coitus was not permitted; so that intense mutual excitement (mutual masturbation) was all that was possible. In this situation his attention was attracted by her very elegant boots. . . . In the society of the opposite sex the only thing that interested him was the shoe, and that only when it was elegant, of the French style, with heels, and of a brilliant black, like the original. In relations with prostitutes, Mr. v.P. required a shoe that was elegant and chic, carefully washed and starched petticoats, and black hose. Nothing else in woman interested him." And as if to emphasize the power of the symbol, Krafft-Ebing states in italics: "*He was absolutely indifferent to the naked foot.*" As this patient's fetish took hold over him he "was so under the domination of his boot-ideas that he would even blush when boots were talked about." In case 114, we hear of a patient who could reach orgasm only when he "revelled in the memory of shoe-scenes (the shoes of his schoolmistress)." He married, but in spite of lively erections when he thought of his wife's shoes, he was absolutely impotent. To cure this, his doctor advised him to "hang a shoe up over his bed, and look at it fixedly during coitus, at the same time imagining his wife to be a shoe." This, we are told, freed the patient from epileptic attacks, and made him potent "so that he could have coitus about once a week."

But despite Krafft-Ebing's emphasis on a purely sexual root for fetishism, the data he offers as evidence does not sustain his sexual theory. As he points out, it is not just any shoe or dress material that makes sexual expression possible, but only special dress materials such as fur, velvets, and silks. The use of these materials to increase sexual feelings cannot be explained on a sexual basis alone. "These cases differ from the foregoing instances of erotic dress-fetishism, in this, that these materials, unlike female linen, do not have any close relation to the female body; and, unlike shoes and gloves, they are not related to certain parts of the person which have peculiar symbolic significance."* Moreover, these cases "cannot be due to an accidental association . . . for these cases form an entire group having the same object." What is this object? Krafft-Ebing resolutely rejects a linkage between status and sex as an explanation of the power of furs, velvets and silks, as symbols which stir sexual desire. He tells us that Sacher-Masoch (whose novel *Venus in Furs* supplies us with the description of dominance and submission in love which was used to develop the concept of masochism) "explains that fur (ermin) is the symbol of sovereignty," but that this explanation is "unsatisfactory and far-fetched." "Unsatisfactory" to Krafft-Ebing, a good mechanist, because for him the sex act was a matter of stimulus and response, not of action

* Richard von Krafft-Ebing, *Psychopathia Sexualis* (New York: Pioneer Publications, 1947), pp. 268-9.

and passion. As in so much psychiatric writing, sex could condition a social relationship, but a social relationship (*how* we play our sexual roles) could not condition sex.

○

THEORETICAL PROPOSITION 23
Victimage is the basic form of expiation in the communication of social order.

(a) The basic social function of atonement, in religious as well as social drama, is the re-establishment of communication with authorities who are believed to sustain social order. We do penance for our sins, as others appointed by the society do penance for us, to cleanse our spirit of disobedience so that we can communicate in purity of heart and mind, and thus live again in order with our fellows because we are living in obedience to authority. Disobedience destroys communication with our gods and authorities, and when we cannot communicate with them we cannot learn to act in the name of the great social principle of order which binds our gods and ourselves alike. In Psalms, 22:1, in the Gospels of Matthew and Mark, and in Bach's *St. Matthew's Passion*, we hear in the cry of Jesus—"My God, my God, why hast thou forsaken me?"—the desolate cry of those whose lives have lost all meaning in the silence of their gods. This moment, the climactic moment of the Passion of Christ, and one of the great moments in our art as well as our religion, is a moment of terror over desertion by God.

(b) It is not fear of punishment, but fear of being out of communication with those who create a sense of order in our world which is unbearable. We must communicate with our rulers and gods to discover what they want us to do as expiation for our sins, just as we must keep in communication with them to know their commandments. The power of our priests is based mainly on their ability to communicate with our gods; but in this priests are no different from any group of officials who know how to communicate with authority. The ward boss in an American city has little power in his own right, but as one in communication with the "boys downtown" he has great power. Petty officials in a bureaucracy are of small importance as individuals, but they have the power of initiating a message to the head officials. Go-betweens of all kinds—brokers in modern business, marriage brokers, negotiators, arbitrators—all have power simply because they are able to keep channels of communication open.

Since the power of all go-betweens vanishes once they open communication, it is to their advantage to increase difficulties in communication, or at least to create the impression that only the greatest skill and effort can overcome difficulties in communication. Thus whenever we must "go through channels" we soon find that we can reach "higher-ups" only through intermediaries who alone can send our communication to the "higher-ups." Yet at the same time we find that intermediaries increase difficulties in communicating by increasing the mystery and glamour of superiors with whom we must communicate. Wonder and awe increase the majesty and sublimity of our superiors, but they also make communication more difficult. As Gracian admonishes his monks who seek to win friends and influence people in the world outside the monastery: "You imitate the Divine way when you cause men to wonder and watch." The art of ruling in the world, as in heaven, is the art of mystification.

(c) The first step in seeking to re-establish communication with authorities whose silence cannot be borne is purgation through victimage. We create victims whose degradation, suffering, and death are a kind of petition to the gods to open themselves to communication. Victims sacrificed in horrible and fearful ways also serve as a communication of power among men. When we offer something or someone as a victim of sacrifice, we petition our gods to attend to us, and in sacrifice of something we value we prove to our gods that we are humble and obedient to them. When authorities mount public dramas of victimage in which they inflict horrible tortures on victims, they make a show of power to inferiors whose obedience is necessary to their power. Right cannot exist without might, and those who would rule must see to it that their control of might is staged in terrible and awesome ways, so that inferiors will be convinced of their power and majesty. Those who believe in the power of authorities to sustain social order must be assured through acts (as well as arguments) that their authorities are keeping their majesty and power in good repair. In the mystery dramas of feudal times God descended to earth amid sounds of thunder, as the devil lept from a pit belching the fumes of hell amid the terrible cries of the damned. Tyrants who would rule us through the charisma of their person, or the awesome power of a social principle "beyond reason," often dramatize their power in order to strike terror in us.

(d) Symbolic victimage in tragic and comic art differs from social victimage as we experience it in war, the execution of criminals, or other forms of staging power through violence. Society uses art as well as religion to create attitudes which dispose us to act in certain ways. We see this in the creation of attitudes toward manners and fashions as well as in the great conflicts wherein we seek to destroy enemies whose death guarantees our survival. An enemy who is shooting at us is not only a symbolic victim; his bullets are very real, and if we are to survive we must shoot back. The enemy becomes a victim only when he is symbolized through sacrifice as a means of propitiation—as when prisoners of war are tortured and killed to assuage the anger of the gods, or when the enemy is depicted as an evil monster who will rape our sisters, wives, and mothers, kill our children, and torture civilians. Art "conditions" us by giving us symbolic villains we can revile, curse, and hate, just as it gives us heroes we can praise, bless, and love. But the symbols of art are human symbols, for they deal with the concrete individual acting his part in the community of the world in order to achieve order among men.

(e) The "perfect" victim is one whose power is so great that we must summon all our energy, cunning, skill, luck, and piety, to defeat him, or one so beloved that in sacrificing him we give up something of great value. In struggle against the perfect villain, or in struggle within ourselves to give up pleasures we cherish most, we must subordinate individual desires to the common good. In community ritual drama the death of the perfect victim is the death of a total threat to our community. As villain, devil, or demon, the victim must be so powerful and cunning that his suffering and death will be a total purgation of the community. Thus, Hitler "perfected" the Jew as a victim. For only if the Jew could be made into the "most diabolic creature in existence," as Hitler described him, could his suffering and death purge the German community. The more monstrous the crimes imputed to the Jew, the more virtuous it was to hate, torture, and kill him, and the greater the burden of German sins he could carry. Streicher prepared the Jew as a symbolic scapegoat who could be used for symbolic cleansing by any German community, or any community that wished to identify with Germany. Hitler made the Jew a real scapegoat whose torture and death cleansed the German community of sin because it made possible the confrontation in reality of what had been possible before only in fantasy. Beside the villain whom we hate stands the hero whom we love. Abraham's sacrifice to God of his beloved son and Jesus' sacrifice of himself for man, like Socrates' sacrifice of himself to Athens, are total sacrifices which speak to the gods of total obedience and love.

(f) Beside the "perfect" victim stand many "imperfect" or partial victims, and in a highly competitive society such as ours, one man's hero may be another's villain. Thus the ideal customer, the business-man's hero, who spends his way to heaven at Christmas, may be a villain to those upholding holy vows of poverty. The soldier, who obeys orders blindly, will be stupid and even "sinful" to the intellec-tual, who believes that reason lives in doubt. The priest's leap into the supernatural, like the technologist's faith in technique, horrifies the humanist, who believes in keeping relationships between means and ends open to constant criticism. And since social action takes place in agonistic forms, the hero must find an antagonist who will serve to bring to light the good qualities of the hero in his struggle for mastery. The intellectual cannot dramatize the virtue of doubt as a way of wis-dom without showing the social disorder which arises from the busi-nessman's submission to the "iron law of profit." The businessman, in turn, shows how the intellectual's dedication to doubt and question destroys capacity for action. We make our opponent's principles dark and evil in order to throw our own principles of order into brilliant relief.

O

THEORETICAL PROPOSITION 24
Victimage of the self is determined by social victimage.

(a) Victims exist within the self, as well as in society. But for the purposes of constructing a model of human relationships based on communication, the "inner victims," the inner selves whom we punish and mortify in various ways, may be considered re-enactments of "outer" or social selves. Where there are "total" victims available to us, we turn inward only to marshal our strength against a known enemy. We turn inward to prepare for outward action, not to stay within the self in reverie or fantasy. Thus if we believe, like Luther, that Satan produces all the maladies which afflict mankind, we do not brood over whether Satan exists; we know he is our enemy, and we buckle on the armor of faith to attack him. To fight without fear we must overcome the "mystery" of our enemy; he must be reduced (through some kind of "desanctification") to human proportions so we can act against him with confidence.

Thus Luther advises us to seek out the society of boon companions, and to drink, play, talk bawdily, and amuse ourselves. One must sometimes commit a sin out of hate and contempt for the devil, "so as not to give him the chance to make one scrupulous over mere nothings, [for] one is too frightened of sinning, one is lost. . . ." And then like a doughty warrior who knows his enemy and longs to come to grips with him, Luther cries: "Oh, if I could find some really good sin that would give the devil a toss!" It is only in struggle against sin that we become strong, and know God's blessing, for "God gives to the devil and to witches power over human creatures in two ways: first, over the ungodly, when he will punish them by reason of their sins; secondly, over the just and godly, when he intends to try whether they will be content in the faith, and remain in his obedience." As we struggle, we prove our strength to audiences—sacred as well as secular—whose approval we must have to sustain social order.

(b) The "outer" victim can be brought into consciousness only if he can be confronted. Such confrontation makes possible conscious communication with real others, for only in such confrontation can we communicate and thus act together. The "inner" victim can be brought into consciousness only through processes of mortification in which we create an "inner" victim whom we can punish. We act inwardly to discipline a self that threatens order within the self. When the "inner" and the "outer" victims are the same, that is, when the qualities of the self we punish correspond with those punished by the society, we experience profound integration of our private and public selves. Hitler's Germans were taught that profit motives were ignoble, since the highest calling of man was that of the soldier, and that, in the perfect

German soldier, Germans, and, indeed, the world, would find their soul. At the same time the Nazis personified Jews as devils who corrupted through money, and Marxists as devils who corrupted the German soul through reducing "spiritual" motives to economic motives. Nazi punishment of the Jew and the Marxist was a punishment of profit motives which conflicted with noble "soldierly" motives within the German soul. Since "inner" and "outer" enemies were the same, attack on one was attack on the other.

(c) We learn to act toward the self as we learn to act toward others. We address inner as we do outer selves. When I stop writing this page to read what I have written, I take the role of an audience over against the self which has just stopped writing. I address myself, and, as in all address, what I say to myself is said in rhetorical expression within a dramatic structure. Even the dream has many moments of address. The dream is often a kind of dumb show, a pantomime, but it is a drama; just as the pantomime itself is a form of drama (and a very ancient one), and an important part of every face-to-face communication. We learn to address our various inner selves in terms of how we are taught to address others who personify our sins. If we are taught that lust and gluttony are sins, we punish such desires within ourselves, as we punish them in the others. If, as the ideal courtier, La Rochefoucauld, teaches us, envy is an ignoble emotion, we guard ourselves against expressing it, and experience shame when we feel it arising within us. If, on the other hand, we are taught that envy of other's possessions is a virtue, as we are in a society based on individual spending, then we must be made to feel inferior for not being envious of our betters. In a society of heroic spenders, we communicate our success through spending. As modern Christians we become guilty over the poverty of those who cannot spend, just as Christians of Wesley's time were guilty over the wealth of those who could spend.

(d) But when private and public victims do not match it becomes very difficult to act. If I must punish in public what I really admire in private, I am soon in deep trouble with myself. There are many incongruities, and much disorder, among the roles we are asked to play in our community and institutional life. Bankers, the sacred officials of a society where money is a symbol of community, exhort us to save so we can spend. As trained killers returning from war we must learn that to kill a civilian is a crime, even though only a few short weeks ago killing and wounding other human beings was a virtue. No society or institution is without incongruities of this kind. It is not the absence of incongruities between ends and means, but how they are resolved which determines social integration. They can only be resolved through destruction (private, within the self; public, within the community) of what we believe to be the cause of disorder. This is the role of the ancient and ever-present figure of the victim upon whose back we load our own evil in the belief that in sacrificing him we destroy our evil. Such victims, like the Jew in Hitler's Germany, are sanctioned victims, and when there are enough of them, and they are sufficiently powerful as "total" victims, they can be used to purge our social order, and thus ourselves, of fear, anxiety, and guilt. When our society fails to supply us with such victims, we must find them within ourselves. Until we have destroyed our guilt and fear, we cannot communicate openly and freely, and thus cannot act as citizens of a democratic community.

IV
METHODOLOGICAL PROPOSITIONS

Methodological propositions are supposed to demonstrate how we know what we say we know. If we say that social relations arise, and continue to exist, in the sociodramas of everyday life, how can we observe these relationships? The test of these propositions is simple. Do they tell us anything about concrete human acts in society? What forms of social life can we distinguish through their use? How do these forms affect social integration?

METHODOLOGICAL PROPOSITION 1
All statements about the structure and function of the symbolic act must be demonstrated to exist in the symbolic context of the act.

(a) Sociologists must do more than apply a model of association to symbolic expression and then "discover" that what we say exists in society does so because it exists in the model, or that what we discover in symbolic expression exists because it exists in society. When we say that social order arises in communication in which we relate as superiors, inferiors, or equals, and pass from one position to another, without, at the same time, showing how this really occurs in a given body of symbols, we are using symbolic contexts for illustration, not demonstration. For if we know the social meaning of a symbolic expression before we examine it, the expression tells us nothing we do not already know. Thus, if we "know" that images of climbing a stair are really images of social climbing, or that all images of authority are really images of the father, the context of the social drama we are analyzing merely illustrates what we already know. But how do we know it?

(b) The "social facts" of symbolic action (in either purely symbolic acts, as in drama, or phases of action where symbols are used, as in business or war) are the symbols themselves. Unless we assume that symbols simply fall into random patterns, or that symbolic meaning is determined by extra-symbolic factors (biological, economic, or religious, as the case may be), we must explain how symbols function as symbols. This is not to say that meaning in society is the same as meaning in symbols, but only to stress that the function of symbols as symbols must be taken into account whenever we discuss social relationships in any context of experience.

(c) Symbols are the most easily, and the most directly, observable "facts" in human relationships, for they are the forms in which relationships take place. Extra-symbolic explanations of social aspects of conduct require a much greater degree of "interpretation" than do symbolic explanations. We can only infer what a gang of juvenile delinquents did, even though we cite as "facts" reports (as in case histories, interviews, life histories, etc.) of what they say they did, or an interviewer says they did, or what others say about what interviewers say about what delinquents said. Often there is no verbatim record of interviews. We know only what the interviewer "reports." In the "non-scientific" study of literature, data such as texts and art works does not depend on what someone says about them. We are not told what is "in" *Hamlet* without reference, or with small reference, to the text. Literary analysis of symbolic work is a demonstration; sociological analysis is often nothing more than an illustration, or a report of how a study was conducted. Yet, sociologists (certainly American sociologists) think of the symbols gathered in interviews as "clear" and "factual," while the highly public symbols of communication are subjective and hazy! But if we use symbols as our "facts" (and a good many sociologists do) then we must admit that we get our sense of acts as facts from our sense of symbols as facts, rather than vice versa.

(d) Symbolic facts, just as other facts, do not leap into our minds simply because we stare hard at them. They become facts because some kind of sociological relationship among symbols is inferred. It is easy to smuggle interpretations into our use of symbolic facts, as we do when we talk about rites as a way to achieve perfection in conduct through relating what we do on earth as but a step toward what is done in the supernatural realm of heaven. But as long as there is a symbolic text available to which we can return, possibilities exist of methodological improvement. For then *how* conclusions were reached —that is, in terms of what data interpreted by what methods and techniques—can be studied.

(e) In using symbolic material as proofs of hypotheses, three steps must be taken. Proof must always be grounded in reference to symbolic usage as it exists within the symbolic material used as reference; inference and interpretation added to such usage must be clearly indicated; and, finally, reasons must be given for selecting and interpreting in one way, and not in another. We must clarify our interpretations so that others will know what they are.

(f) Analogies must be used carefully in sociological interpretation of symbolic material. The proof of analogy is *not* what we know about its analogical source, and *certainly not* what the technique used in the non-social field from which the analogy was drawn tells us; the proof of analogy is what it tells us about the social aspects of the symbolic material under consideration. If we discover the term "rite" or "class" used in two contexts, we should not begin by asking what esoteric "symbolic" meanings a rite might have in religious, economic, psychoanalytic, or physical terminology, but begin with the observable "fact" that the term "rite" bridges two or more contexts of meaning. And even if we do begin with a set meaning for rite, and describe just what rite means, the hard facts of research will show that this symbol has been determined by a certain set of associations in a given context. These sets are forms of symbolic relatedness which must be studied in different and changing contexts. These forms (like the forms noted in concordances familiar to us in literary studies) must be noted initially without inference or interpretation. We must avoid the temptation of making them into purely terministic correlations which can be used so easily for analogical exegesis. Such correlations sometimes leave us with no way of fitting our symbolic clusters, or associations, into an over-all scheme of interpretation. But, at least, in this empiric notation we have the factuality of a symbolic chart to which we can return at will as new questions arise.

(g) "Ideal-type" constructions are useful in the interpretation of applied symbolic material. But we must be careful to indicate their range of usefulness. Weber's ideal Puritan who earns to praise the Lord and finds grace in his calling, tells us very little about this Puritan's American descendants who now fulfill their calling through heroic spending as well as pious earning. Freud's patriarchal family tells us little about American matriarchy. Simmel's image of sociation as "being-with-for-and-against each other" tells us little about the communicative context of such interaction. Malinowski's "context of experience" does not include symbolic experience as a part of the context. We must not derive social meanings from "constructs" which we have already ascribed to experience. A sociolinguistic methodology stands or falls by its usefulness in showing *how* to find, in various kinds of expressive contexts, the social meanings we say exist in such experience. Expressive contexts have many meanings. The sociologist must distinguish clearly just which is "social" about his analysis of symbols. If he uses class, status, institution, style of life, custom, as his element of social analysis, he ought to say so, and, further, he ought to construct clear models of sociation based on these elements.

(h) Symbolic expression is determined by the function of language as language, as well as by its function as communication in society. Men communicate to create social order through hierarchy, but how they communicate is also determined by hierarchy. Whatever we say about hierarchy is said by abstracting hierarchy from communicative contexts, just as what is said about communication as a social fact is said in terms of a hierarchal or some other social context. But if we are to create a sociological methodology of symbolic analysis we cannot allow linguistic concerns to overshadow sociological. The canons of dramatic form used in Shakespeare's historical plays are not the same as the canons used in mounting a drama of hierarchy in the coronation of the Queen of England, or of the investiture into office of the President of the United States. Shakespeare was writing a play; the citizens in charge of the coronation, or the presidential inauguration, are upholding the majesty of a social office.

(i) If we say that forms of interaction are determined by role-taking, we must have a model of role-taking which can be applied to concrete social experience. When we say that statuses and roles are analogous to the particle of mechanics, and are not attributes of the actor, we cannot form hypotheses for dealing with sociation in terms of actors playing roles. For if our model is constructed to deal with motion, it is a mechanical model, and such a model cannot be applied to the kind of non-mechanical qualities of experience common to the symbolic experience of emotions. Forms of sociation which function "like" play, games, conversation, or drama cannot have a mechanical structure. For if interaction is like drama, it is not like a machine, and on the other hand, if interaction is mechanical, it is not dramatic. Descriptions of the structure of an act which are not taken from the same field of experience as the function of the act cannot serve as a sociological model of human relatedness. We cannot say that roles "gear" or "mesh" without reducing emotion to motion. A combination of mechanical and dramatic images becomes a kind of monstrous chimera. Mechanical images of interaction simply reify techniques taken from the study of motion in nature, not of man in society.

O

METHODOLOGICAL PROPOSITION 2

Sociological explanations of symbols must be grounded in the analysis of social drama as a drama of hierarchy.

(a) The social "fact" of a symbol is both social and symbolic, but its factuality, and certainly its observable social factuality, can be derived from how it is used as a symbol of hierarchy. In social drama there is a statement of principle which, in the purely social realm of symbolic action, becomes a statement of a principle of social order. This principle can be analyzed as an "idea" of order, and we can show how this idea is "structured," but this structure must be described in terms of a social function which arises, and continues to exist, in communication. A drama of hierarchy unfolds as an act; it has a beginning, a middle, and an end, the tension of rising and falling action, which is expressed in images, as well as ideas. We emote in images; we think in ideas; we act in social dramas. We look, then, for ways in which social contents of experience (class, family, religion, politics, art) are given form as actions as well as images and ideas of hierarchy.

(b) The drama of hierarchy must be analyzed as a drama of passage from lower to higher, higher to lower, and of submission to principle of agreement (equals to equals). Social passage is a transformation of roles, and while we must note the static interrelationships among and between class, ranks, or status groups, we note also the principles of social order which are invoked to legitimize transformation. Transformation (from the sociological view) is a change of identity which occurs in role change. Identities change as we create new roles and as we destroy the old. We watch for the ways in which ostracism, sending to Coventry, banishment, cashiering and drumming out (as in armies), the "cut" (in purely social moments), and all variants of the "social kill" are expressed, just as we watch for the ways in which individuals are integrated within a group. Birth and rebirth of roles are two social modes of symbolic integration; confrontation of the incongruity between old roles we are not yet ready to kill off, and the new roles struggling for birth, is another.

(c) Symbols of order are used to integrate the development of hierarchy in symbolic action as well as in action proper. We look, then, for terms for superiority, equality, and inferiority and the tensions which arise from such distribution of authority. We look also for approved and disapproved ways of passing from one rank to another. How are these related to "statements of policy," or adapted to the typical problems of the society? What strategies, and, specifically, what symbolic strategies in dealing with superiors, inferiors, and equals, and of passage among them, are used?

(d) We watch for all types of hierarchies, and the ways in which classes, status groups, styles of life, and social roles are related to them. Five kinds of hierarchies can be distinguished in symbolic expression: (1) physical nature, as in Darwinian evolution; (2) human nature, as in the psychology of Freud and the *Maxims* of La Rochefoucauld; (3) language, as in the work of Kenneth Burke, where the dramatistic nature of words affects the quality of social experience; (4) spiritual hierarchy, as in the work of Frazer, where we move through "ritual" from lower, or natural, orders of experience, to supernatural, or celestial, realms; and (5) social hierarchy, as in sociology, when we describe how we move upward, and downward, in some scale of social distinctions, and relate as equals in status honor or in agreements deemed necessary to common action. Social and linguistic hierarchies are closely interwoven, and their effect on "natural" and "supernatural" hierarchies is a basic concern of the sociolinguist in his search of methods of analysis.

(e) No hierarchy can last without purges of some kind. We must note modes of catharsis, rites of purification, sanctification and desanctification, movements of transcendence, sanctioned ways of confronting incongruity (as in comedy), and all variants of symbolic cleansing used to purify a hierarchy. Victimage (the "kill") offers many clues to social catharsis. In the name of what principles of social order is the victim sacrificed? Moments of purgation and victimage are moments of transformation, and as such they offer many clues to shifts and changes in legitimation of power in society. In the name of what social principle of order is purgation conducted? Who invokes what name, under what condition, and in what kind of purgation?

(f) When analyzing how symbols are used in social drama, we ask: What goes with what? We have noted, for example, how courtship is depicted. That drama has its own internal structure. Other social dramas also have internal structures. Do superiors "stalk" their inferiors? Do they merely "clarify" the voice of the people (as they are supposed to do in democracy), or do they quell the voice of the people to make their own firm and majestic voice heard, as they do in authoritarian states? Do we make money to serve God, to play a game (the "money-game"), to win prestige, to serve the community, or to "uphold the American way of life?" Such linkages offer clues to the social meanings of trite and hackneyed phrases used in social drama as stereotyped themes of social action. The enemy within is cunning, venal, hypocritical, treacherous, lacking in honor, or obscene; the enemy without is ruthless, inhuman, boastful, or untrustworthy. It is from such typical clusters of imagery that stereotypes emerge from the drama of role enactment in society.

(g) We do not only ask what goes with what; we ask: What does *not* go with what? What is in opposition to what? Agreement with authority, veneration for the principles of social order to which leader and follower alike subordinate themselves in their community roles, can be communicated easily enough, but disagreement, doubt, and dislike of authority are always difficult and often dangerous to express. Disobedience and doubt are not dropped or forgotten in the drama of community life but are transformed in many ways. We may, for example, be taught that it is "wrong" to take the name of the Lord in vain, or to degrade the image of the lady in obscenity, or to express dislike of the great American game of baseball. We may be taught, too, that we must respect the valor of officers, the holiness of our priests, the wisdom of our teachers, the purity of our college girls, but what we are taught and what we experience may be very different. It may be, too, that we live in such a controlled community that we can express doubt over virtues only with great difficulty, if at all. But it would be meaningless from a sociological view to say that we do not express opposition, doubt, and ambiguity over the virtues of our leaders, or the efficacy of the social order itself.

(h) Obscenity, cursing, blasphemy, and all dark and secret expressions of opposition exist in every group. The youth who struggles to satisfy sex and status drives in a social world where he is not allowed to satisfy them in the same manner as adults, but must honor and obey adult ways, must express in forbidden ways what he cannot express in approved. But in cursing, writing obscenities on walls, telling dirty jokes, mocking his teachers behind their backs, drawing caricatures on the blackboard, or lampooning the pompous dress and manners of his elders, the adolescent does not repress, but expresses, his hostility. We note then how conflicts are expressed. The dreamer muttering in his troubled sleep, the sleepwalker striding in ghostly silence, the schizophrene spinning out his mad tale, the paranoid describing his angry persecutors, are trying to say something. Oppositions to authority range from approved public institutionalization of such opposition, to opposition so private and secret that it can be expressed only through elaborate disguise, or in moments hidden and secret from the world. Villains, clowns, and grotesques (as in caricature) are obvious examples of how we institutionalize opposition within a society. In our generation hot and cold war has become a "normal" way of life. There is nothing hidden, clandestine, or repressed, about our hatred for Russia.

(i) Private enemies, the enemies locked within the self who cannot be reached in reality, can be confronted only in fantasy and guilt. The prisoner indulging in auto-erotic fantasy, conjuring up visions of a sumptuous dinner, or recalling the image of his wife through fondling her stocking, must have in fantasy what he cannot have in reality. As his rage mounts, he turns it against his captors, not himself. When he cannot turn his anger against his captors, he expresses his fantasies in conversation with others or with himself. Guilt occurs when we cannot face by ourselves, or can face only with great difficulty, disobedience of inner commandments which coincide closely with those in the world outside of the self, those commandments which are believed to sustain social order. Guilt of this kind cannot be repressed for long. Like murder, it will out, but the ways it comes out in expression can be as devious, twisted, and grotesque as the struggle to form the images of the nightmare or the dream.

(j) In grotesque and absurd forms of communication, opposites meet, sense becomes nonsense, and acceptance becomes rejection. All sorts of hidden and secret forms come to eerie light in absurd dreams and nightmares. But these strange hierglyphics become public when they assume a communicable form. We may say that the grotesque in art and play, and the "meaningless" symbols of nonsense, are not real, any more than a children's tale of make-believe in an enchanted castle of their own contriving, is real. But what we really mean is that we do not know how to interpret such symbols. The terrible symbols of the nightmare may not be "real," but few symbols have such profound somatic effect. Like the precursors of Freud in psychology, sociologists must wait until some great mind lights a path to understanding the riddles of identification with authority which make us monsters screaming for the blood of our fellowmen or saints who suffer and die in compassion for our brothers.

(k) We do not doubt in dreams, nor do we experience much comedy, or at least comedy of the kind we know in waking life. In dreams, we accept or reject; we pursue or we are pursued; we kill or we are about to be killed. We know dread, anxiety, fear, and horror, and as these mount within us we struggle to awaken so we can regain consciousness. For in consciousness there are *real* others who will respond to us, and tell us what our fear and horror means, and how we can face it. In dreams, nightmares, panic, fear, dread, anxiety, and deep shame, we are cut off from communication from real others. We must bear the burden of our anguish alone. But to be alone is to be in much company, the company of fantastic others. If we live in a society where we can communicate well in the social drama of life, our solitude is serene. We have learned how to communicate with real others, and in the responses of real others we have learned that we are a member of a group whom we love and cherish. My fellow scholars judge my work, and in this judgment I reach decisions about the value of my work. But the book I now write has been judged by no one save myself. As I sit here typing I am like a god (or a devil) creating a world. But the moment I settle back in my chair to read what I have written I become an audience to myself. I am no longer shaping a world, but struggling as a member of a human community to identify through communication with significant others.

(1) Our yearning for real others, the struggle to consciousness in the nightmare, the grotesque and horrible ways we communicate in rage, hysteria, and madness, the puzzle and bewilderment of doubt and anxiety, all these can be controlled only so long as we can give them form. It is only in form that they become what we call "real," and it is only in communication with real others, that is, public others, that the meaning of action emerges. When our world falls apart we cannot communicate because we do not know how to communicate. Our symbolic systems fail, or they become grotesque, and can be borne only in alienation or madness. But even this stage of social consciousness can be endured so long as it can be communicated to real others. Picasso depicts the horror of war in his painting of the bombing of Guernica, but in giving horror form he made it communicable. Beckett finds men absurd, but in *Waiting for Godot* he gives form to the absurdity so at least we can face an absurd world where, like stricken animals, we huddle together in our doom. Perhaps when we understand better the shadowy figures of the dream, we will discover them to be a struggle toward form, an attempt of a repressed self to express in the privacy of sleep what cannot be expressed, or can be expressed only with great difficulty, in the public world of communication. The dream might then be analyzed as the result of difficulties in communication among superiors, equals, and inferiors.

(m) It may be that Freud was right in teaching that adults seek to return to childhood satisfactions. But what, precisely, are "childhood satisfactions" if they are not social, and, if social, how are they related to the Freudian libido? Does the child wish to kill his father and sleep with his mother *only* to enjoy sex? For is not the kill a moment of dominance? The content of dominance is familial and sexual, but the *form* of the act, the kill, is social. If we seek sex only, why must we *kill* the father? Our parents are our first, and probably our most profound, experience of authority. For a time in childhood we believe they can right all wrongs, just as they alone can cause our joy and sorrow. The destruction of this belief, the discovery that our parents are not gods, is the sociological trauma of childhood, and, perhaps, of social life itself. When we lose our gods where can we turn? How are we to satisfy our yearning for authority? How are we to still within us the longing to return to the past serenity of childhood when we could run to our parents for safety against others, and for expiation of guilt against ourself?

O

METHODOLOGICAL PROPOSITION 3
The staging of an act in society is a social drama of authority which we analyze by asking: where, or under what conditions, is the act being presented? What kind of act is it? What kind of actors are selected for what kind of roles? What means or instruments do the actors use to communicate authority? And how is the expression of hierarchy related to a principle of social order?

(a) Social drama involves every art and science of symbolic expression. The staging of a social act, like those of the drama in art, is designed to create certain effects, as we see in the art and science of designing stages for drama, games, political conventions, and public meetings. Audiences are always arranged in certain ways, and how they are arranged tells us a great deal about hierarchy in the actor's community, and the position of the actor within it. People of different classes, conditions, and status groups enter, sit, and leave in ways which are thought proper to their position in the community. And just as all serve as an audience to the actors in the social drama being mounted on some kind of stage, so do they serve as audiences to each other. "Seeing and being seen" is a strong motive for attendance at all drama. Even in great and pure performances of art drama, intermissions are provided so that members of the audience may promenade before each other.

(b) Audiences are stratified in various ways. First, there is a general public; then classes or orders within this public; community dignitaries and visiting dignitaries who are assigned places of honor; performers such as actors, speakers, dancers, or musicians; and some exalted personage (or his delegate) who represents the ultimate audience in the community hierarchy. In play, games, festivals, ceremonies, rites, and drama proper, some such indication of hierarchy exists. The art and science of architecture offers many clues to hierarchy, for the architect must allocate (according to accepted "rights") the space and materials available. He must express hierarchal differences, and, at the same time, create stages whereby different conditions and classes become audiences to each other as well as to the actors on the stage. The honor and majesty of being an important public person must be communicated to be kept alive. The king and queen have a royal box which separates but does not hide them from the audience. Indeed, there is nothing more public than a "private" royal box. The persons of their majesties may be private, but the social role of kingship, its staging, is played in a constant glare of publicity.

(c) The actors on the stage, whether in drama proper, or in the social drama of play, games, festivals, ceremonies, and rites, are stratified by the design of the stage itself. The ways in which actors and audience enter, meet, talk, and depart are infused with a hierarchal radiance that is accentuated by art, but the aura of hierarchy as staged in drama rises from the community role of the actor as well as from the magic of art. In every staging of drama (art or social) there are at least three levels on the stage where the action takes place. The common people play their part on the lowest level, the next level is given to people of quality, but on the highest level only the gods of the community, or, in more secular times, those raised to great power, appear.

The same is true of community presentations in parades and pageants. Those in the parade march by three types of audience, the common people who watch from the same level as the marchers, the elect of the community who watch from stands, and finally the community guardians who watch from the highest point of all, the reviewing stand. In classical Greek drama, as in the ecclesiastical drama of the Middle Ages, the gods appeared (quite literally) from on high. The roof of the Greek scene-building provided an upper story which was used to represent the heavens in which gods and goddesses appeared. In American musical comedy of the Ziegfeld era, a grand staircase, on which expensively gowned statuesque beauties paraded down to the stage, added much to the dignification of these expensively draped goddesses of love.

From ancient to modern times there have been many kinds of stage devices used to indicate the hierarchal position of the actors. The Greek *mechane*, a large crane, was used to lower characters from above to indicate their heavenly origin, as when gods and goddesses appeared in chariots from the sky. Indeed, this device for indicating heavenly intervention was so common that it became known in Roman times as the "god from the machine," and the Latin phrase, *deus ex machina*, is now part of our language. Even by the time of Aristophanes the descent of the gods to settle complicated points in dramatic action through sheer hierarchal mystification was evoking criticism. The sudden intervention of the gods, as Aristophanes pointed out, was not a very humane or rational way to settle human difficulties. But if gods no longer descend upon the stage, supernatural powers still dwell in the clouds above nations in "ways of life," ideologies, and other transcendent virtues which are depicted in dark and mysterious figures who descend upon discussion to banish reason from discourse. At some time in social drama, as in the popular art drama of the community, there is a final descent of the gods (or an ascent of the actors) in response to invocations of the great heroes who protect the community. The gods who crowned ancient hierarchies have not died; they have simply taken new forms. A Greek who died for Athens seems strange to us. Few of us would die for Chicago, but many of us have risked our lives to uphold the American "way of life."

(d) The class, rank, or station, of actors and their audience is seldom created by art alone. The artist, however great he may be, does not create the glory of a king, the majesty of a president, the love of a mother, the mystery of a lover, the bravery of a soldier, the wisdom of a scholar, or the holiness of a priest. These social roles have their own magnificence and radiance, a *social* radiance, which is kept alive in the many institutional and community dramas in which these roles are enacted. Through intensive and frequent repetition these roles become traditional roles in the symbolic life of the community. For the Christian there is nothing greater than the cross, for the soldier nothing greater than courage in defense of his country, for the scholar nothing greater than wisdom. At the sign of the cross, the devout kneel in profound obeisance to God; at the sound of his regimental pipers the Scottish soldier charges with the glory of a nation of warriors in his heart; as scholars rise to chant their invocation to wisdom in the school song, the hope of wisdom among men, and love of the young in the paths of wisdom, is born again. But if the artist, and all those staging our social dramas, do not create the radiance of these roles, they certainly create the forms in which we communicate them, and in great art sometimes create roles which become community roles. The artist, as artist, does more than communicate what exists already in the community. But even though he creates forms to make sense to himself, his forms may be used by others in social drama which is used to create and sustain order in the community.

In social drama proper, great stress is placed on the communication of the majesty and glory of rank. In the coronation of Great Britain's king the sceptre of kingship is placed in one hand, and the orb, representing the world, surmounted by the cross of the Christian church, in the other. Sometimes the radiance of these symbols is so great that it almost overwhelms the man who holds them, and great care must be taken to see that he carries his symbols of office with dignity. In democratic, as in authoritarian society, we are careful to uphold the dignity of office. The President of the United States may be a "man of the people" when he campaigns, but when he becomes President his public appearances assume a solemn and majestic air. When he appears on television the Great Seal of the United States flashes on the screen. Behind the President is his seal of office, the flag of America, and sometimes the flag of the Christian Church. The President, as befits a democratic leader, reports to his people by stating in solemn and earnest tones the problem we must face, how we have tried to face it in the past, why our opponents or enemies have made it difficult for us to solve it, and why, as a result, we must work together. He then states the decision he has made in the name of the American people, recalls our great heritage of freedom, asks his people to help him in striving to attain a perfection of our principles of democracy, and ends by humble invocation of God's help. As the President finishes, the strains of the national anthem ring through the air.

(e) Public presentations of leaders offer many clues to the ultimates, or combinations of ultimates, which are invoked in the name of social order. In applying our model of dramatic action, we ask: What kind of act is glorified? In what kind of stage is it placed? By what kind of actors is it to be carried out? Through what means is it to be achieved? And, finally, what is its ultimate value or purpose? We watch particularly for all steps from lower to higher values. A hierarchy is communicated through the staging of a progression of steps from lower to higher, in which each step is determined by a higher step, until finally the hierarchy ends in the final step, a transcendent ultimate which is the principle or order on which each step rests. These ultimate meanings infuse the beginning as well as the end of a hierarchy, and their glory and mystery is felt in each step.

A hierarchy is therefore a progression, a way up and down in which each class of being strives toward the kind above, until the striving of all ends in some great perfection, such as God, country, wisdom, idealogy, or love, which is beyond struggle and is the end of all desire. Methodological study demands concentration on the formal aspects of ascension and descension, for if we are to show how hierarchy functions and what kind of structure this function assumes, we must observe the ways in which rank is symbolized in the communication of social order. This can be done only if we believe that the social data of status consists in how it is symbolized in social drama. And in this belief in an action frame of reference for social drama, we search for symbols which give us clues to the hierarchies of conditions, actions, actors, means and ends, that are accepted by the institution or community we are studying.

○

Stage, act, role, means, and the principle of social order invoked as a determinant of social order, are linked in various ways in social drama: ten types of linkage may be distinguished.

(a) *Stage-Act*. All statements which ground social motives in conditions, backgrounds, environments, natural laws, "objective situations," existential conditions, historical necessity, equilibrium, or any spatio-temporal image, and the act are defined in terms of each other. Whenever "trends" are discovered in space or time, species "evolve," empires "take the course of destiny," or the "nature of society" makes social solidarity "inevitable," we ground social integration in scene or staging. Such explanations of social order are often deterministic and horatory, with exhortation smuggled in under the guise of scenic determinism.

(b) *Stage-Role*. In this linkage, social conditions are said to call for roles in keeping with the stage, and the stage in turn, is depicted as in keeping with the role. Thus, we hear of politicians who are "prisoners of the situation," movie stars who are "forced" to live up to the public image of their press agents. We hear too of motivation in physical and biological nature where men do not enact roles but are "moved" to action. All theories of human nature based on drives, instincts, homeostasis, stimulus-response, and other "physical laws of nature," are derived from belief in the "conditioning" of the actor by the scene or stage of action—the environment, as it is called in physical and biological science.

(c) *Stage-Means*. This linkage is common to all beliefs in "ways" of acting, "styles of life," or "media of communication" (as when we say, following Marshall McLuhan, that "the medium is the message"), as determinants of social motives. Customs, usage, tradition, magic, how we "condition" ends through social "process" or communication as such are characteristic of this linkage. When we say manners make morals, or that proper observance of rites sustains social order, or that certain forms of prayer and sacrifice propitiate the gods, or that a more advanced technology will create a better life, we are saying that certain means will, in and of themselves, produce a certain social environment.

(d) *Stage-Principle of Social Order.* When the principle of social order is made part of the situation under which we act, stage and principle are linked. Thus we say it is "natural" for men to work for money because money "determines" the "law" of supply and demand. Or we say that animals and men, and, indeed, all nature, is determined by God because God created the world and continues to infuse it with his glory and love. Or we say that since man as a biological organism struggles to satisfy his needs for food and sex, all principles of social order are conditioned by such needs. Or we say that nature is red in tooth and claw and that conflict and war bring out heroic qualities in men, hence war is "natural" to man in society, and to animals in nature. Or the Nazis said in excuse for their monstrous crimes, only the "leadership principle" guarantees order. In sum, whenever we discover a principle of social order conditioning the scene through some kind of immanence, incarnation, consummation, essence, intrinsicality, inherence, substance, character, disposition, trait, etc., we are in the realm of grounds for action which are conditioned by the purpose the action is supposed to serve.

(e) *Act-Principle of Social Order.* When a soldier tells us war is necessary to purify the race, or a scientist teaches that science alone can save the community, or we are told that any kind of act will in itself insure community survival, and will do so "inevitably," it is assumed that some principle of order, as invested in a certain kind of action, will itself determine social integration without the intervention of the actor playing social roles, or conditioning by the environment or scene, or the effect of certain forms of communicaiton.

(f) *Act-Role.* Here we explain an action by the character of the role, as in the religious "charisma" of the holy man. Weber's types of religious authority where the personal qualifications of the religious leader and the power and glory of his religious office are distinguished, offer other examples. Religious leaders, such as the prophet, seer, magician, diviner, saint, priest, and organizer, create religion in keeping with their roles in religious life. Whenever we say that the sheer nature of an office, i.e. the official acts performed by those holding such office, modifies a man's character ("the office makes the man"), or that the power of vestments or uniforms transforms the wearer, we are assuming a reciprocal effect between act and role. We are saying that there is a reciprocal relationship between what the actor does (his act) and the roles he plays in society.

(g) *Act-Means.* When means, or how we do something, is said to determine the act, we assume a reciprocal relationship between how we do something and what is done. Thus science is not an act of being, but a means of doing, for the scientist's method, not his character or "being," determines his acts. How the worshiper performs the sacred rites, not his intention or the purity of his soul, determines the success of his prayer, in this view of motivation. All views on the efficacy of proper observance of customs, usage, manners, or fashion as a way to sustain social order belong here.

(h) *Role-Principle of Social Order.* In this linkage, we say that some quality in the social role of the actor determines a principle of social order. *A priori* theories of social order, and all determinations of social experience by the "nature" of social roles, and not by the nature of the problem the actor is trying to solve, belong here. Thus when we say that some kind of social ladder must always exist because it is in the "nature" of society to "regulate" social order in terms of hierarchy, we are explaining social relations by roles whose enactment creates social order.

(i) *Role-Means.* Here we say that roles and the tools, instruments, means, and agencies used in role-enactment determine each other. We are told that the role of the politician is determined by how he communicates. Theories of war as determined by machines, or business by television, are other examples. Whenever we say that how a man plays a role determines order, or, in turn, that a role "requires" certain forms of expression in social dramas, we are linking role and social order.

(j) *Means-Principle of Social Order.* When instruments or techniques become ends, as when we hear that operations determine concepts, that is, how we record temperature *is* our concept of temperature, or, in social action, as when we say "manners make the man," means become social ends. Thus when we say that money, which is intrinsically a means or agency, exists to satisfy a profit motive which alone energizes social relations, we make an end or purpose out of a means.

When we say art exists for its own sake, we are making means its own social end. In social relations in America we extol social climbing, how we move up the social ladder, as a principle of democracy. To be discontented with our social position is not an indication of flaws in democratic society, or of the cardinal sin of envy with ourself, but an indication of our fitness, not only to increase our standard of living, but to increase it forever. For it is not arriving at some plateau as a step to a higher level that determines our democratic virtue. *How* we rise in democratic society becomes an end in itself, a principle of order.

○

METHODOLOGICAL PROPOSITION 5
In symbolic analysis of social drama we ask: in the struggle for power within an institution, who evokes what symbols of authority? In what kind of action? By what means? Under what conditions? And in the name of what transcendent power is authority legitimized?

(a) We must distinguish agonistic qualities in social interaction, and since social order is always a resolution of competition, rivalry, conflict and war, we must *begin* our analysis at moments where such agonistic elements are open to observation. Sometimes this is very difficult because institutions always present their principles of social order as *beyond* struggle. Thus, God is beyond and exists outside of time and space, money "works the same" for all because it is a "law" of the market, wisdom will cure men of evil for once they understand the misery of evil they will turn from it, a classless society will bring a good life to all because such a society is above the selfishness and greed of those bound by class interests. But in the social drama of the world which we can observe, every such absolute is conditioned by struggle and contest. That is, even transcendence is born in struggle to legitimize power of a certain kind, under certain conditions, by certain actors who use certain means to achieve a certain end.

(b) Thus, our methods of analysis must be developed to clarify, not to deny, ambiguity, doubt, struggle, competition, rivalry, conflict, and war. Freud has done this in his family psychology, and in so far as institutions can be thought of in terms of the family, the Freudian struggle between the Id, Ego, and Superego possesses great methodological value. But where the family model of analysis does not fit completely, as it does not in many aspects of community life, or in societies where the Freudian patriarchal family is not common, then we must develop another model. Like Freud and Burke, we propose drama as a source for such a model, because in drama, and particularly comic drama, we expose incongruities between means and ends in action. The structure and function of games (where games are considered in terms of symbolic interaction, not, as in modern "game theory," as a form of signaling) offers further clues to the ways in which action is determined by struggle. And finally, war with all its variants of killing and victimage shows us how institutions, communities, and societies use conflict as a means to legitimize their use of violence as a "crusade" to uphold a "way of life."

O

METHODOLOGICAL PROPOSITION 6
Themes and plots in social drama may be studied by noting moments of transformation as well as fixed moments of belief in the drama of social hierarchy.

(a) Social hierarchy is always marked by stages of some kind, but we must distinguish stages of movement upward (with a downward counterpart) toward some final state of perfection which is "beyond" hierarchy. As a principle of social order democracy is not a perpetual ascension or descension, but of stages, just as a life is not simply a progression from the womb to the grave, but a progression marked by stages we name childhood, youth, adulthood, etc. The symbolic phase of every act, as well as of fully developed social drama, is marked by similar stages. These may be very crude, as a beginning, middle, and end of a parade, or very complex, as in a High Mass. Stages in progression toward an end cannot be analyzed unless we know what principle of social order gives them coherence. That is, given the separateness of acts, scenes, parts, or movements in symbolic expression, we must ask of *what* they are a part.

(b) Our best clue to the consubstantiality of parts in social drama lies in names. A name is a title, and a title, in turn, is a way of essentializing characteristics and qualities deemed necessary to a social end, just as a nickname is a way of summing up (either negatively or positively) some characteristic quality of an individual. Thus, all striking and colorful names for acts, attitudes, ideas, images, and all the nuances of hierarchal relationships, must be watched carefully, for they are clues to the social values that individuals use to identify with each other in the process of transformation from one condition to another in society.

(c) Depictions of community origin and utopian perfection offer clues to the meaning of public imagery in community organization. Thus, we invoke the "Founding Fathers," or the "original Constitution," not to recapture a past but to solve problems in the present. We invoke perfect communities, under the guise of utopias, heavens, and ideal commonwealths, as "final" values or purposes in the drama of social order. Even when we invoke a past, we do not seek to return to the past we have invoked, but to press toward the goal which the past "illuminates" and which we were reaching before we "lost our way," or "abandoned the right path." Futures and pasts are symbolic constructions which we use to guide us in action, or to lead us to accept, doubt, or reject some course of action in a present. Symbolic constructions of social order in the past or the future are always fictions because means-ends relationships can only be tested *in* action. Doubt and ambiguity are realms of change. They are like bridges which we use to cross from the old to the new, or to return from the new if it does not help us solve our problems in acting together.

O

METHODOLOGICAL PROPOSITION 7
The ways in which audiences are addressed in social
drama offer many clues to the distribution of authority.

(a) Do superiors cajole, threaten, request, demand, bully, tease, scold, inspire, or discuss with their inferiors? How people are addressed tells us how they are regarded, and since forms of address, and the social drama in which address occurs, can be observed, such communication offers us many clues to relations between superiors, inferiors, and equals. Thus if we believe that the voice of the people is the voice of God, we address them very differently than if we believe them to be fools, children, or beasts. Address is not limited to speech or writing alone. Communication in any form is an address so long as we are using it to persuade others to believe in our majesty, loyalty, or devotion. Gods are worshiped in dance, song, speech, and writing; inferiors are reminded of our majesty through the pomp and circumstance of parade and ceremony. Equals meet in contests, games, debates, and legislative argument, as well as in the private moments of intimate talk where friendly laughter over the arrogance and stupidity of superiors, or the hypocrisy and pettiness of inferiors, lightens the burdens of hierarchy.

(b) The ways in which the "I" addresses the "We," "They," "Thou," and "It," and holds dialogues with itself, take many forms. In a caste system, the "I" may address its "It" only through intermediaries. It may even be forbidden to utter the name of "It." Or what cannot be said "seriously," in tragic and solemn modes of address, must be said in comedy. We watch for all of blasphemy, cursing, and obscenity, for they tell us much about the strains of hierarchy. Whom we curse —when, where, and how—tells much about our hate because through cursing hate reaches forms which we can observe. We watch, too, for ironic modes of address, since these tell us of moments in social courtship that no longer make sense, or do so only through a kind of complicity between actors and audiences (both inner and outer) who let each other know what they are doing is not very sensible yet (for want of something better) must be done in hopes of sustaining social order. And, finally, we watch for moments of sheer horror in address. In horror the world is not simply senseless, or to be endured through irony, or evil, to be purged through sacrificial victims, but grotesque, as in the dream when we move into the nightmare. There is no way to make sense out of horror. Like Lear howling on the heath, we address a monstrous and evil world, a world in which madness is the price of survival.

(c) The mystery of a social order is like romantic love: No one can define it, but everyone knows what it is. Or it is like money, which in itself means nothing and yet as a symbol can mean anything. Every society has such mysteries, and expresses them in many ways. The savage believes in garden magic, the feudal aristocrat believed in a great hierarchal pantomime of courtship, the bourgeois (as Carlyle reminds us) believes in the sanctity of clothes as insignia of hierarchy, while the socialist is moved by the mystery of a classless society, reached through the rigid class structure of a bureaucracy which is to melt away. These mysteries affect us through their embodiment in individuals whose beauty, elegance, wealth, wisdom, skill, or holiness moves us deeply because we believe that there is nothing beyond such expressions. In them desire ends and a world "beyond meaning" which is yet the source of meaning, begins. They are, as we say, ends in themselves.

○

METHODOLOGICAL PROPOSITION 8
There are seven basic forms of social drama: these are games, play, parties, festivals, ceremonies, drama, and rites.

(a) Random play is the earliest attempt at social drama, but social drama, like art drama, has many forms. In such play each player does about as he pleases, with little regard for the other. Random play becomes formal play (as in the game) through rules, for games have rules which are codified and are subject to ratification by all those concerned with the game. These may range from the members of local amateur clubs to great national games like American baseball. The game is essentially a contest. Players compete against each other under the guidance of rules in terms of skill, strength, cunning, perseverance, or luck. The party is purely social. We *play* society at a party, and this kind of play gives us a specific kind of grace, "social grace." The festival takes us into the community realm of social drama. Here players act in social, not individual or institutional, roles, and in doing so they subordinate themselves to the community. In these great public ceremonies private roles become public roles, or what we call social offices. One sociopsychological basis for play, games, parties, and festivals is the creation of social euphoria, a joy in being together in staging ourselves playfully for others, as they are staging themselves for us.

173

(b) In social play, differences in rank, skill, sex, or class becomes a source of pleasure. As we play the flirt, the mysterious and strange power of sex, whose expression separates us as it increases our desire for each other, is lightened by a new spirit, the spirit of play, fun, and comedy. We play at sex by facing openly the burden of strangeness and mystery we experience in our serious and solemn communication of sex. We reduce sexual superiority and inferiority to equality, for only equals can play, and thus in play we discover and recapture the joy of sharing the tensions of difference. In many games players are assigned handicaps, as we see in golf and tennis where players are matched according to their skills, or as we see when stronger boys assign one of their best players to the weaker side, or when a good checker player gives his less skilled opponent a certain number of his own pieces. We struggle to win the game, but honor in winning comes from overcoming opponents under rules agreed to by all.

(c) Equalization in competition also occurs in moments of purely social life when we play an incognito role in what we call the "social game." An exalted personage requests that he be allowed to appear incognito, as when he requests the toastmaster at a banquet not to use his titles, or asks his hostess at a party to introduce him as "one of the boys." He may even go so far as to invert his rank by assuming an inferior role, as when the rich appear as beggars at Mardi Gras, or a great lady masquerades as a coquette, or when the boss allows himself to be teased at the office party. In all these we make hierarchy a game; we *play* at hierarchy, just as the child who dresses in adult clothes plays at being grown up. In such games it is not the absence of hierarchy, but playing with it that draws us together. We know that the opponent who gives us ten strokes could defeat us at will, just as an old man knows that the girl with whom he flirts so gayly would not respond to a serious expression of sex.

(d) Ceremonies, rites, and ritual drama are the most formalized types of social drama. They must be performed in certain ways because the efficiency of their appeal depends on their form of expression. In sacred rites, as in magic and art, form becomes a power in its own right. How do we know we have reached the gods with our invocations? There is really no way of "knowing" in the scientific sense of the word, but we know whether we have communicated in the form considered proper to the occasion. In ritual and ritual drama these forms become fixed through tradition. We do things a certain way because "they have always been done that way." Change is not only disapproved, it is considered dangerous. This is very different from games whose rules may be changed easily, and where all that is required is the consent of the players. In such games it is the agreement that is sacred; each player binds himself to play the game according to rules he has agreed to follow. But the rules can be changed at will by agreement of the players.

(e) Rites are comic as well as tragic. Every society has its comic gods and heroes, who, like their tragic counterparts, are worshiped because they bring order into life. Comedy allows us to confront problems and vices that we could confront in no other way. Some of these problems are local and particular, others are universal. Avarice, gluttony, envy, cowardice, lust, lying—these sins threaten any social order, while the confidence man, the man who measures all by money, the "gold-digger," the lazy bum, the wily salesman, or the windy promoter, are indigenous to our society, just as the flatterer, the litigant, the panderer, the courtesan, or the hier, were indigenous to Roman society and comedy. Vices destroy order, but if we are to combat vices we must know what they are, and how they work in a given social order. Comic gods, like all truly social gods, remind us too that vices are often caused by an excess of virtue. Thus, arrogance stems from pride, avarice from prudent use of money, gluttony from the art of eating, and envy from ambition. In comedy we seek to correct the abuse in the name of a social norm of conduct. In American society, where ambition to earn and spend money is a virtue, we cannot mount civic tragedies in which the sin of ambition is punished. We must do the opposite. The villain who strikes fear in the hearts of our businessmen is the able-bodied consumer who wants little, does nothing to increase his wants, and envies no one. Thus, while we punish vices in the use of money, we do not attack the principle of money as such.

Huckleberry Finn, Charlie Chaplin, the elegant but seedy tramp, or W. C. Fields, the phony whose bland middle-class mask poorly hides a drunkard who swindles and cheats his inferiors and beats children, warn us in laughter that too much devotion to money makes life very dull and inhuman. In great community comedy of this kind we do not invoke a supernatural beyond reason, but a *social* principle of reason to protect us. Instead of torturing and killing those who personify our evils, we mirror our vices to show how they destroy the humanity of our relationships with one another. We seek to purge ourselves of attitudes and acts which keep us apart from each other, as well as from our gods. We remind ourselves that before we become gods we must be men, and that even as gods we are beasts and men still. We strive to kill the "old Adam" in us through religious rites where victims suffer and die for us. But we can laugh at our bestiality, as the Athenians did in their satyr plays, or as we do in American burlesque, cartoons, and our "low" and "high" forms of comedy. We laugh at ourselves to purify ourselves as social beings, just as we laugh at others to rid them of peculiarities which keep them apart from us.

O

METHODOLOGICAL PROPOSITION 9
Childhood play is the first experience of social address.

(a) Very early in life we begin to play roles. Such roles are sometimes purely inner roles, as in the imaginary playmates children create, or the imitative roles in which the child copies those about him, as when he plays at being a mother, a father, a policeman, or a teacher. In playing such roles the child creates within himself the stimuli which call out the particular response, or group of responses, that go with such a role. As he plays at being a storekeeper, the child takes the role of salesman and offers something to himself. He then becomes a buyer to himself, and haggles over the goods and their price. Finally he buys it and puts it on the shelf. These forms of play-acting are his earliest experiences in address.

(b) The child addresses himself as he would another, and thus learns to call out in himself the responses that actual address to others would call out in them. He takes such responses and organizes them into a role, for in role-taking within the self we say something in one character and respond in another. As we respond in the character of the other, we stimulate the first self to respond. In such inner dialogue and role-taking the social self is born. As conversation with the imaginary other takes the form of dialogue, it becomes organized, and in such organization we discover that there is a proper way—that is, an approved social way—to play storekeeper. As the play continues, we may even hear the child criticizing the self or the imaginary other for playing the role badly.

O

METHODOLOGICAL PROPOSITION 10
Games teach us the power of rules as a form of social order.

(a) A game is organized through rules. The player enacting his own role does so through his ability under rules to take the role of all the other players. He must know what others are going to do before he can play his own part, just as others must know what he is going to do before they can play theirs. Rules become internalized through our capacity to call up in ourselves responses which are being called up in the other, and thus enable us to anticipate the responses of others. The game teaches us one way, the way of rules, to order social relationships. We act with confidence because we expect others to act in certain ways, and we are able to respond to these ways of acting because the game has a form, a set of rules, which determines how the other must act toward us.

(b) The power of rules lies in consent and agreement that is freely given. The best rules, those which bind us together simply by their power as rules, are so constructed that very little is left to the decision of those who judge them. Rules are upheld by those who agree to be bound by them, not by the decisions of judges. Unlike the English judge, who makes the law through legal decisions which are carefully codified and often become law in turn, the umpire makes no decisions about the rules but simply applies them. When a rule is broken, he stops the game and penalizes those who have violated the rules, but penalties too are determined by rule. Thus rules are both positive and negative. When they are broken the game must stop, for the players are bound only by rules which are clear to all, and which must be applied in the same way to every play and to every player. There is no hierarchy in the application of rules. We speak of divine law, or the law of God, or law itself as a kind of supernatural entity, but we do not speak of rules of God, or the rules of a king.

(c) Disobedience of rules stops the game because infractions of rules destroys the equality under rules which is necessary to the game. Where we are not bound as equals we cannot act together under rules. The child who disobeys his parents does not destroy the family, and the sinner who breaks God's laws does not destroy God, but the player who breaks a rule destroys a game. The penalty paid for infraction of rules is not like the ransom paid by the weaker to the stronger. Penalties under rules are intended to equalize the score so that the game can go on as a game, that is, as a contest in which all are bound by the same rules. Honor in winning under rules comes from scrupulous observance of the rules. To take advantage of the rules may be cunning and shrewd, but it is dishonorable to use rules to gain an unfair advantage over an opponent. Advantages in skill, power, experience, or luck are equalized through handicaps because the honor in winning under rules is in victory over an equal, not over an inferior whom we crush with the weight of our power, or a superior whom we outwit with cunning or guile.

(d) The use of rules offers many clues to relationships between equals. As children we learn to be equals through relating under rules; as adults we struggle to perfect rules and to widen their application. As we extend what Jefferson called "umpirage," we create new opportunities for men to act together as equals. For citizens of a democracy, the will of equals is the strongest will of all, but equality under rules exists in all societies and in all institutions. In our analysis of authority we ask: Under what conditions are rules, rather than tradition, custom, law, nature, or some form of the supernatural, invoked? And within the framework of the act as developed here we ask: When and where are rules used, by whom, in what way, and for what purpose? We note carefully the relationship of rules to authority (keeping in mind that European social theory—and sociological theory even in America—does not admit rules as a social bond equal in power to the bonds of religion, politics, economics, or the family).

○

In parties and social gatherings we learn to relate on a
purely social basis through manners.

(a) Manners bind us to each other through their power as an expression of purely social bonds. The power of a "society leader" is the
power derived from skill in social forms of address. The power of the
public official in charge of protocol lies in his knowledge of the rules
prescribing etiquette in ceremonies of state. Every group creates good
and bad manners. The specific interests of a group may be political,
economic, sexual, educational, ecclesiastical, criminal, or familial, but
in all such groups there is a proper and improper way to *express* such
interests. These proprieties are social proprieties, not simply economic
or political ones.

(b) Basic social interests are expressed in official as well as individual
roles. All such roles involve expression in address; a criminal gang
leader, as much as a bishop, is expected to talk, dress, and act in ways
considered proper to his role. Few are capable of judging the skill of
the gangster or the bishop, but all know the public image of the gangster and the bishop (or at least that of the gangster) as they see it on
television, in the press, and in the movies. Manners are, therefore, the
daily rhetoric of society. They are forms of address which we use to
establish various degrees of social distance between ourselves and
others.

(c) If we are to identify with people, we must have the right to their
company. Once in their company we watch manners carefully to
discover who accepts and who rejects us. We watch, too, for other
kinds of expression, such as irony. We assume that those who are cold,
aloof, or "formal" hold themselves superior, while those who wait on
us hand and foot, laugh long and loudly at every one of our jokes, or
listen in fascination to what we say, think themselves inferior. But
those who address us playfully through irony, gentle teasing, or light
mockery, demand that we regard them as equals. We must uphold the
dignity of our superiors, and respect the devotion of our inferiors. Because of this we cannot tease or mock them. Nor can we be ironic,
for there is an air of complicity and familiarity in irony, as indeed
there is in all moments of laughter and fun. As we laugh together, or

as we snicker furtively at a comment over the confusion between majesty and pomposity which so often inflicts our superiors, or between servility and loyalty which we find so often among inferiors, we lighten the burden of our roles as superiors and inferiors. The kinds of play and irony, and indeed the whole range of comedy permitted in manners, tell us much about the strains of hierarchy. They tell us much about equality too, for as the aphorists on manners remind us, we must be careful to jest and play only with peers. Joking with superiors (and inferiors) is always risky.

(d) Manners are also a weapon, as we indicate in common speech when we say "he cut me dead." No power is more formidable than the power of making men ridiculous. La Rochefoucauld held that ridicule dishonors more than dishonor itself. Even majesty cannot survive ridicule. As Frederick the Great wrote Voltaire (a master of the art of ridicule): "Ridicule is more deadly than all the arguments in the world. Few men can reason, but all fear ridicule." To be ridiculous is to be grotesque, and thus placed beyond communication. After ridicule comes cursing, obscenity, blasphemy, and all forms of malediction. Between the poles of using manners to destroy the social role of a person, and using them to uphold and augment his self-esteem, there are many gradations.

(e) In the realm of manners nothing can be forced or taken, all must be given. We court each other in positions of superiority, inferiority, and equality, but those positions must be given by those with whom we seek to identify. In this sense, manners are of more importance than laws, for they establish scales of social distance and assign individuals to positions on this scale. Manners vex or soothe, corrupt or purify, exalt or debase, barbarize or refine us by a constant, steady, uniform, insensible operation like that of the air we breathe. Confucius teaches that: "It is good manners which make the excellence of a neighborhood. No wise man will settle where they are lacking." In the Confucian view, manners integrate us because, far more than law, custom, tradition, or regulation, they create the social order of daily life.

○

Festivals increase social integration by creating joy in
fellowship.

(a) In eating, drinking, dancing, and singing together at communal
feasts, individuals strengthen their social bonds. There is an intense
feeling of unity, as individuals lose themselves in joyful celebration.
Under the stimulus of food, drink, song, dance, play, and all the arts
of merriment, our love and devotion to each other mounts as we re-
joice in our fellowship. For if the community is sustained in the solemn
concourses of tragic drama, and the rites of sacred ceremony, it is also
refreshed in the joy of feasting together in laughter and fun.

(b) Festivals give form to social life because they create rhythms in
community life. The dead time of the clock gives way to the living
time of communal drama. We celebrate changes in seasons, the origins of our community (as in the merrymaking of the Fourth of July),
the birth, death, and resurrection of our gods. On a more private level
we feast within the family on birthdays, homecomings, and other occasions important to family fellowship. Fasts follow feasts, just as
feasts follow fasts; the burial of the dead is followed by feasting over
the memory of the dead. These rhythms of joy and sorrow break the
tedium of life. They add excitement to our lives because they give
social relations dramatic meaning. We look forward to Christmas, plan
for it, set stages for its celebrations, announce its advent with great
parades, keep its spirit alive with song, personify the drama of gift-
giving in the figure of Santa Claus, gather together around decorated
Christmas trees to give and receive gifts. For one day at least we are
brothers in joy. Through the gifts we give we share in each other. In
the merriment and feasting of the season, we break up the rigidity of
rank and station, and in doing so discover the pure fellowship of our
social bonds.

(c) In American society we celebrate through joyful spending on
food, drink, and gifts. For a few days we treat money lightly, even
playfully, as if to poke fun at our seriousness over money at other
times. But in spending we also sacrifice. As we spend we show that we
are willing to give up something we cherish. Gifts of price are the

sacrifice, small and great, of a plutocratic society. Who has a right to our gifts, on what occasions, and for what purpose, tells us much about social bonds. Festal spending in our society may seem to be mere display, but in the joy and merriment of the feast our bonds of fellowship are strengthened.

(d) What is celebrated in festal gaiety, how, by whom, where, and when, tell us much about community organization. In what a community finds joy, how this is communicated, in what roles, in what kinds of social stages, and when, offer many clues to the distribution of authority. In play and merriment we become equal; the burdens of rank, and whatever separates us, are lightened. "Carnival," the festival which precedes the great fast by which the Roman Catholic Church prepares for Easter, is recognized. Exuberant mirth, unrestricted freedom, combined with masquerade, jesting, and burlesque, prevail. *Fastnacht* (in Teutonic countries) is likewise celebrated as a feast of folly, revelry, and license. In such festivals the gods themselves are mocked.

(e) In many festivals there is an inversion of rank. In the Bacchanalia of Athens, as in the Saturnalia and Lupercalia of Rome, raillery mounted until there was a temporary subversion of civil order. Slaves ate with their masters, just as during one day of *Fastnacht* women exercised absolute authority. In the spring feast of the Mundas (of North India) servants were allowed to forget their duty to their masters, children their reverence for parents, men their respect for women, and women all their notions of modesty, delicacy, and gentleness, until they became raging bacchantes. We read in Frazer (*Spirits of the Corn and the Wild,* London, 1912, ii, 62), that at the Pondo festival of first fruits, there is no one in authority to keep order. People are even permitted to abuse their chief to his face, an offense normally met with summary vengeance and death. Among the Hos of North India, sons and daughters reviled their parents in gross language as parents in their turn reviled their children. In the Roman Saturnalia, Frazer writes (in *The Golden Bough,* part VI, "The Scapegoat," p. 307): "No feature of the festival is more remarkable, nothing in it seems to have struck the ancients themselves more than the license granted to slaves. . . . The slave might rail at his master, intoxicate himself like his betters, sit down at table with them. . . . Masters actually changed places with their slaves and waited on them at table."

(f) But nowhere was the inversion of status more marked than during the Feast of Fools, or various Christmas revels presided over by the Lord of Misrule in England and France. During these feasts, mimic dignitaries represented the highest authority of the Church. They masqueraded in the vestments of the clergy, and exercised for the time being some of the functions of the higher clergy. Priests dressed as clowns or women, as in Carnival festivities where men dressed up as women, and women as men. The inversion of status was especially marked by such offices as bishop, pope, and king, whose exalted positions were assumed in mockery by clergy of the lower ranks. Rag days in Scottish universities, gridiron dinners in American politics, like the office party at Christmas in American business offices, carry on the ancient tradition of the Saturnalian feast. Normal life is suspended, the usual order of social relations are reversed. For a few days the rigid bonds of rank, sex, age, family, and all authority are broken in fun and laughter. As we laugh together, the fellowship mounts, for in such laughter the incongruities of status and rank are confronted and mocked.

O

METHODOLOGICAL PROPOSITION 13
Ceremonies are social dramas in which we seek to uphold the dignity and majesty of social roles believed necessary to social order.

(a) Ceremonies enhance official social roles. In parades, processionals, as in all the pomp and circumstance of social life, we stage ourselves in solemn majesty. At commencement ceremonies we are careful to behave as the public of students, parents, and townspeople think we ought to behave in our role as professors. We know they are not capable of judging how wise or learned we are, but they are capable of judging how well we carry ourselves as professors during the ceremony. We exercise little individual choice in dress, in position in processional line, in how we walk, sit, rise, sing, or talk. We are (as we tell ourselves) playing at being a professor. Our play is solemn and controlled because we are playing a highly traditional role which is believed to uphold order within our profession and, indeed, the community. In the eyes of students and their parents we are (literally) "clothed with authority," the authority of the professor who personifies the principle of wisdom in society.

(b) A ceremonial role is always a group role, and it is an expression of rank within the group just as the institutional ceremony is an expression of rank within the community. In ceremonial drama we watch for indications of rank and honor. At military, academic, political, or ecclesiastical ceremony we watch dress, staging, and action, to discover what determines honor and rank. The insignia of a soldier tell us his branch of service, his rank, how long he has served, and how well he has served. We watch too for ceremonial linkage among institutions, as when we see musicians dressed in evening dress and white tie, the evening uniform of gentlemen. In Haydn's time musicians dressed in the livery of servants; in our time they dress as gentlemen and ladies. We watch too, for indications of how social offices are ordered from low to high within the institution, just as we note what position of honor is given an institution in all great community ceremonies. For while each institution has its own honor and dignity, it derives these from whatever social principles are accepted by the community as final and transcendent. In the Germany of Kaiser Wilhelm, as of Adolf Hitler, great homage was paid to the military. Military dress was affected by large numbers of Germans, and to be in any kind of uniform was more honorable than to be in civilian dress.

(c) As Marx and Carlyle (although for very different reasons) point out, all clothes are a kind of ceremonial dress. Carlyle tells us: "Clothes give us individuality, distinctions, social polity; clothes have made men of us." Once in uniform, we feel the power of the collectivity to which we now belong. Our longing for authority can at least be expressed. We indicate to others without and within institutions (and to ourselves) that we have enrolled in a group, and that we have a certain rank within the group. But in gaining social power we surrender the right to act freely and spontaneously as individuals. Now we must subordinate ourselves to the customs and traditions of the group. "He that puts on a public gown must put off a private person." But in doing so we discover a social self, a *role*, and as we play our part in institutional and community ceremony we discover the strange luster and aura of social office. Who among the students, parents, and townspeople are really competent to judge my competence as a sociologist? Yet in the presence of the dark majesty of my doctor's gown, and the weight of my insignia of rank, all bow before me. They are not bowing to *me*, but to the social office I fill as a guardian of wisdom in society.

O

METHODOLOGICAL PROPOSITION 14
Rites are social dramas in which collective sentiments are fixed through communication with supernatural powers who are believed to sustain social order.

(a) Anthropologists tell us that all regular collective expression of social sentiments tend to take on "ritual form," but there are many regular collective expressions in society. We have already discussed play, games, parties, festivals, and drama, as collective expressions. Even in an informal gathering such as a party, a group sauntering down the street, the play of children, or the ephemeral realm of fashion (where what we are wearing today we would not be "caught dead in" tomorrow), there is a regular collective expression of social sentiments. It is not such expression that distinguishes ritual, but its use as a means to fix collective sentiments through communication with some great supernatural power believed to sustain the principles of social order on which the society is based.

(b) Religion offers the purest examples of communication with a supernatural "beyond reason" whose meaning is not believed to be dependent on communication. Priests make explicit what others are content to leave implicit. *Any* term for social order whose meaning is not believed to be dependent on communication is a supernatural term, and whether we call it god, nature, man, society, science, or art, we make such terms "god-terms." For if how we communicate does not determine but simply "reflects," "indicates," "discovers," the laws of god, nature, man, society, how do we know these laws? Religion at least faces this question by teaching that we know them through revelation from some supernatural source.

(c) It does not help matters much to repeat in some new way what has already been said by Radcliffe-Brown (among others): namely, that rites are symbolic expressions, and that such expressions have a "social function" because their proper enactment is believed to create and sustain social order. *All* forms of social drama (as the term is used in the propositions given in this book) are believed to do this by those who take part in them. We must ask: What distinguishes ritual expression from other forms of expression? and how does ritual become social? For those seeking to construct a model of symbolic action based on communication in society, the question is no longer one of what ritual does (its "organization of sentiments," "maintenance of that order of the universe of which man and nature are interdependent parts," etc.) but one of how it does what we say it does. Malinowski and Radcliffe-Brown define ritual action through metaphor and analogy (or through extra-symbolic "referents"), not through analysis of the structure and function of symbols within the ritual act. In his discussion of taboo in the Frazer lecture of 1939, Radcliffe-Brown argues against Durkheim's distinction between the religious rite as obligatory and the magical rite as optional. He finds it difficult to accept Frazer's argument that all rites are at base a propitiation of superhuman powers which are believed to control nature and man. He argues that the distinctions made by Durkheim, Frazer, and Malinowski are difficult to apply to concrete actions in society because the simple dichotomy between magic and religion does not help much in the analysis of concrete acts.

Radcliffe-Brown proposes that we use the term "ritual value" rather than "ritual," so that we can remove the concept of ritual from a purely religious context. The basic question then (according to Radcliffe-Brown) becomes one of the relation between ritual and ritual values to the essential constitution of human society. He rejects Malinowski's theory which explains ritual actions by their referent in work and technology (although Malinowski admits that ritual acts differ from technical acts in having "some expressive or symbolic element in them"). The proper study of rites, Radcliffe-Brown argues, is the study of their real effects: not the effects that a rite is supposed to produce by the people who practice it, but the effects that it does actually produce. We must study the effects of rites upon the network of social relations binding individuals together in an ordered life.

How is this to be done? We begin by accepting the symbolic function of rites. We discover in them a "ritual idiom," and, since each rite has a myth associated with it, we have similarly to investigate the meaning of myths. As a result, we find that the meaning of any single rite becomes clear in the light of a cosmology, a body of ideas and beliefs about nature and human society. We must take into the account the whole body of cosmological ideas of which each rite "is a partial expression," because the continuity of society depends on keeping them alive by their regular expression in rite and myth.

How do we study this "regular expression"? Radcliffe-Brown refers to classical Chinese thought on ritual. Confucius, Hsun Tze, and the compilers of the *Li Chi* (*Book of Rites*) taught that rites are the orderly expression of feelings appropriate to a social situation. In the classical Chinese theories of social order, rites serve to refine and regulate human emotions. The performance of rites cultivates in the individual sentiments on whose existence the social order itself depends. How do they "refine and regulate human emotions"? Not by religion, but by art. *How* rituals were performed determined the welfare of the state, the fertility of its lands, the fruitfulness of its trees, the fecundity of women and of herds and flocks. The fulfillment of rites in China was a fully developed act, what we call a *dramatic* act, in which what was done, where, how, by whom, and for what purpose determined the efficacy of the act. Each rite required an appropriate attitude, and a correct expression of the attitude.

Reverence, eagerness, reluctance, joy, gloominess, and, indeed, all attitudes were believed to exist in their expression. They were not "states" but "forms" of conciousness. A high standard of expression was required, gentility implied great elegance in the niceties of bearing; a wide range of gestures and attitudes were developed, beside which our humble stock (hat-raising, hand-shaking, bowing, and the like) seems very meager. Hierarchal gestures were refined through constant practice. Thus we read in Book X of the *Analects:* "When the ruler summons him [a gentleman at the Court] to receive a guest, a look of confusion comes over his face and his legs seem to give beneath his weight." This is followed by advice on bowing, scraping, nodding, kneeling, and all the arts of "shrinking," or "making oneself small." We read of three hundred rules of major ritual and three *thousand* minor observances which had to be mastered by the Chinese gentleman. The expression "to know" when used by itself in China meant to know the rites, and indeed the whole idea of knowledge was that knowledge was gained in action in society, not in the perception of ideas in the mind.

(d) In Confucianism we have a cosmology which is based on aesthetic norms of conduct whose end is harmony between man, nature, and the gods, and whose means for the achievement of such harmony is ritual based on art, not religion as we know it. Our view of art as an agreeable arrangement of forms to be used solely for enjoyment (to give "delight") is a very limited one. In the greater part of man's history, and even today among many millions of people, art is regarded as something far different. Among primitives, as well as among non-European peoples, art exercises power over nature, man, society, and even the gods themselves. Confucius taught that the soul of man must be "incited to virtue by the *Songs,* then given a firm footing by the study of ritual, and finally perfected by music." (See Book VIII, 8 of the *Analects,* the Arthur Waley translation in the Modern Library Paperback edition.)

The Greeks shared this belief. Art, and particularly poetry, had a direct moral purpose. The primary function of the poet in Athens was that of teacher. As Shelley said in his A *Defense of Poetry:* "But poets, of those who imagine and express this indestructible order, are not only the authors of language and music, of the dance, and architecture, and statuary and painting; they are the institutors of laws, and the founders of civil society, and the inventors of the arts of life, and the teachers [of men]." Thus, in saying that ritual determines social order, and that ritual is expressed in art as well as religion, Radcliffe-Brown merely restates in another context, the context of primitive life, what has been said before by Confucius, Plato, Aristotle, and Shelley (to mention but a few) in the context of civilized life. But what he fails to do, and what the functional anthropologists following in the steps of Malinowski and Radcliffe-Brown must do, is to show *how* ritual creates and sustains social order.

(e) It is not enough to argue, as do Malinowski, Loisy, and Durkheim, that ritual based on religion gives men confidence, comfort, and a sense of security. Ritual also gives men fear of black magic and evil spirits, of the Devil, and of Hell, as well as fear of God. If social order depends on harmony between nature, man, and God, and harmony is not a religious but an aesthetic concept, and if, as we have argued, ritual is an attempt to communicate with supernatural powers who fix collective sentiments in forms which are believed to be an expression of the principles upon which the social order is based, then we ought to discuss the forms ritual assumes in communication.

188

(f) The social function of ritual is to uphold authority. In ritual, God *commands;* the kings of the earth rule by *divine* right; supernatural principles, like Platonic essences, are "pure" spirit beyond time, space, and motion; gods are beyond desire as well as thought. In celestial communication there is no discussion, because there is no need to overcome difference. The word of God, as Luther tells us, does not discover but creates the spirit. Rituals of social order based on religion equal (and sometimes surpass) in sublety and power those based on beliefs about nature, man, man in society, or art as a principle of order. For religious drama, as Kenneth Burke points out in *The Rhetoric of Religion,* is both circular and linear. In the cosmic drama of religion man sins but returns to good through atonement and sacrifice; man dies but is reborn in another cycle of life; man is born in a lowly status but is purified through progression upward in the hierarchy of the world which ends finally in God.

(g) In a secular frame of mind it is easy to point out how curious it is to believe in something that continues to circle on itself. But every society uses some variation of the "eternal return" as a principle of social order. In America we believe in an "ever-increasing" standard of living. Here there is not even a return, but an infinite spiral into some kind of orgiastic future where we will have ten cars and three homes instead of one. But where does the spiral end? Does the good life occur at the tenth car or the fifth home? If not, then where does it end? It never ends, because the ever-increasing standard of living is a principle, an absolute which is both cause and effect of its own being.

O

METHODOLOGICAL PROPOSITION 15
Drama depicts social action as symbolic action to be judged by principles of order believed necessary to order in society.

(a) A dramatic action is the depiction of a concrete act by certain kinds of actors, performing a certain kind of act, under certain conditions, by certain means, to achieve a certain end. Reason in drama and narrative is very different from reason in the sciences of space

189

where how we *perceive* the world, not how we *act* in it, determines truth. Dramatic truth also differs from ritual truth. Drama, and especially comic drama, seeks to keep action open to reason in discussion among men, not, as in religion, between men and the gods. Even in traditional drama, appeals to belief are appeals to reason in action; certain ways of acting lead to certain results in human relationships. As spectators we learn on a purely symbolic level, but on this level, attitudes (which are incipient acts) are formed. We do not have an attitude and then seek forms in which to express it, but in the experience through form provided by artists of all kinds, and by ourselves in communication with others, we experience attitudes.

(b) Art is a socially sanctioned realm of change, ambiguity, and doubt. There is no "truth," but many "truths" in the art world. The artist presents his own vision, fully aware that other artists will do the same. Art institutionalizes change in society, just as religion institutionalizes "eternal" and "fixed" principles of social action. Change cannot exist without permanence, nor can truths be changed without confidence in change as a form of order in society. Doubt will not lead to controlled inquiry but to fear and terror, unless we develop means to perfect doubt as a sanctioned method of inquiry. Inquiry into the ends and means of social action assumes, of course, that the principles of inquiry upon which are based art, science, and, indeed, all the probings of the human mind, will lead to some kind of truth; just as the devout worshiper of a god assumes that the proper performance of his rites will put him in communication with a god who will then open his mind to truth.

(c) The social truth of art is found in communication among men where there are many voices, not one powerful supernatural voice, raised in search for truth. Dramatic reason is born in dialogue among men who bicker and contend, as they curse and bless, yet who believe that in such contention truth can be reached. There are aesthetic myths, and aesthetic mystics, just as there are religious myths, and ascetic mystics. Terms for beauty, like terms for God, can easily become vested with supernatural power. When there is only one form of beauty in art, reason in art dies. For reason cannot live unless in the life of dialogue. But neither can reason in dialogue exist unless there is belief in dramatic form in art as a form of community. When our leaders no longer believe that the forms of drama and narrative have any effect on human relationships we turn to those who do believe in the efficacy of some kind of symbolic order to create and sustain social order. Whatever we say about the "illusion" of beliefs in the power of ritual acts in religion to sustain social order, they at least depict men in action in time, not simply in motion in space.

(d) Sociological methodology must show how dramatic form, purely as form, functions in the symbolic context of social action. But we must show, too, how the social context of experience in the community is used by the dramatist, and, finally, how the artist's forms are used by various institutions in the community or by the community as a whole. The hero of art drama is first of all a hero taken from the traditions of his own art, but he is also taken from the many social types already extant in the community. The new and unique hero depicted by the great artist is taken by the community as a model for action, because the community needs heroes who can solve problems in action. The clue to the meaning of an art work, or at least its *social* meaning, lies in how the different and conflicting claims of the actors are resolved. In the name of what principle of order, as vested in what institution, class, party, or status group, do actors resolve their differences, assume new roles, or, ultimately, face death? These moments of transcendence offer us clues, in art as in society, to beliefs about the form and content of principles of action which are supposed to create and sustain social order.

○

METHODOLOGICAL PROPOSITION 16
The staging of an act in society is a social drama of authority in which the relationship between ends and the means must be kept under constant review through criticism.

(a) Every institution, sacred or secular, must judge the efficacy of its acts. Superior, inferior, and equal alike must be constantly alert to how well they are communicating with each other, because it is only through communication that they relate. In this we are all like orators who scan the faces of their audiences for clues to the success of their speeches. Even when we talk to ourselves we listen and reply to what we say. In dreams and nightmares we judge ourselves. Even an animal must judge his environment (that is, select the stimuli to which he will respond). Criticism is, therefore, a constituent part of all communication; and in the development of community life, as in the development of the individual, criticism becomes a necessary phase of social action. The decisive questions in the analysis of the expression of social order are: Who expresses what kind of criticism? when? under what conditions? by what means? and for what purposes? How are critics selected, trained, and rewarded?

(b) To construct a sociological methodology of criticism we assume a perfected, critical institution in which those who mount a social drama of social order, those who are audience to it, and those who are responsible for creating the form used in the drama are in open, free, and close relationship to the critic (as he is to them). When we consider criticism from such an institutional view, we distinguish between the artists (and all symbol manipulators), the social drama they create, the kinds of dramas authorities mount to legitimize their power, the publics and their reception of these dramas, and, finally, the selection, training, and patronage of critics who pass judgments on the social efficacy of such dramas. The critic exists in authoritarian as well as egalitarian societies. Five-year plans fail, and some explanation must be made of why they failed. The differences in criticism among various types of institutions does not lie in the function of criticism, but in how the critic communicates. We ask: How does the critic communicate with those in power, with artists and symbol manipulators who are responsible for creating symbols of power, with audiences whose response determines the success or failure of the authorities who seek to rule them, and, finally, with other critics?

○

Relationships between authorities, symbol manipulators, public, and critics, may be determined by asking to what degree communication between and among them is open or closed.

(a) Authoritarian critics communicate only with their rulers and other members of the ruling class; democratic critics communicate openly and freely with any audience they can reach. The final value in democratic criticism is the enlightenment of the whole community through open, free, and informed discussion. We ask, then, of the critic: With whom may you communicate your judgments over the relationship between means and ends in the various kinds of role enactments which are supposed to uphold a social order? What may be communicated by the critic? when? under what conditions? by what means? and for what purposes?

(b) Since no society is wholly open or wholly closed, there will always be a mixture of all types of communication. Thus, in the authoritarian society of Louis XIV, the court could be criticized so long as such criticism was "in fun" through art (as in the comedy of Molière), and confined to courtly audiences—those at Versailles and Paris (when "properly" controlled). In any society, political questions are closed, as well as open, to criticism. If we discuss defense secrets in public we give aid and comfort to the enemy. In an authoritarian institution, such as a hospital, the pathologist must not communicate his findings to anyone but a few members of the staff. An army officer must not criticize his superiors or inferiors in public, for this is "washing dirty linen in public."

(c) Between the extremes of open and closed critical communication there are many circumlocutions in communication. We use many euphemisms, substituting particular words, phrases, and names for others. In common speech we say that a person "passed away," "has gone to his reward," or "kicked the bucket," when we mean that he has died. Or, in satiric allegory, we talk about animals when we are really talking about men. Such coyness extends also to slang, in which we are allowed to criticize acts we could not say much about—or say anything about—without great difficulty in proper speech. Every institution provides means for expressing ambiguity in slang, obscenity, nicknames, and jokes over the wisdom of superiors, the loyalty of inferiors, and the good sense of friends. Supernatural powers, like all authorities, are given familiar names which allow us to talk about them. Satan, the Prince of Darkness, becomes Old Nick, while money becomes boodle, buck, bundle, cabbage, chips, dough, gelt, jack, kale, wad, or green stuff.

(d) While our dreams have many more disguised meanings than the circumlocutions we use in public, we do use hidden and secret communications in public communication, too. Thus, we read that among the Greeks it was thought unlucky to use the names of divinities of the underworld because of their connection with death. Among the Hebrews the Tetragrammaton, or Sacred Name, could not be uttered; only *Adonai* or *Elochim* could be used as the name of God. Even today in our secular society we often admonish each other not to speak of the devil, for this might make him appear. And certainly in America we speak carefully of death, so carefully indeed that in such cemeteries as Forest Lawn the dead are embalmed (sometimes with their pet animals) in lifelike poses, so that their loved ones may remember them "as they were in life."

○

METHODOLOGICAL PROPOSITION 18
The primary type of relationship between authority, symbol manipulators, critics, and audiences exists within face-to-face groups.

(a) When criticism takes place in small, intimate groups, the purposes of the criticism are understood by everyone present. Authorities, symbol manipulators controlled by authority, the audience, and the critic, all know the meaning of each other's responses almost immediately, because they are using symbols which they share in common and frequently use in their daily lives. In such relationships there is no segmentation of institutional or community life; the speaker speaks to the group as a whole. Such criticism is not considered to be a specialized or "expert" statement derived from some specialized and abstract standard of justice. Here there is no office of criticism apart from the authority of the group itself, and while the audience in this type of criticism is the group as a whole, the critic knows the group will be bound by authority's interpretation of custom and tradition. The "way it always has been done" is a binding norm, because in primary groups tradition is not simply usage, habit, or custom, but an enactment of social order.

O

METHODOLOGICAL PROPOSITION 19
A second type of relationship occurs whenever a status group, class, institution, or society seeks to monopolize communication.

(a) Whenever symbols of social order are monopolized by a caste, a priesthood, a profession, or any closed group, the critic cannot communicate to general publics, but only to the ruling group. Communication with general publics is considered heresy, not criticism. The task of the critic in communicating with general publics is to justify the faith, not to question its efficacy. The critic reaches publics through censors, judges, or other critics superior to him in a hierarchy of critics whose rank and social office determines the power of their critical office. In such criticism, means, but not ends, may be opened to criticism.

(b) Criticism within an elite is always difficult. For if those in power are brave, wise, and intelligent, how can there be need for criticism? The principles of action, their ends as social order, have been established, often by divine or supernatural powers, and communication with these powers entrusted to a priesthood "elected" by the gods themselves. Yet even in such autocracies wars are lost, kings die, people revolt, and famine stalks the land. Questions over what went wrong must be answered. Criticism, as judgments of action, must be undertaken in autocratic and democratic states alike, but the ways in which this criticism is communicated to various publics will be very different.

O

METHODOLOGICAL PROPOSITION 20

A third type of relationship occurs whenever critics
judge in terms of craft principles.

(a) Critics often consider themselves to be guardians of a craft skill.
This easily passes into belief in the craft skill as an end in itself, and
domination of the craft by publics who use it for power over fashion,
style, and art in terms of standards of judgment set by taste and con-
noisseurship. Critics become advocates for specific groups such as the
gentry, the connoisseur, the salon, the publisher, the school, or crafts-
men and artists. We hear of "art for art's sake" in the world of art, and
manners as the "poetry of society." This type of critic often communicates only with other symbol manipulators, as in the highly
specialized role of the "play doctor" of our theater. The public is
"known" to exist, but the critic conceives of his public as the con-
noisseurs, the men of taste, or other symbol manipulators. The general
public is "vulgar" and "low," and it is considered demeaning to criticize
for them. The public may be "pleased," its taste "instructed," but it is
only permitted to "overhear" what the critic is saying, for he does not
communicate directly with the general public.

○

METHODOLOGICAL PROPOSITION 21

In a fourth type of relationship the critic conceives of
his role in terms of communicating directly to the
public, and acts as a delegate of this public to the artist.

(a) A critic who acts as a delegate welcomes the public, and assumes
a role as spokesman, teacher and "literary priest." He strives to communicate to the widest possible audience, and to enlarge his audience in
every way. In a final variant of this type of relationship, the critic may
consider himself to be speaking to the people as a prophet, or a great
cultural leader. For him the voice of the reader, or the voice of anyone
who uses the artist's symbols in whatever form, is the voice of God. He
relates to authorities, as well as to the people, in the role of an interpreter of what artists "really" mean, or what they "should mean," and
he shows how the artist's intentions should be carried out in terms of

the taste of the public and the principles of social order upheld by those who seek power over general publics ("the people").

○

METHODOLOGICAL PROPOSITION 22

In a fifth type of relationship, authorities, artists, publics, and critics assume a mutual responsibility for the creation, distribution, and use of what they consider to be the best kinds of symbolic expression.

(a) The critic who assumes that men in society have mutual responsibilities tries to weigh the competing claims of authority, artist, public, and the critic himself. He seeks to maximize ways in which each can enter into relations with the other. As a critic of social drama he tries to make clear in what the congruity between ends and means in community expression consists. He struggles to achieve a methodology. He tries to interpret symbol manipulators and their publics to each other on the basis of their relevance to the struggle for order in society. At this point the critic is no longer an apologist for some existing authority. His ideal now becomes that of free criticism, and the development of criticism as an institution where the critic will have the right to say what he likes to any public he can reach. In this democratic ideal of criticism, discussion of men and issues reach maximum power when criticism is informed, open to all, and carried on among people who have been made aware of the problems which engage the critic, and are well enough educated to follow the deliberations of the critic.

(b) Measuring critical practices against the democratic ideal of free, open, and informed critical discussion gives many clues to the analysis of social hierarchy. When we apply our democratic model we discover at once that even in institutions and communities where there is great freedom there are many blocks to free communication of criticism. All authorities agree on the need for criticism, for even the most authoritarian leader must know why he failed if he is to try again, but authorities do not agree on how criticism should be communicated. The Defense Department does not want its officers to discuss military planning before the people, for this will give the enemy information vital to our security. School authorities do not want free, open, and informed discussion by members of their staff on the sex life of students because this might offend parents and the church (the people are "not yet ready" for such discussion). Businessmen do not want students trained to doubt the virtue of money as a symbol of community life, they want them trained to know how to make money "work better." Professors do not want public discussion of their teaching, or student's ratings of their classroom performance published. Urban planners do not want the values of their plans discussed by those who "do not understand" the problems of planning. In this planners, like most experts, want their critiques discussed by those who are "competent" to judge their work as experts. As children we are taught that it is not polite to discuss religion or politics in company, and as the proverb admonishes us, we must not discuss rope in the house of a man about to be hanged.

(c) But however institutions may disagree on the freedom of the critic to communicate his judgments, all are agreed on the need for criticism. In our methodology we ask then: Where is criticism open, where closed? We search, too, for types of ambiguous, veiled, or hidden criticism, which is neither open or closed, as we see in all forms of comedy where we are permitted to say in jest what we cannot say openly and directly. Make-believe, and all the variants of wishing we see in fairy tales, fantasies, and day and night dreams, often contain veiled criticism. We ask, then, what may be criticized? by whom? how? when? where? and for what purpose?

(d) For our purposes of sociological inquiry we ask: What access does the critic have to the various means of communication which exists in his society? For whether criticism is open, veiled, or closed, it must be communicated, and the control of criticism tells us much about authority. Even societies planned by the wisest rulers must plan for criticism. How this is done, and who plans criticism, are decisive questions for an understanding of the social drama of authority, democratic and authoritarian alike. If there are to be guardians of our community, who shall guard the guardians? If there are to be appraisers, investigating committees, inspectors general, and other types of critics, who shall criticize the critics?

○

METHODOLOGICAL PROPOSITION 23
Basic functions in society must be dramatized before they can be communicated as actions.

(a) The basic social dramas occur when men come together to find mates; to rule and be ruled; to provide for material wants; to defend themselves against enemies at home and abroad; to transmit and create ideals, purposes, values, and skills believed necessary to the preservation of their society; to enjoy each other's company on a purely social level; to entertain themselves through play, games, and art; to cure themselves of physical, mental, spiritual, and social maladies; and finally, to uphold and create cultural values, goals, and purposes through religion, art, and science.

(b) Rulers who seek to legitimize their authority over us always do so on the basis of "service." In our methodology, we ask: How are the family, government, social welfare, defense, education, entertainment, health, and religion symbolized? What social roles are assumed by those who carry out these functions? What kinds of dramas do they mount in their presentation of themselves to their institutional and community audiences? For whether such rulership is invested in kings, presidents, dictators, tyrants, emperors, managers, leaders of management or labor, chairmen, ward bosses, parliaments, legislatures, or courts, they must administer these basic functions so as to persuade inferiors, equals, and superiors alike that they are administrating well. For if they do not, someone else will, and he will gain power in doing so. Thus, the study of administrative communication is necessary to an understanding of power in society.

(c) For most people, it is how a role is played, not critical discussion of the social principles involved in the role, which determines the success of a leader. There have been many revolutions in history, but few have destroyed the social drama, or even abolished the leading roles, of the society they attacked so bitterly. The actor, not the role, is abolished. Indeed, when the community drama itself is attacked, we have what is called a reign of terror, a time of *no* order, which, like profound anxiety in the individual, cannot be endured long. Sometimes, indeed, the panic ensuing from this reduction of a community to a mob is so frightening that tyrants far harsher than those thrown from power are accepted as leaders, if for no other reason than to bring anarchy to an end. Revolutions which escape such terror (like individuals who escape deep and prolonged anxiety) leave intact the basic social role-structure of their society. Thus, the British revolutions of the seventeenth century, and the American revolution of the eighteenth century, left the social life of their respective communities nearly unchanged. George Washington replaced George III and the American Congress replaced the British Parliament, but the social roles and social offices common to British and American life changed but little.

(d) To understand how a society achieves social order, we ask, then: How are basic social functions staged and communicated? For example, who is the American mother? Is she old, young, holy, wise, sophisticated, maternal? Is she a housekeeper, a homemaker, a career woman, a wife, or some combination of each? Is her "femininity" maternal, erotic, poetic, or economic (as the Great American Customer)? That is, in the symbolic life of the community, how is she depicted? by whom? how? on what occasions? and for what purposes? We ask, too, how she is *not* depicted. What kinds of acts are forbidden her, what uses of her image are proscribed by custom, law, tradition, and taste? We then inquire into the problems of the American mother, as these are depicted in various types of communication. Is there a typical mother of the smart set magazines? How is the mother depicted in the slicks, the popular family press, and the pulps? How is the mother's image used in advertising? How is she honored in community rites and festivals (as in the American Mother's Day)? What are her rights in law? Is any provision made for her in education as a teacher or a student? And, finally, in what way is her role related to the great principles of the society which are believed to uphold social order?

(e) The legitimation of authority is based on persuasion. The political leader goes directly to his people, both in his struggle for power and in his attempts to stay in power. Force may put a leader in power, but it will not keep him there, for, as the proverb reminds us, we can do everything with bayonets but sit on them. And even when we use force, we assume that one way of using force, and not another, is proper and just. No one can force us to die for a leader or the cause he represents: we must be persuaded to risk our lives, and once persuaded, our beliefs must be kept alive. We ask then: From what symbolic source does the leader draw his power? In what *name* (God, country, ideology, defense of our homes and families) does he ask us to fight and die? Does he present himself as a military leader, and if so, of what rank? If he presents himself as a civilian leader, what kind of civilian is he?

○

METHODOLOGICAL PROPOSITION 24
Authorities relate family life to social order through the depiction of courtship, marriage, and parenthood as a preparation for citizenship in the community.

(a) Authorities seek to subordinate sex to their own principles of social order. This is done through creating dramas of courtship and marriage that serve as norms for "proper" and "right" ways to court and to conduct a marriage. For American businessmen, the ideal drama of courtship and marriage is a drama of spending. The woman must be taught to become the "Great American Customer," and she must, therefore, become highly adept at spending, or what we call shopping. For churchmen, the courtship must become a sacrament which leads to union with God. For artists, courtship must be subordinated to aesthetic canons, as in the "love story." Statesmen want the family to produce citizens devoted to the state. The army wants virile sons whose parents and teachers will inspire children with the virtues of military life. Leaders of high society want families to raise children who will become skilled in the arts of the "social game." Thus, each authority has its principle of family life. These principles often contradict each other; indeed,. sometimes they are in such deep conflict that they cannot be resolved by the individual as he acts in society.

(b) Our first and our most important experience of authority comes from the family itself. How we are ruled at home will have much to do with how we rule others and how we regard the ways others rule us. Authoritarian parents produce authoritarian children, who, in turn become authoritarian adults. Whatever else we learn in the family, we learn to love and to hate as superiors and inferiors. The Freudians have made experience within the family so central to their theory that Freudian psychology is really a family psychology, not an "individual" psychology. The essence of the Oedipus complex consists in the simultaneous operation of hatred and incestuous impulses, accompanied by tender love impulses. This mixture of feeling gives rise to what the Freudians call ambivalence. The son wants to express his hatred for the father, but, at the same time, he feels also a tender love for him. Normally the child realizes that his hatred and incestuous impulses were wrongly displayed emotions and incompatible with his happiness. The resolution of the Oedipus complex is of crucial importance since it determines the mental health of the individual.

(c) The sociologist recognizes the sexual and aggressive roots of behavior in the early familial experiences of the child, but he is also interested in how the structure and function of the family affects economic, religious, protective, educational, and prestige-giving functions. The major sociological function of the family is the socializing of family members so that they will perpetuate the cultural achievements of the group. The family is a miniature community in which members must submit to a common discipline. Social solidarity is based on habits and sentiments learned in the family. The biological interdependence and co-operation of the members of the family, which give rise to intimacies of the closest and most enduring kind, have no parallel among other institutions. The interplay of the attractions, tensions, and accommodations of personalities in the intimate bonds of family life, and above all, the ways in which we learn to express ourselves, make the study of the family basic to all social study. Parents are our first and most intense experience of absolute authority, an authority who can make us miserable or happy, and make all things right by command. Our parents are also our first audience. We play before them, bring things to them, entice them to play games with us, in hope of learning how to attract and hold their attention.

O

METHODOLOGICAL PROPOSITION 25
Symbols of government must be dramatized as symbols of social order.

(a) Rulers who seek to legitimize their authority over us often do so on the basis of service to a "higher" ideal of community life. As sociologists we ask: What social roles are assumed by those who carry out these functions? What kinds of dramas do they mount in their presentation of themselves to their institutional and community audiences? For in all societies, egalitarian as well as authoritarian, someone must rule. And in whatever role such rulership is vested, we must be persuaded as inferiors, equals, and superiors that our leaders are administering well. No matter how powerful the leader may seem, his power rests on how he relates his goverance to the satisfaction of physical, biological, social, and spiritual needs. And no matter how charismatic the leader may be, once he begins to communicate his charisma to followers who are striving to create a community, he must convince us that he can not only inspire, but *organize* a community. He must, as we say in America, know how to boss. When we give a man power over us, we expect him to know how to use it. He must rule in love and reward his loyal followers, just as he must punish the disloyal, and use his power to overcome enemies at home and abroad. He may do this in the name of God, country, social order, or the family, but however he symbolizes or names his acts, he must satisfy the community's basic social needs.

(b) We observe carefully how rulers stage themselves before different audiences, ranging from the office staff of the boss of a small local institution to the elaborate social dramas in which an emperor, king, or president acts out principles of social order. All rulers, small and great alike, enact a drama of authority. Few, very few, create the social roles in which they mount the stage as administrators. Any surgeon, priest, manager, labor leader, gang leader, officer, or director finds that a certain way of playing the role of leader has existed long before he plays it. These traditional roles, or social offices, stabilize institutional and community life because they are forms of enactment which are well understood and can be responded to easily by others who must act together with those who occupy the role. For if a leader must judge the loyalty, courage, and devotion of his followers, his followers, in turn, must judge that leader's majesty and power. When the followers have been taught to believe deeply in great transcendent principles which uphold social order, they watch carefully to see that their leaders play their roles in keeping with such principles.

(c) Force in arms is always carried out by the people who are governed. Thus force is always on the side of the governed. Governors have nothing to support them but opinion, and thus opinion becomes the basis of government. Political opinion is the result, not of a "social force," but of an enactment of a "way of life." People want to be ruled in certain ways, and just as there are religious, aesthetic, economic, and scientific "ways of life," so too are there political. How we are addressed by our leaders, in what kinds of action, by what means, in what roles, and in the name of what grand purpose, determines political action. Beliefs in authority are not abstractions, but dramatic rules of conduct.

(d) A political leader must see to it that the political system which sustains his power is upheld, and he must also play his role as leader in such a way that his office within the system is honored. Every state is founded on force, as Trotsky, Bebel, and others remind us. But even force must be organized, and this can be done only when people are persuaded to undertake the sacrifices and the risks which the application of force entails. Long before battle we must vote money to raise armies, allocate men and material to the production and distribution of arms, and convince men to fight and die. And even when we fight, we do so not simply to wound, kill, and destroy our enemy, but to make him accept our will as his will. As we say, war is a continuation of politics in which we must be careful to win the peace as well as the war. Force, like any power in society, depends on a distribution as well as a possession of authority. Who has the "right"—by birth, skill, or possession of land, money, or rank—to become an officer determines how a war will be waged.

(e) In politics the glory of what we call the system of politics must be kept alive. The basis of this glory varies among societies, just as it shifts from one expression to another in a given society. Kingship is based on the *relation* of the king to the gods. Thus we hear of the "divine right of kings." Weber has much to say about status honor as a "typical component" of life that is determined by a specific—positive or negative—social estimation of honor. Status honor is expressed by a specific "style of life" which can be expected from those who wish to identify with each other. What Weber meant by a "style" is illustrated by his discussion of the Chinese literati who ruled China for so long. The literati were, above all, "keepers of the rites." They were careful to glorify the *ways* of ruling, the rites, ceremonies, and staging of political power. In their practice of governance the performance of the office, not the man, was "sacred."

But even the most skillful "official glorifier," as Spencer called those responsible for keeping the glory of office alive, must decide on some *form* of glorification. We watch then for the kind of social drama mounted by those in power over us. Is it a family drama, in which our leader plays the role of the "great white father"? Is he "above the battle," in a remote realm where his judgments are not swayed by the vulgar passions of men? Is he partisan and skilled in vituperation ("Give 'em hell, Harry!")? Is he cold and calculating, a "walking computer?" Does he surround himself with military symbols, and if so, in what military office? Is he resplendent with insignia of high military office (as Kaiser Wilhelm) or with the mock-modesty of humble rank (Stalin and Hitler)? The drama of politics, like the rhetoric of political appeal, tells us much about the sources of power in society. A style, whether of status, art, religion, or science, is an identification, a way of expressing desire to belong to one group and not to another.

(f) In American politics, where campaigning was born in debate before the people, it is important that the rules of debate be honored and dignified. The candidate for office must "go to the people," he must address himself to issues which are considered crucial to the community, he must stand ready to debate his opponent (either in person or in replies in speeches or newspaper and television interviews); he must mount a drama of contest and struggle between himself and his opponent. This must be done with a certain playfulness and humor. American politics must be "fun" as well as "serious." We expect to enjoy political drama, and indeed it may be said that our frequent political campaigns are the great drama of American life. For us, politics is also a game, the "great game" of politics, and we expect our candidates to play hard according to the rules, and to be good winners and good losers. The political candidate must "run a good race." He must "put up a good fight," and "take the issues to the people." And above all, he must fight fairly—that is, he must not "break the rules of the game."

(g) In democracy, autocracy, constitutional monarchy, or whatever form of government, there are two elements which must exist side by side. These are glory and efficiency. Glory is a dignification achieved through style (a "way of life") which inferiors use to identify themselves with superiors. Superiors, in turn, use styles of performance (their "presence") to move the hearts and minds of inferiors to loyalty and reverence. It is also used to dignify equality through enhancing the mystique of playing fair according to the rules of the game. Among equals it is necessary to play fair to gain the honor of one's peers; indeed, it is by playing fair according to rules that one indicates to an opponent that he is being treated as an equal. In play among equals we can give or accept a handicap (as in golf matches), but we do this so that we can begin our play as equals under rules. Once the play is under way, we ask no quarter and we give none. We do not want our opponent to withhold his strength, nor do we want him to be so unequal that we cannot pit ourselves against him. We are bound by rules of our own making, and we win or lose according to rules which make the game a clear test of skill, stamina, and courage.

○

METHODOLOGICAL PROPOSITION 26
Authorities must create and sustain ways of making, distributing, and consuming food, clothing, and shelter, according to beliefs in the right of superiors, inferiors, and equals to share in these services.

(a) How we raise food, produce goods and services, and transport them is determined by who has what right to how much food, clothing, and shelter, and what facilities exist for the transportation of symbols necessary to the operation of the organizations which supply our goods and services. Before wheat can be sown, harvested, and transported, there must be some kind of decision about who is going to get how much wheat, when, where, and how. And this decision must be explained to the community at large. If it cannot be defended—if slum dwellers must forage among Gold Coast garbage cans for food the rich have thrown away—then some "reason" for such injustice must be given. Before a businessman can order goods he must know how much he will pay for them, what his costs will be in holding them for sale, how long he must wait for delivery, and how long it will take him to sell them. Before the consumer shops, she must have some idea of what she wants. Before the manufacturer can produce goods, he must plan and design his goods on paper before he actually produces them.

(b) The provision of goods and services is a social act, and a communicative act. Goods and services are distributed according to rank and power; at the same time, the kinds of symbols available to us, and their control by various institutions, determine the kinds of goods and services we have. As Veblen said, invention is the mother of necessity; and invention, the creation of wants, is a symbolic process. Markets, our advertising men remind us, are not "discovered," but "created." Goods and services cannot be transported without symbolic control through messages to interested parties about when they are shipped, who is transporting them, when they will arrive, in what condition, and at what point of destination. A "transportation net" is a communicative net, and the transportation of things depends on the transportation of symbols which stand for the things. The American economic system now functions in terms of a symbol called money, whose symbolic properties have made possible the American way of providing services for the community.

(c) Socialist economies are no different in their dependence on communication. The economy must be planned, and the planners must communicate their plans to the people. For no matter how grandiose the plans, the will to achieve them must be created, just as critiques over the success and failure of past plans must be communicated to those in power (if not to the people). The symbolization of plans, in the socialist state, then, becomes something like the dramatization of the market in a society such as ours. Just as we create daily and hourly dramas in the press and on television about the earning and spending of money as a means toward an ever-increasing standard of living, so must socialist authorities dramatize their present plans in visions of glowing futures of these plans.

(d) Money as such is not a very useful symbol of hierarchy. Unlike other insignia of hierarchy it means nothing in itself. The right to keep wheat we have harvested, to keep a certain number of skins taken from animals killed in the hunt, to own land, to use roads, to marry, all depend on symbols too, but such rights are not wholly symbolic. Wheat may be eaten, skins dressed into clothing, and land may be used to provide a home. But money cannot be eaten, used to clothe the body, or used as shelter from the elements. It cannot even be used, like land, to indicate hierarchy. A man who simply accumulates money is called a miser, while a man who builds up a great estate of land is considered a public hero (or villain). The death of a wealthy man who dies in simple surroundings, or of a miser worth many thousands who dies in a cheap boarding house, is a front page story in our press. A man who has money and does not put it "to work" to make money, or who does not spend it to communicate his success, is really considered slightly mad. For if we do not put money to work, how can we earn more money? And if we do not spend, how can anyone know how rich we are? Thus, money must be transformed into something other than what it is, and this process of transformation involves a great share of our time and energy in America.

○

METHODOLOGICAL PROPOSITION 27
To understand authority we must observe what kind of social drama is mounted by the military, the police, and the intelligence services used by each.

(a) Institutions, communities, and societies must defend themselves against enemies within as well as without. In large communities this is done through two kinds of armies: the police who are used against enemies within, and the military who are used against enemies without. Every institution must also develop its own intelligence service. In the symbolic analysis of defense institutions we watch for ways in which symbols of the military, the police, and the intelligence services affect communication of other social functions, just as we watch for the ways in which defense institutions present themselves to various publics. This may range from the "garrison state" with its complete subordination of all social life to the military, to peaceful societies which defend themselves only against attack. We ask, too: In the name of what power, or combination of powers, are we asked to uphold military virtues? That is, *what* are we defending? and in what kind of social drama are we trained for defense? and what institutions in the community are involved in defense? We examine carefully any linkage of symbols of war with other symbols, as when we are told that war is a means of preserving the peace, or, as when the Air Corps dispatches a squadron of planes on what we are told is a peace mission, or as when we are told that a peace-loving nation has resumed nuclear bomb tests. We were told once that we must go to war to end war; now we hear again that soldiers are really guardians of the peace. In 1956 we saw Russian tanks with the dove of peace painted on them moving into Hungary. Here, as so often in the social use of symbols, opposites meet.

(b) In the symbolization of war we see the essential paradox in the relation between force and the great transcendent ideas of social order that are used to legitimize the use of force. If the "dictatorship of the proletariat" is "inevitable," why is Russia an armed camp? Why has it been necessary for Russia to imprison, torture, and kill so many of her citizens in purge trials? Why has the Russian government imprisoned, tortured, and killed the citizens of subjugated states now under Russian "protection"? If the voice of the people is the voice of God, in whose eyes all men are equal, why then are Negroes in America prevented from making their voice heard at the polls? If nature is "red in tooth and claw," and war is but a state of nature, what is the use of talking about abolishing war? If war "purifies" the spirit through the sacrifice it requires, what is the good of a spirit that lives in blood and misery, and feeds on violence? And, finally, why is it necessary to defend through violence and war social principles which are just and reasonable, and emanate from an all-powerful God who created the laws of society? Defense is an admission of weakness, for in saying that we have to defend our principles, we admit them to be in danger.

(c) Defense against the enemy within the state offers crucial points of inquiry for an understanding of the communication of social order. As we ask how it comes about that an all-powerful and loving God permits evil, so we ask how it happens that a powerful and just ruler must contend with disobedience and crime. And, finally, we ask why it is that principles of order produce so much disorder. For, obviously, there can be no crime until a law is passed to define it ("Laws make crimes."). Questions of the same kind must be asked about the defenses individuals create within themselves to deal with their own suffering and guilt. For if we have chosen the quite solitary life of the scholar because we delight in creating order in imaginative forms through which we make sense out of the world, why are we so often racked by melancholy and depression? If we believe that love and compassion are the great principles of order within the self, as in society, why then must we struggle so hard to conquer hate and indifference? And, most terrible of all questions directed to the self, if we believe that love and brotherhood are the laws of community life, why do we enjoy hate, violence and killing on symbolic as well as motor levels of expression?

(d) In social drama, as in art drama, we depict villains (the "bad guys") who, like the devil among the devout, embody the evil principles we must fight. Sometimes we derive the principles of the villain from nature, when we hang a criminal who committed a crime "against nature." Or we say that man sins "against himself." Or we say a man sins against the community, as when we execute a traitor. Or we banish a man from our company because he lacks tact. Or we hunt down, torture, and kill heretics because they are possessed by a devil who must be driven from our community. Or we condemn people for ignorance, because virtue consists in the struggle to "know thyself." And, final irony of all, we find that we must defend ourselves against our virtues, for are we not warned in proverbs that the wise man must know when to stop being wise? And do we not hear from Luther that we must sometimes commit a sin "out of hate and contempt for the devil" for "if one is too frightened of sinning, one is lost." Thus, we must learn to defend the self as well as the community. Our dramas of defense within ourselves against our vices and excesses of virtues, like the great community dramas of defense mounted by the military, tell us much about authority, because in the depiction of the enemy within, as well as without, we confront the weakness of our principles of order.

(e) Intelligence services range from syping on enemies within and without to critical appraisal of our own performance. The intentions and capabilities of our enemies must be assessed and reported. The criminal world within the community must be watched. We must know whether we are achieving ends good for the group, and that we are using means appropriate to such ends. As we become more skilled in propaganda we can be taken in by our own publicity. As superiors we must be wary of sycophants and "yes men." As inferiors we must guard against rulers who delude themselves, as they seek to delude us.

We must recognize the seeds of revolt within the community, just as we must face unruly selves within the self.

○

METHODOLOGICAL PROPOSITION 28
The basic function of education is the transmission of traditions, customs, and sentiments which are believed necessary to social order and, at the same time, the creation of methods of inquiry which will help us to solve problems we must solve if the community is to survive.

(a) Every authority seeks to educate us to his view of social order, and to teach us skills considered necessary to the preservation of such order. Education ranges from training in how to criticize our gods to producing a "sales pitch" which honey-tongued salesmen seek to use to convince us that success in love depends on the kind of hair oil we use. We have to be educated to want the things money will buy, just as we have to be educated to love wisdom. The purest form of education creates and sustains inquiry on the relations between means and ends in human conduct. When ends are not open to inquiry, we are in the realm of magic, and its modern variant, advertising. In magic, means alone—*how* a thing is done—determine success. What those in power want done can be checked easily enough by examining the allocation of community resources to education. And, since all allocations are legitimized by beliefs in the relation between a certain kind of education and social order, who gets what in education tells us what kind of social order is desired.

(b) The first task of education is to pass on the traditional lore upon which social consensus is based. The second is to create methods of inquiry that make possible systematic questioning of traditions and goals in all cases where they no longer work. We act together in the name of traditions that lie in a past, but we also act in the name of goals that lie in a future. So long as tradition serves to create consensus, and we can act together without much difficulty, we do not question. But where tradition does not work, and action becomes problematic, we must question the principles of action we have taken for granted. And even when there is a high degree of consensus, we must still experiment with our tools of inquiry to keep them in good working order. There are, then, three modes of education: first, formal education in tradition; second, the construction of social goals; and third, the invention of methods of inquiry we can use to test relationships between means and ends in conduct.

(c) We note in education how tradition is sustained. Who are the guardians of the past? Are the "founding fathers" of the community priests, warriors, businessmen, politicians, artists? Is the way to the perfect commonwealth economic, political, military, religious? How will it be reached? What forms of communication will be used? How can we judge the efficacy of tradition, and how do we know if we are making progress in our journey to our ideal commonwealth? Who controls education? On what basis are teachers, administrators, boards, and students selected? How are various publics communicated with by educational institutions? How are funds allocated for education? How is the critical function of education preserved? How is the creativity in the school rewarded? Who speaks for education, and to what publics?

○

METHODOLOGICAL PROPOSITION 29
Forms of sociation in themselves become transcendent
ultimates in social relations, as we see in manners,
etiquette, and play.

(a) One final court of appeal which determines how we relate to each other exists in forms of sociation themselves—what we call "good form." We come together to satisfy sexual, economic, political, religious, and aesthetic needs, but none of these can be satisfied unless they are expressed in "proper" social forms. We must have sex, but we must have it in ways determined by social as well as sexual needs. We come together to buy and sell, but *how* we buy and sell, the social form of trading, is not determined simply by economic motives. Even when we face death in war we do so in styles of fighting considered proper to the honor and glory of our community. We must even die "in style."

Thus, while the social bond has many strands, and human motives are determined by many things, the social bond, as a social bond, derives its power from purely formal elements such as those we see in play, games, parties, talk, fashion, style, and all the ways in which we stage ourselves in purely social moments in society. The forms of manners, like the forms of art, are created to achieve certain effects. We see this clearly in dress and adornment. Dress, we are told, is always highly practical, but when we come to define what we really mean by "practical," we discover that practicality ranges all the way from protection of our bodies to the expression of the most fanciful kind of play (as in the Santa Claus costume). Dress is also a communication of social order; in the army dress is used to communicate hierarchy. We are of a certain regiment, our regiment belongs to a certain division, our division belongs to a certain army, our army belongs to the armies of the United States of America, and our ministers assure us (in time of war) that our army belongs to God.

(b) Dress communicates individual as well as social roles. While army insignia indicate that we belong to a certain branch of service, and our rank in that service, they also tell something about us as individuals. We have been a certain number of years in service, we have fought in certain battles, or served in certain campaigns, we have suffered certain wounds, we have achieved certain honors. But beyond all these clearly marked insignia there is another kind of indication, a purely social indication which has little to do with official military symbols of rank, station, length of service, merit, or skill. This is the cut of the uniform, the way the uniform is worn, and the manner of the wearer, the whole range of military "bearing" we see in individual expression of military manners. The soldier is not alone in this. A cursory glance at clothes of any kind tells us that they are intended to relate us to each other on a social basis, and whatever interest they symbolize, clothes are used to produce purely social effects.

(c) Tact emerges in social drama where we struggle to achieve "good form." Whenever people meet, a struggle begins between individual or group interests that are extrinsic to the gathering and purely social demands that are intrinsic to the moment as a moment of pure socialization. We enter a gathering as businessmen, teachers, parents, scholars, deans, professors, students, administrators, parents, or simply men and women, who are rich or poor, beautiful or ugly, stupid or wise. But after a few moments the purely social form of the occasion creates a new stage, the stage of manners, and we play our parts accordingly.

O

METHODOLOGICAL PROPOSITION 30
In play we learn to subordinate ourselves to rules, and to "internalize" the meaning of roles.

(a) Whether we watch a game or take part in it, we are conscious that play is determined by rules. Childhood play is our first experience with rules. Without experience in conduct guided by rules we cannot become selves, for it is through rules that voluntary and free selves find characteristic expression of their freedom. In playing a game the child must be able to take the attitude of all the others involved in the game. The attitudes and movements of the other players are organized into an act under rules, and it is these rules which control the response of the individual. Thus in playing a position in a game, or a part in a drama, the child learns to assume how others will play theirs. What he does is controlled by his ability to take the part of others who are playing with him. By means of rules we organize the attitudes of those involved in the same process.

(b) We "internalize" social roles through arousing in ourselves the response we arouse in others. We can do so because the forms of expression used by the self (the spoken word, the physical gesture, architectural space, etc.) are experienced by the actor as they are by his audience. I hear what I have said, and see what my hand does, as others do. Their response is a response to a symbol we experience in common. The same is true for the spatial symbols we use in staging acts, as in architecture. The room in which we meet and talk is common to both; what the other person does in it determines its meaning to me, just as what I do in it determines its meaning to him. Thus, social meanings arise in moments in which a symbol means what it does to the self because of what it means to the other. The self and the other are bound by a third element, the symbol, whose meaning, in turn, depends on the possibility of reciprocal responses of actor and audience.

(c) We watch for acts that are bound by rules, as well as for acts where rules cannot be used. The sacred is not the realm of rules. We do not speak of God's rules. There is little mystery about rules. Rules cannot be secret. On the contrary, it is their clarity and public codification which characterizes their use in social relations. Rules are the same for all. Once king and commoner enter a game they subordinate themselves to the same rules. When the gods of Greece visited the earth to compete with men they accepted the rules set by men. Divine intervention could save a god from losing the game, but in appealing to his fellow deities for help, he lost honor among men as among the gods. For the mystery of rules, the honor of the players, is determined by adherence to the rules, in both victory and defeat. If we are to win or to lose honorably we must do so under rules that we create, or agree to, before we enter the game.

○

METHODOLOGICAL PROPOSITION 31
Health is symbolized by authorities as a means to increased group participation.

(a) We ask of those who would keep us healthy: Who has what kind of stake in what kind of health? The army wants one kind of health; church, business, the school, another. The healthy soldier has quick reflexes, great endurance, and must be able to live in the midst of violence and death. The church wants sensual drives disciplined. The businessman wants "live-wires" for salesmen and people with vast appetites as customers. The scholar who must sit for hours does not want the active body of the soldier. The muscles of the dancer must be very different from those of the weight lifter. In America the heroine of health is the young matron who is an eager and happy consumer of all the goods and services that money will buy.

(b) Health practitioners of all kinds link themselves with symbols of authority, as in institutions devoted to health like the Red Cross, Blue Cross, and White Cross. Before their adoption of white robes, doctors operated in formal dress. Now they operate in white gowns, interview patients in white coats, and in their greatest stage, the hospital, are surrounded by many grades of inferiors who dress carefully in gowns which indicate their rank in the hierarchy of the hospital. Many gestures of deference are given the doctor as he makes his rounds. His entourage of nurses, interns, residents of the hospital, follow him at a respectful distance, nurses do not speak unless spoken to, voices are lowered, and as the door of the sick room is opened, all draw back in silence to let the doctor enter. In America, the American Medical Association actively aligns itself with private enterprise, and medical orators tell audiences that private medicine alone can serve the public good.

(c) Each civilization has its own kind of sickness, which can be cured only by reforming the civilization itself. The prevalence and severity of many diseases have changed in the course of history. Malnutrition in one society means hunger; in another (such as ours), surfeit. Filth diseases attack the poor; diseases resulting from overeating attack the rich. There are diseases specific to occupations: chimney sweep's cancer, miner's phthisis, wool sorter's disease. There are diseases peculiar to certain types of social organization. Smog kills and disables many city dwellers. Within four and a half days during late December, 1952, in London, almost five thousand persons—as well as prize cattle being held for the Smithfield show—died of smog. Efficiency itself, the prized norm of mass production, leads to monotony and boredom. Monotonous environments have their own deleterious effects on the brain. We read in modern medical research that as a result of prolonged exposure to a monotonous situation the thinking of an individual is impaired, his emotional responses become childish, his visual perception is disturbed. As the efficiency of industrial production increases, a pathology of boredom sets in.

(d) The sociologist seeks to discover the pathologies of group relations which cause disease. The locus of psychobiological events is not in the soma of the individual but in a nexus of persons and their relations. Neuroses and some of the psychoses are not a characteristic peculiarity of some "fraudulently isolated patients," but the result of malfunctioning of relationships within a group. We thus enter a new realm of medicine, the "sociosomatic." Here we seek to understand how social relations produce negative as well as positive emotions. As sociologists, we believe that emotions cannot exist until they are expressed, and that their expression depends on communicative forms which can arise only in relations between the self and others. Such forms are the locus of our relationships and hence of our emotions. There are pathologies of social forms as there are of the body. As we torture, wound, and kill in war, as the horror of concentration camps haunts our thoughts, as we waken in nightmares of trembling and fear, we know that *how* we relate as social beings determines our health. We deal with the sociopathology of daily life as best we can, but our knowledge of the relationship between social organization and health is very limited.

○

METHODOLOGICAL PROPOSITION 32
Religious invocation of the supernatural, the way in which we communicate with our gods to infuse social order with supernatural power, is a basic form of social integration.

(a) From the sociological view taken here, religion must be studied as a social drama of integration. And since religious groups are noted above all for the high degree of consensus which they achieve in their fellowship, the nature of the consensus achieved in religion must be studied if we are to understand consensus of any kind. In *The Rhetoric of Religion* Kenneth Burke proposes that we treat God as an "Idea of Order." He interprets Genesis as an account of the Creation interpreted as a statement of *"principles of governance,"* in which the account of Creation may be interpreted as saying, in effect: "This is, in principle, a statement of what the natural order must be like if it is to be a perfect fit with the conditions of human sociopolitical order (conditions that come into focus in the idea of a basic covenant backed by a perfect authority)." He accepts Hobbes's dictum that: "He is only properly said to reign, that governs his subjects by his word, and by promise of rewards to those that obey it, and by threatening them with punishment that obey it not." In so far as order in religion is related to order among men in society it involves the idea of a command, and its proper response, "obey." Thus Order "is to Disorder as Obedience is to Disobedience."

(b) What, then, is involved when we say that religious action may be studied as a paradigm for all social action? How does religion integrate men? How does religious integration differ from other forms of integration, in art, play, and pure social moments? Institutions are powerful to the degree that they help men to face what cannot be cured but must be endured. Death must be faced, and even though we face death in fear and dread, we must learn to live with our fear of it. In human society death does not just happen, it is organized. That is, while many die what is called a natural death, millions also die at the hands of other human beings. On this terrible level of his being, man is not simply a beast of prey but a social beast of prey. We socialize to torture, wound, and kill, as well as to heal, protect, and create life. Modern wars are now called "people's wars," and the predatory aristocracies once blamed for war are now matched by predatory peoples who wound and kill each other by the millions to uphold ideologies in place of thrones. Ideologies, not kings, are now divine. The horror of being human begins once we confront this need to hate and kill. For we must confront suffering and death if we are to live together in society. And we must confront them in action. It is not enough to "think about" death; we must do something about it.

(c) The deep sense of social communion experienced in religious rites is reached in four crucial moments in religious expression. These are an admission of sin, the expiation of sin, the invocation of a supernatural power through a hierarchy based on power to communicate with the supernatural power, and the use of a victim whose suffering and death becomes a vicarious atonement for our sins. Whatever our belief about their divine origin, religious rites are human expression. The communicative and social aspects of the religious act do not in themselves explain the religious content of the religious act, but neither do the dogmas of a religion explain social order. When we create an "ideal" religious rite as an aid to the construction of an "ideal" social act we take a middle position between religion and society as constitutive elements in sociation. We find our middle ground in communication which we narrow further to dramatic communication. We do so because we believe that *how* religious experience is communicated will tell us much about how society arises and continues to exist in all communication.

(d) Societies are integrated by efficient and mystical symbols of social order. Money must be banked securely, distributed safely, and spent wisely, but there must be beliefs over the value of earning and spending money as a "way of life" so that people will discipline themselves, and others, in the pursuit of it. Social theorists use different terms for mystification. Walter Bagehot speaks of dignification (those elements in political communication "which excite and preserve the reverence of the population"); Herbert Spencer tells us that the "government of ceremonial observance" precedes other kinds, approaches nearer to universality of influence, and has the largest share of influence in regulating men's lives. Max Weber argues that social strata and status groups sustain their power because of the glory of their "style of life" (as among the Chinese mandarins) which is upheld through status honor. Marx speaks of the "fetishistic character," "mystifications," and "social hieroglyphics" of value in capitalism (but not of socialism). Carlyle describes clothes as "emblematic" of social order.

(e) In our time Kenneth Burke argues that all notions of "rights" and "obligations" must be discussed in terms specifically suited to the treatment of symbolism as motive in human conduct. "Rights" cannot be derived from "nature," but must depend on the resources of language for their form. And since language is a social product we must study the reciprocal relations between symbolic usage and the distribution of authority as a hierarchal form. For this hierarchy to function it must be "inspirited" by a "condition of mystery." Mystery arises out of difference, and it is because of different modes of living and livelihood that classes of people become "mysteries" to each other. Like Durkheim, Burke believes that this condition of mystery is revealed most perfectly in primitive priestcraft which promotes cohesion among disparate classes and yet, at the same time, upholds the mysteries of the differences it seeks to overcome.

(f) Priestly mystification rises to great social power when celestial hierarchy is imagined as an analogy to human social order, and social order, in turn, is imagined as a secularization of celestial order. In this style of thought we ascribe social order to a celestial order and then, somewhat later in our utterance, writing, or dramatic unfolding of social order, "derive" social rights from this ascribed order. Mystery begins with the distinctions we make in conduct between "thou shalt" and "thou shalt not," or, more simply, in obedience and disobedience. We obey through resolving differences (God's commandments as against human desires: woman as sexual object as against woman as friend or madonna), and differences are accentuated by those who stand in authority over us as resolvers of the very differences they stress (or, sometimes, create).

(g) Mystery begins and endures in the strange and forbidden. As infants we are made aware that we must not do many things. We do not know why we must not, and since our remote and awesome authority, our parents, admonish us to obey, not to question, we try to make sense in fantasy out of what we cannot deal with in reason (as question and inquiry). The realm of disobedience becomes so persuasive in infancy that in our relatedness with adults we live far more in terms of "do not" than "do." As priests supplant our parents we enter a new and equally mysterious realm of "do nots." These are called, quite literally, commandments, and whatever the Temple of God is called, it is for the small child (or, at least, the small child of Calvinistic faith), a Temple of "Thou Shalt Not." As Kenneth Burke has pointed out, on the sociolinguistic level the infant encounters its first negatives as sheerly extralogical contradiction. Harry Stack Sullivan describes the pain and shock of punishment over pleasurable infantile ways of satisfying the demands of the alimentary canal.

(h) Mystery, then, lurks in negation. The trauma of life in society begins (and continues) in disobedience. For if our parents and priests are right, and they certainly mount awesome dramas of their rightness, why do I want to disobey them? In disobedience I separate myself from them. But no one, not even an adult, can live long in separation from his parents and priests. Social hierarchy, even in childhood, cannot exist only in negation. A hierarchy must be positive in what it is, a way from a lower to higher realm of social being. But once "do" and "do not," "shall" and "shall not," "is" and "is not," becomes "mine and thine," then all the power and radiance of the forbidden arises. The neighbor's wife we must not covet becomes glamorous because she is forbidden, a strange and mysterious creature who haunts us in acts which to her husband are familiar and even tedious.

(i) In early life we meet with "do" and "do not" on a simple but profound motor level. We obey or disobey parents, who in turn, are warm and loving when we obey, just as they are cold and distant when we disobey. The reward of primal obedience is love, the very personal love of the parent who fondles and strokes us. Affection is born in smiles and laughter. We are tickled and teased into smiles. Unlike the grasp of the hand, or sucking with the lips, the smile is the response of an other. This "other," unlike the things I reach out to grasp, or to stuff in my mouth, must be communicated with, *persuaded*, to give me what I want. In such persuasion symbolic experience begins. Communicating with an other, a parent who can accept or reject us, is done through gestures whose meaning is established in common responses to the same gestures. The smile means what it does because it evokes reciprocal responses of love and warmth. We learn that a gesture (such as the smile or the cry) creates and sustains a relationship between ourselves and an other.

(j) The social expression of religious experience is always both positive and negative; there is a negative, destructive, disintegrating influence, and there is a positive, cohesive, integrating influence. As we say of drama, there is an agonistic quality in religious action. The core of religious experience, and the moment of its mystery in communication, is the moment of communion with God. This relationship takes precedence over all other conceivable relations among men. But this moment of communion, however deeply experienced by the individual, is a communication. It comes to the individual in some form. Even if we assume that all forms of expression originate in God, they are forms of expression still, and their success or failure as communication depends on how well or poorly they are used as symbols. Thus in discussing religious fellowship we must be careful to distinguish the reciprocal nature of the communicative process by which the spirit and attitudes of a religious community are created and sustained. A religious group develops through the development of a specific terminology through which habits, customs, and traditions of religion are expressed in worship.

(k) Forms of prayer, sacrifice, and ritual do not simply "articulate" religious experience, they also shape and determine the organization and spirit of a religious group. This is as true of sects who preach that religious experience of the holy is beyond communication as it is of those who stress the importance of liturgy in communication with God. Even those who stand silently in fear and trembling before their God stand with other worshipers who are related in their silence. Thus while the holy may be ineffable and thus beyond communication, it is not beyond sociality. For if silence is "corporate," this corporation assumes characteristic social forms. However silent Quakers may be in their worship they are related (as are all worshipers) in certain social ways.

(l) From a sociological view it is not a question of whether guilt is indigenous to man, but of what *forms* guilt assumes, and how these affect social relationships. Rulers arouse guilt over disobedience of their commands. There are many sources for the greatness of religion as a social institution, but paramount among these is the recognition by the organizers of religions that guilt must be defined explicitly, and once defined must be expiated. In short, if a religion makes us guilty, it offers us ways to rid ourselves of the guilt it has caused.

O

METHODOLOGICAL PROPOSITION 33
Art creates symbolic roles which we use as a dramatic
rehearsal in the imagination of community roles we
must play to sustain social order.

(a) Our consciousness of being bound together in a specific kind of social relationship is determined by the forms of expression used in the communication that takes place in the relationship. These forms originate in our attempts to relate to each other, but as forms they are perfected in art. Our relationships, to be relationships, must have order. In art, order is called form, and it is to the achievement of form that the artist directs his energy. The musician struggles to order time in the creation of rhythms in tones; the dancer orders movement in space; the architect orders space; the writer orders words in communication; while the painter orders perception so that we see the world in certain ways. We are powerless without art, for without the forms supplied by art we cannot communicate, and when we cannot communicate we cannot relate as social beings.

(b) Aesthetic experience offers enjoyment characteristic of consummation, the outcome of an undertaking. It suffuses the objects that are instrumental in the undertaking, and the acts that compose it, with something of the joy and satisfaction we feel in its successful accomplishment. The artist attempts to interpret complex social life in terms of goals. It is not simply because of its capacity to envision a future that art affects a society—religious, political, educational, hygienic, and even technical institutions establish goals to direct their activity in a present. The peculiar quality of aesthetic experience is the appreciation and satisfaction of a sense of the finalities of action that it gives us.

(c) Art performs its social function when it is used to interpret experience to the individual as the shared experience of the community of which he feels himself a part. Art forms determine the interpretation of social experience; without them we could not share experience because we could not take the roles of others, or evn bring much of our unconscious fantasy into conscious form. Through art we bring private reverie into public meaning, and depict ends in conduct which deepen and enlarge shared experience. The power of art (popular and fine art alike) lies in its capacity to break down the walls that separate men. Through art we are able to take the role of others, and thus break down the unrecognized and unconscious barriers that isolate the individual in modern society.

(d) To say that great art is concerned with the conscious exploration of action in such a way that an object, an art work, is created which can be used to develop attitudes so that action can go forward toward desired goals, presumes a theory of the imagination as part of action (not "thought"). Imagery within the act gives action form, just as rules give form to the game. Great art is the conscious exploration through symbolic forms of the possibilities of human action. It is a form of imagery which we use during the symbolic phase of action.

The symbolic act of conscious expression is a directed process, an effort directed toward a certain end.

(e) Great art creates forms which enable us to explore conciously symbolic phases of experience; magical art inspires us to practical actions believed necessary to social order. Reason in art also moves us to action by placing imagination in the service of reason, and imagination so used opens ends, as well as means, to analysis. In magical use of symbols we do not question ends. People using magical art know what they want, but they do not know how to get it, or, if they know, are not sure they can endure the hardships necessary to obtaining it. Popular art makes heavy use of magic. There is never any question of the value of riches in the American rags to riches story, nor is there any doubt about how to get rich. The goal and path are clearly marked (so clear and well understood that Horatio Alger could write such stories for juvenile readers). What is problematic is whether the desire for riches will be strong enough to carry the hero through the hardships of seeking wealth.

(f) Make-believe art (from a sociological view) dissipates emotions which, if developed into action (as in magical art), or brought into consciousness (as in great art), would threaten those in power, or create great pain to the individual in his attempts to create order within himself. Make-believe art serves as a "wish-book." Symbolic presentations are not used to explore consciously the meaning of action, or to inspire us to act in forms held proper to our rank or station in life, but to satisfy longings and yearnings which we cannot satisfy in reality. It is not so much the form of symbols which determines make-believe art, as their use. In the Middle West of America the lavishly illustrated Montgomery Ward catalogue, containing thousands of items, is called "The Wishing Book." The most efficient description of items known to modern business thus becomes sheer fantasy, a kind of merchandising poetry, to poor, lonely, and frustrated readers. Even those who cannot read can enjoy the illustrations. Sexually starved readers can enjoy lingerie ads. Poor farmers can ride imaginary tractors. All—young, old, male, female, educated or illiterate —can wish for what they cannot have.

Make-believe art creates as well as satisfies desires. The great art of one group may become the make-believe art of another, just as, conversely, make-believe art may become great art. *Huckleberry Finn,* read as a make-believe story of the lost boyhood of frontier life (whatever Make Twain's intentions), is now enshrined as an American classic. Classics, such as the tales of Henry James, may be read for sheer snob appeal. Art here becomes part of a ritual of elegance. The book is a "conversation piece," or a "coffee table book." The elegant doings in high society of the heroes and heroines of James and Wharton are not read as art, but as a means of identifying vicariously with a glamorous upper class. When there are few discussions on the relevance of art to contemporary problems, or, as in much teaching of the humanities in our schools, when only the formal characteristics of an art work are studied, or, when modern art is, by virtue of its contemporaniety, deemed ephemeral, we are in the realm of make-believe. We are using art to satisfy status longings in fantasy that we cannot, or will not, satisfy in reality.

(g) One great social function of art, particularly comic art, is to expose (through conscious confrontation in public symbolic forms) incongruities between means and ends in conduct. Much has been said in anthropology, psychoanalysis, literature, and sociology, about the similarities between religious and social integration. When social bonds are discussed in classical social theory, religious imagery is often used to illustrate the nature such bonds (as in anthropology where we hear a great deal about the "sacred" and "ritual"). When dramatic imagery is used, as in the phrase "ritual drama," tragic drama is invoked, as in Freud's use of the Oedipus legend, Jane Harrison's description of ritual drama as tragic drama, and Kenneth Burke's discussion of social bonds as tragic bonds in the chapters on Genesis in *The Rhetoric of Religion.*

The sociologist who turns to comedy can at least be sure that what he says about comedy is not something he could just as well say about religion, or magic, or ritual. This is necessary, because if we say that art determines society, then we must be sure that what we are saying about art really is about art. And even when we do say that art determines society, and use only tragic art as our example of art, we leave a great amount of art out of our scheme. Art is *both* tragedy *and* comedy, and if tragedy was admitted to the sacred festivals at Athens, so too was comedy. And if the tragic hero becomes a god, the comic hero is not without deep and demonic powers of his own. Who is to say that Hawthorne's tortured Puritans tell us more about America than Mark Twain's Huck, Tom, and Jim?

(h) Freud argued that jokes serve as a resistance against authority, and as an escape from its pressure. Freud's elaboration of this hypothesis must be taken into account in any theory of comedy, but it must be revised for use in social theory. Comedy *sustains* authority as well as resisting it, by making ridiculous, absurd, or comic whatever threatens an established way of life. American laughter at her immigrants (German, Irish, Scandinavian, Italian, Jewish, and Mexican, in turn), like Molière's laughter over parvenus, is a form of social discipline. It kept these newcomers in their place until they could behave like established Americans. The German farmer was teased for his "dumb" ways of acting in the city, the Irishman for his "blarney," the Scot for his thrift, and, as befits a nation of "go-getters," the lazy and shiftless (of *any* background) were ridiculed as bums.

(i) But comedy has another face. This is irony, in which we expose and clarify doubt over what we cannot, or will not, change. In the profound and searching irony of La Rochefoucauld man is locked within himself by self-love. He needs others, but only as audience to his own glory. To satisfy self-love man will commit crimes so monstrous "that when they are brought into the light of day, [he] fails to recognize them or cannot resolve to own them." (Maxim 564.) He will disguise vice as virtue, or even parade his vices ("We would rather speak ill of ourselves than not at all." Maxim 138), to gain and hold the center of the stage. But the paradox of self-love becomes painfully obvious as we strut and preen before audiences whom we really despise and who, we know, hate and despise us. The social grace of ironic comedy is the use of reason to search out hidden vices, and to confront them clearly. Perhaps we will never cure our vices, or soften the miseries of life, but in irony we are not dupes. We have *chosen* to confront our vices and our misery. If we cannot will our fate, we can decide how to meet it.

(j) Faith in the reason of irony, and, indeed, all comedy, is possible only when doubt is considered a way to truth. When doubt is thought of as weakness or heresy, irony cannot be used. When there are wide gaps between social classes, or when status groups become strange and mysterious to each other, irony fails. When reason in society has no value, irony easily offends authority, as the fate of Socrates, the god of irony, warns us. Irony exists in one type of social bond, the bond of open, free, and informed discussion as a means to truth. The ironist cannot predict the future, nor can he tell us of heavens and utopias he alone has visited. Nor can he believe in laws "discovered" by reason which are beyond reason in some kind of nature whose "laws" can be known but not created nor changed. He believes in critical intelligence created in free discourse among men who believe that such discourse creates and sustains social bonds.

(k) Irony must end in acceptance of authority. Vices may be disguised, but their disguises can be seen through, after all. Whoever sees through them is the "true" authority. Clues to such authority abound in moments of address, or presentation of the self. The authority in the courtly act is the king, whose authority in turn comes from a principle of nobility, which in turn is derived from God. But the principle of courtship addressed by La Rochefoucauld, the great analyst of kingly courtship, is not the noble as warrior, priest, or statesman, but as *grand seigneur,* the great gentleman, who rules through manners that are based in the authority of God *in,* not beyond, society.

(l) Art, and especially comic art, is a sanctioned expression of doubt, ambiguity, and disrespect. The girl, in *Alice in Wonderland,* or the boy, in *Huckleberry Finn,* is used to express, quite innocently, problems that could not be raised in any other way. Those in power may attend to the child's innocent complaints with no loss of majesty. The ingenue, the country cousin, the farmer's daughter of American burlesque, and the king's fool are all "innocent." We permit the child to ask questions that would be considered rude, insulting, or heretical if asked by a responsible adult. The wide-eyed wonder of the innocent opens up to full view incongruities which have been hidden and suppressed because their expression might subject those in power to mockery, disdain, or open revolt.

(m) In great comedy, unconscious, hidden, and suppressed conflict is brought to light. And if dream fantasy is the guardian of sleep, comic fantasy is the guardian of reason in society because it makes possible confrontation of social disrelationships. Kings *cannot* question, for majesty must be beyond question. A king or god may answer but never ask, for who can know more than a god? But in the laughter of Aristophanes over democratic demagoguery, or Rabelais over feudal mystifications, of Molière over aristocratic hypocrisy, of Swift over contradictions between man's pride and his bestiality, of Shaw over the incongruities of sex and class, or of Mark Twain over the irrelevance of the genteel tradition to frontier life in the West, leaders could risk their majesty and followers their loyalty.

(n) We watch, then, for shifts in art among tragic, comic, and ironic modes. What situations, actions, roles, and values are treated as tragic, comic, or ironic? How do these treatments change in time within the same society, from culture to culture, from class to class? What social types are dignified, burlesqued, reviled, or hated? What transformations are taking place? Which social roles are being desanctified, which made sacred? What new heroes and villains are emerging? What strategies of adjustment to a given social order are being proposed by artists? How does the artist speak to his audience? How does he conceive of his own role? How do the views of the artist in social events, types, and groups compare with those held in religion, science, politics, business, military, institutions, and the school? Finally, what is the place of art in society? How is the artist recruited, trained, rewarded, and sustained? What, in sum, is the function, or use, of art? How is it used by various institutions, and how is it used to create and sustain social integration by the society as a whole?

○

METHODOLOGICAL PROPOSITION 34
Science raises problem-solving to an ultimate value by making methods used in problem-solving a guide to social action.

(a) The sociologist studies religion as a form of conduct based on the belief that social order is sustained by sacred order. He studies art as a form of dramatistic order which is believed to create and sustain social order. Scientists are not concerned with how communication with the supernatural determines social order, or how the drama of art is used as a drama of social relations, but with the discoveries of "laws" of uniformities. While these "laws" are stated in terms of uniformities, the scientist is always ready to change any "law" when it no longer explains certain kinds of events or conduct. Such "laws" are really more like rules. Science constructs a functional conception of knowledge based on how things and events are related within a given field in which events occur in some kind of observable order. But all such knowledge is hypothetical. Even in the sciences of nature, the subject matter is not "nature in itself," but nature subjected to human questioning. The rules of how to conduct this dialogue between man and nature is what we call scientific methodology.

(b) For the sociologist (as Mead stressed), scientific knowledge consists of finding a relationship between an object that lies in the consciousness of people in society and an object, or "thing," that lies outside of it. Scientific knowledge is not a way of going from an object already in experience to something that lies outside of experience. It is rather, a statement of the *relationship* between the mind and whatever it senses or perceives. The world of the physical sciences (the great sciences of our time) is a world of external relations, of what lies "out there" in a reality which is conceived of in the sciences of nature as a kind of physical process in space and time. These processes are composed of such structures as the atom or the stellar galaxies. The analysis of these structures through concepts about them, and the creation of hypotheses to test concepts of the structure of a given process, distinguishes scientific from other kinds of analysis. The scientist faces problems as they arise in experience when some phase of the act in process has been inhibited. The test of a hypothesis is its workability, its capacity to break down blocks in thought and action. A good hypothesis "makes sense" out of what did not make sense, and as a result of this sense, thought about the problem can proceed.

(c) The social sciences are the study of social order. On both practical and ideal levels the social scientist seeks to discover the rules of permanence *in* change. He tries to understand how order and structure in society can exist in the midst of changes which arise when tradition no longer works, and when we must construct new goals so that action can continue. How can we bring change about in orderly fashion, and yet preserve order? Change always seems to threaten a given order, and yet without change, social order would be impossible. How can we incorporate methods of change into the social order itself? The scientific study of this is the study of the social processes involved in change. It is not the recognition of change which differentiates science from religion, but the recognition that all social action is hypothetical. We do not assume in science that change is but another path toward a fixed goal. Nor does the scientist assume that goals (as perfected acts) will not be reached in this world, but in the world to come.

(d) Science regards the "problematic" as natural to conduct in any given social order. We can regard the "problematic" as a sign of weakness, or, as in some religions, as a sign of corruption and sin. Or we can regard it as the area of change in which novel, emergent aspects of social relationships are struggling to birth. Religion challenges science by asking how we can proceed to goals which are not fixed. For, if we do not know our goals, how can we order change? How is society to find a method for changing its own institutions and still preserve the security of these institutions? We want a society that is going ahead, not a fixed order. How are we to change situations that need changing, and yet preserve the stability of the institutions in which change occurs? How can we say we have advanced when we cannot state the goal toward which we are advancing? When we do not know the goal, all we can say is that we are on our way, but we do not know where we are going. Obviously, we cannot act very long in this manner; we must have some method of charting our progress.

(e) Progress as recognized by science is the solution to a particular problem. The social scientist does not look toward his systematic goal and direct movement toward it. He tries to find out why his system does not work. The test of his solution is whether his system starts working again. His interest lies in finding out what the problems in social process are. When he locates the problematic, he asks: How can events and things be so constructed that blocks in process can be removed to let action go forward? In the social problem of art we are aware of certain dangers to social order, particularly in the field of commercialized art. How can we recognize the legitimacy of the expression of the art, the freedom to enjoy art as we like, and yet at the same time admit the dangers of commercial perversions of art? As social scientists, we do not set up an ideal form of art; we begin with the dangers of art to society (or to art as a social institution), ask just what it is that finds expression in art, what kind of freedom art requires, and try to reconstruct a social setting for art in which both danger and freedom can be expressed. We must assume that art (like any expression of need) will go on, and yet we must avoid the dangers to social order in the phases and kinds of art that threaten order.

(f) The social scientist tries to understand the background of a problem and the social processes in which it developed. He states the problem in terms of checked processes, and then tests his solution by seeing whether those processes can continue or not. This kind of method enables us to keep order in society and yet to change this order within the social process itself. It is a recognition of the fact that intelligence expresses itself in the solution of problems. All forms of life must solve problems. Environments change, food stocks diminish, old enemies lose their power while new and fearsome enemies appear. Biologists tell us that nature produces variations which are tried out in the environment until one serves the purpose of adaptation. Scientists make use of trial and error, but they seek to shape this procedure into a conscious method. The social scientist does not simply question; he *systemizes* question-asking until it becomes a tool of inquiry.

(g) Science stands beside religion and art in society as a "way of life." Science is beginning to take on characteristic form as a social institution. We do not yet have clearly marked scientific social types like those familiar to us in the priest and the soldier whose role is sustained (as a social office) through clear expression in dress, deportment, gesture, character, vows (the "sense of calling"), and hierarchy. It is only in the laboratory that the scientist plays a clearly marked role. And certainly in our time the image of the scientist is that of the laboratory scientist. In film, television, and literature, the scientist is usually depicted as a man in a white smock who works in a laboratory filled with a vast array of mechanical apparatus. There he is "conducting an experiment" whose progress is being recorded on instruments which measure according to scales. His experiments are usually being done with physical nature.

This image supplants the older American images of the scientist as inventor (Edison), naturalist (Audubon), surveyor and geologist (Clarence King), or engineer (Dodge, the builder of the Union Pacific). In 1860, science meant engineering, and the engineer was a man who could "build things" not "just draw them." He worked in the field among men as a boss over them. The naturalist plunged into the wilderness where survival demanded the honored frontier virtues of stamina, cunning, and daring. The inventor struggled to bring comforts to the home. He was the popular hero of Veblen's "machine process," what we now call technology. During the Civil War, and particularly in the armies of the North under Grant and Sherman who fought what were called "engineering campaigns," engineering was used in both the statics of siege warfare and the mobility of open battle. The engineer, as surveyor, road builder, and military engineer, emerged as a public hero. He also emerged as a business hero in the years following the Civil War. In his engineering guise, the scientist combined the powerful symbols of war, technology, and money. Not only did our military engineers open up the frontier, they taught the terrible art of mass destruction. In the decades after the war, especially in Chicago and later in Detroit, they joined with businessmen in relating science to the industrial technology so characteristic of our time.

(h) As a "way of life," applied science in our time is expressed in technology. Here everything is reduced to a problem, and to a great degree, a problem of space. How "efficiently" we can do something, when by efficiency we mean how quickly, how cheaply, how easily, or how simply, determines how we live. These are all quantified units, and the expression of "cost" in time or money; it is in terms of such units that our vast apparatus of accounting has developed. But the Industrial Revolution was a revolution in communication because it introduced new ways of transporting symbols as well as talking about work. The economist asked the scientist to describe what the machine could "do" in terms of "units of work." Electricity, light, coal, steam, the dynamo, all were lumped together in very different things, such as plant equipment, land, workers, management, or materials, and were described in terms of the amount of labor necessary to produce a given commodity.

Thus, work and energy in social experience became bookkeeping terms which make possible calculation of costs in time, money, and manpower. It mattered little whether capitalists or socialists were the bookkeepers. Socialists estimated cost in terms of labor; capitalists in terms of money. But both kept organizing their ledgers in symbols expressing units of energy which "cost" so much as units of work. Thus, whether work costs were estimated in terms of "labor value" or "money value" the relationship of science (as "applied science"), industry, and technology, remained relatively stable. "Applied" science (until very recently) meant the production and control of physical energy. Since 1800 three great powers in society have been seeking to control science. The university, business, and government are now in open competition for scientific personnel. Each institution has its own goals for science, and the kind of science we will have in the future will be determined to no small degree by which forces or persuades the scientist to accept his leadership. Physics, the science of movement in space, has taught us how to harness physical energy. Now for the first time in history, men can destroy the world. Without highly skilled physical scientists, we cannot survive, but with them in our midst we can also destroy ourselves. Juvenal asked his Romans: Who shall guard the guardians? Now we ask: Who shall plan the planners? What science shall guard the scientists?

(i) Science in our time is struggling to achieve social, as well as intellectual, autonomy. It is just beginning to exist as an institution in its own right, like the church, or the world of art. "Pure science," the free expression of science, has been most at home in research institutes. Usually these have been connected with universities. Applied science has been used by business, government, and the universities. With the invention of the atom bomb, scientists are now aware that if science is to survive some way must be discovered of preserving the humane values of science.

(j) The greatest danger for science (as an institution) comes from making method an end in itself. For when method (how we know what we know) as such is reified, scientists select problems to suit their methods and techniques, and not to meet the needs of the human community. They are being "scientific" when they "do" a problem according to techniques considered scientific. Techniques derived from the study of space, and time reduced to space, are used to study events which have many non-spatial extensions. If, as we have said, science is the solving of problems, then it is to problems, not to technical exercises, that scientists must direct their efforts.

(k) We ask of science the basic questions we ask of any institution. In what situation is science used? We have developed sciences of external nature to such degree that many believe that only studies of our physical environment can be termed scientific at all. But if man exists in relationships other than spatial relationships, as in religion, art, politics, or economics, then science must tell us how to think about problems in these. The questions: Who practices science, in what situation? by what means? for what social purpose? and where? What is, and what is not considered scientific? How is science communicated to various publics? How are scientists selected, trained, and supported? How do the apologists for science relate it to social order? Who are the adversaries and the allies of science? What are the ultimate values of science?

○

METHODOLOGICAL PROPOSITION 35
The final and most powerful moment in the drama of authority is the invocation of the ultimate power which upholds social order and thus wards off threats to the survival of the community.

(a) Wars, plagues, famine, flood, almost any great community catastrophe, can be endured so long as there is some moment of mystery in the social drama of social order which solaces us, and thus makes it possible to endure what cannot be cured. Belief in the "mystery" of religion, art, or science creates a higher value which dignifies and glorifies our suffering. In holding before us a vision of a life beyond death, or a better life to come here on earth, the priest, the artist, and the scientist offer a passage to another existence, and death becomes endurable as the beginning of a new life.

(b) There is great variation in the ultimate symbols of religion, art, and science, but such symbols share one thing: they cast a halo of eternity about the temporal. In Christianity, nature and man are infused with the supernatural, while in Confucianism, manners and rites uphold the moral order of a universe where even the gods are subordinate to laws of "harmonious" conduct. Science teaches that knowledge is power, and that as we understand ourselves better we will lead better lives. This capacity to infuse the present with the future through the creation of gods who are beyond desire and exist outside of time and space, is described in great detail and awe-inspiring forms by all great religious thinkers in their theories of immanence, incarnation, and reincarnation. For our purposes, we note how the priestly office is used by authority of various kinds to solemnize the social drama involved in birth, marriage, and death. There are few institutions which do not make some use of such solemnization. Universities, ostensibly devoted to critical inquiry of all kinds, make heavy use of sacred architecture, processional hymns, and ask clergymen at various times throughout the year to invoke the blessings of God on students whose teachers train them to doubt God and his blessings.

(c) While it is common to discuss bridging between the temporal and the eternal as peculiar to religious drama, and to stress how authority seeks to link itself with the eternities of religion, we note that all great social institutions attempt some kind of "eternalizing" in their social dramas. The humanist who does not believe in revealed religion, and is skeptical of all supernaturals, still holds that wisdom can cure all social ills. Plato held that rulers should be philosophers because the forms of philosophic thought were eternal, and only a man accustomed to thinking in such essences could rule well. Artists create aesthetic myths in which beauty is a mystery whose worship ends in immortality. The soldier becomes a warrior of God. The mother becomes the sainted Mary, the mother of Christ, and, thus, of all mankind. All of us, priest, scholar, teacher, artist, soldier, and parent alike, strive to perfect our roles until they become not simply parts we play in the drama of society, but an enactment of "eternal" principles on which our society rests.

IV

CONCLUSION

SOCIODRAMA AND POWER IN MODERN SOCIETY

Whoever creates and controls the sociodramas of everyday life controls our lives. For it is in these dramas that acts are *named,* and it is under these names that we *participate* in struggle over principles of social order. In 1914 men marched off to wound, kill, and cripple each other *in the name of* France, Germany, Russia, and England. In 1939 the sons, and even the daughters, of these men marched again *in the name of* Fascism, Communism, and Democracy. Millions more were herded into death camps and slave labor camps *in the name of* racial purity or ideology. Battle-hardened veterans who knew the horrors of war, even senior officers like General Patton, broke down in tears and uncontrollable vomiting at the sight of concentration camp survivors wandering like skeletons among their dead and dying comrades. In these camps death alone stopped the pain of hunger and injustice. There was no way to change identity because there was no way to change names (as there had been in the torture cells of the Inquisition when a heretic could name himself Christian). Guilt was categorical; a Jew could not become an Aryan.

During our century, this terrible century of suffering and death, millions of lives have been wrecked in wars fought *in the name of* various principles of social order. We read of battles like Verdun and the Somme where hundreds of thousands died in days, just as we heard of the bombing of Hiroshima and Nagasaki where thousands died in minutes. Six million human beings died in Hitler's German death camps. The weekly toll of dead and wounded in Vietnam is announced like a box score on television. War is no longer remote and mysterious, a sociodrama of words alone. Television cameras follow rioters in our streets. Violence and death are now part of our daily life in the fantasy of art and play (in our television westerns, crime shows, and football), as in the reality of riot and war. Violence is no longer reported as an event which "really happened" and is "recorded" by the reporter, it is *enacted* as community art drama on television, and as sociodrama in riot and bloodshed on our streets. For the first time in history, all, literate and nonliterate, rich and poor, young and old, participate in great sociodramas mounted by those who own and control means of communication.

In sociodrama we identify in action and passion with heroes who struggle to uphold principles of social order, and in this identification with leaders and causes, anxiety, fear, and loneliness vanish. As workers, students, soldiers, all the "little people" of the world, we feel very small in the daily performance of our tasks. Sometimes we lose all sense of identity; we are not even named, but numbered. But when we switch on television, or step into a great public meeting to join in the roar of the crowd, or march together in song under waving flags, a glory, the glory of community, arises within us. We have found a new self, a *public* role, far greater than the self limited to family, neighborhood, workshop, or classroom. Hitler's *Mein Kampf*, and his human slaughter-houses, are terrible witness to the fact that what we rehearse in imagination, the kind of sociodrama we mount in private as well as public imagery, often becomes the scenario of everyday life. If sociodramas of blood, violence, and war are mounted as rites of purification, then torture, killing, and wounding become not only "necessary," but "noble." These sociodramas are not merely symbolic screens, or metaphors in which we clothe the reality of politics, economics, or sex. They *are* social reality *because* they are forms of social integration.

THE MODERN SOCIODRAMA OF VICTIMAGE

Hitler won people to his cause not by discussion or debate (these Hitler called the "lunacy" of committee discussion), but by mounting great public dramas of struggle which all could follow (as we follow sports in America), and in which all could participate. Hitler's speeches are battles, not discussions. His opponents are never "loyal," or members of a competing team, but persecutors, traitors, and, finally, enemies of

Germany who must be destroyed because only through their destruction can Germany be saved. Destruction in blood and terror (the "final" solution) was a sacrificial act in which the enemy both within and without the state was transformed into a victim for sacrifice on the altar of "Germanity." Hitler warned us in *Mein Kampf* that inferiors are not moved by discussion and arbitration which ends in mutual handshakes, but by symbolic, as well as real, participation in the victory of the strong and the annihilation or the unconditional surrender of the weak.

Hitler understood well that when people are habituated to domination and submission in their social relations, dramas of gods and devils who lock in mortal struggle over sacred principles of social order will have a peculiar fascination for them. Hitlerite sociodrama became a tragic drama of racial purity (the sacred principle of social order in Nazi Germany), copied after the greatest sociodrama of our age, the Christian drama of salvation. This is *not* to say that Christianity leads to fascism, but that, as our greatest salvation device, the religious drama of Christian salvation is peculiarly liable to perverse and grotesque imitation as a social drama of salvation. Whether we accept, reject, or doubt Christianity, we must accept the fact that the social psyche of Western man and the psyche of the Christian have much in common.

And what are we to say of the Russian purge trials? In an avowedly "godless" state, public confession of sin against the state, if not against God, was the most powerful sociodrama of Stalin's regime. Stalin became a god-king, his commissars priests who carried out their terrible drama of salvation "for the sake of the masses." Party members who could not believe in the confessions offered in public trials defended them as a "necessary" way to affect "mass opinion." For if the people were not moved by fear and veneration, how could they be moved at all? The purge trial was a sociodrama of guilt, atonement, redemption, hierarchy, and sacrifice in which prisoners were transformed into sacrificial victims whose suffering and death purified the sacred principle of communist society, loyalty and devotion to the "Party Line."

Until the rise of Hitler, Americans assumed that the great sociodramas of feudal domination had lost their power. Hitler's death camps and Stalin's purge trials soon taught us that many Europeans equated social order with the kind of order established in relations between superiors and inferiors. We had forgotten Veblen's ironic warnings in his discussion of the dynastic state in *Imperial Germany and the In-*

dustrial Revolution. The suppression of public opinion in Imperial Germany by police power, "free recourse to juridicial excesses," the censorship of education, and the unremitting propaganda of "Germanism," all this, Veblen said, "reflects the highest credit on the Imperial statesmen and their agents for admirably thorough work and single-minded devotion to duty,—a singlemindedness obstructed by no consideration of law, equity or humanity,—in effect leaning on the principles of martial law."

The burning question of our time becomes: How did man become so evil? How were Auschwitz and Belsen possible? Our survival hangs upon our ability to answer. It may be that we cannot answer in our time. But we must try. The sociologist must ask: What is the nature of social integration? What do we mean by a social bond? How are we to distinguish various types of social integration? What do we mean by social order? Disorder? And we must begin this task at home. Is equality a social bond like inferiority and superiority? If so, what are the specific integrative factors in relationships among equals? And if we believe that Belson and Auschwitz were the result of mystifications based on caricatures of religious sociodrama, how are these mystifications to be exposed and destroyed, and what other forms of integration are to replace them? If we say that German social thought produced Auschwitz, can we create ways of thinking about society which will produce a community of free men?

THE CONFUSION OF SOCIAL INTEGRATION WITH RELIGIOUS INTEGRATION IN EUROPEAN SOCIAL THOUGHT

As I have pointed out in previous writings, notably in *Communication and Social Order,* European models of social order as developed in social theory were often derived from religious models. And since the religious models used were tragic models of violent and mortal struggle between superiors who represent good principles of social order and inferiors who represent the bad, it is not surprising that sociodramas of equality are lacking in European theory. Nor is there much equality in the Christian drama of salvation. We are saved by superiors who forgive us our sins, just as we fall into sin because we disobey the commandments of our superiors.

It would be pleasant to record that British social thought which produced the great aristocratic sociodrama of debate in Parliament had also produced a public drama of social order of comparable power and glory. The familiar pronouncements of Bacon and Hobbes that religious bonds of order are the best modes for social order are sometimes dismissed as feudal styles of thought. But even Walter Bagehot, a founder of modern liberal thought, argues in his classic work of 1867, *The English Constitution,* that the "ruder sort of men" (that is, the people) will "sacrifice all they hope for, all they have, *themselves,* for what is called an idea—for some attraction which seems to transcend reality, which aspires to elevate men by an interest higher, deeper, wider than that of ordinary life."

Bagehot distinguishes between what he calls the "useful" parts of the structure of government (the rational and efficient ends) and the "theatrical." He argues that the common people do not in the least comprehend how the "plain, palpable ends of government . . . should be attained." It is only "natural" therefore that "the most useful parts of the structure of government should by no means be those which excite the most reverence." The elements which excite the most easy reverence will be those which appeal to the supernatural. "That which is mystic in its claims; that which is occult in its mode of action; that which is brilliant to the eye; that which is seen vividly for a moment, and then is seen no more, . . . this, howsoever its form may change, or however we may define it or describe it, is the sort of thing—the only sort—which yet comes home to the mass of men."

Mystic claims and occult actions lead easily into the supernatural, as expressed in religious ritual, or to tragedy, as expressed in art drama. It is true that Bagehot uses dramatic images ("the theatrical elements") for his image of social integration, and it would, therefore, be wrong to lump him together with Bacon, Hobbes, Tocqueville, Fustel de Coulanges, W. Robertson Smith, Émile Durkheim, Bronislaw Malinowski, A. R. Radcliffe-Brown, and Max Weber, among others, who make such heavy use of religious forms of integration for the construction of their forms of social integration. But Bagehot's theatrical images are grounded finally in religious images. "If you ask the immense majority of the Queen's subjects by what right she rules, they would never tell you that she rules by Parliamentary right . . . They will say she rules by 'God's grace'; they believe that they have a mystic obligation to obey her." Bagehot is careful to stress this point in his discussion of the monarchy. Parliament, the laws of the land, the press, these were human institutions, but the monarchy was a "Divine institution in the eyes of the people."

Even the human (*very* human) institution of sexual love has not escaped the European confusion of all integration with religious integration. In the "Fragments of a System of Psychology of Sexual Life" which serves as Chapter I of Krafft-Ebing's *Psychopathia Sexualis,* sexual love is explained after analogies drawn from love of God. The feeling of dependence, according to Krafft-Ebing, is the basis of sexual love since "religion as well as sexual love is mystical and transcendental." "True love," we read also, commands "sympathy, respect, and even fear." Perverted love, as in sadism and masochism, is explained after the analogy of religious sacrifice. "In religious life . . . [the expectation of unfathomed bliss] may assume of self-sacrifice or self-destruction, prompted by the idea that the victim is necessary for the material sustenance of the deity." The sacrifice is brought "as a sign of reverence or submission, as a tribute, as an atonement for sins committed, as a price wherewith to purchase happiness." Religious and sexual "hyperaesthesia" show the same degree of intensity and the same quality of excitement, and may therefore under given circumstances "interchange." And both "will in certain pathological states degenerate into cruelty."

Freud's use of religious models in his psychoanalytic constructions is apparent in such statements as "an obsessional neurosis is a caricature of a religion . . . ." In his later works Freud argued that social order was founded on renounced aggressive forces which were "handed over to the deity and were still permitted in his name, so that the handing over to him of bad and socially harmful instincts was the means by which man freed himself from their domination." Only the enlightened few can live without religion as their prime source of social integration. The analyst must not make the mistake of belittling the need of common men for religion by calling it a piece of infantilism which "only a few are capable of overcoming." Freud's elitism shows clearly on his insistence on the importance of ruling figures as common objects of identification. In *Group Psychology and the Analysis of the Ego* he warns his readers that America is threatened by "the phychological poverty of groups." The great man must hold the people in bondage through reverence, awe, and fear. Moses did not rise from the Jewish people but was an Egyptian aristocrat. God did not choose the Jewish people to worship and obey Him; Moses chose the Jewish people in order to perpetuate an earlier Egyptian monotheism. Not Shakespeare, the glover's son, but the aristocrat Edward de Vere, Earl of Oxford, wrote the plays of William Shakespeare.

The tribal man of the anthropologists is another example of the confusion of social integration with religious integration. Radcliffe-Brown, Malinowski, Durkheim, and their master, Frazer, discover in sacred bonds the source of all social bonds. Society functions through symbols, but in order to understand symbols and learn how they function we must turn to religion. Little (if anything) is said in anthropological theory about other symbols systems, such as art, nor is there much sensitivity to discussions of other grounds for social integration. The sociodrama of primitive life is a religious drama, and even when treated as a community "ceremony" as in the work of Radcliffe-Brown, the power of the ceremony is not derived from the drama of social life but from the relation of this drama to the sacred. Tribal man is tragic man. The "grim figure" of Frazer's priest of Nemi stalks his sacred grove in terror. "He was a priest and a murderer; and the man for whom he looked was sooner or later to murder him and hold the priesthood in his stead." This was the sacred law and the basis for all social integration. "A candidate for the priesthood could only succeed to office by slaying the priest, and having slain him, he retained office till he was himself slain by a stronger or a craftier."

THE PROTEAN POWER OF MYSTIFICATION

In moments of despair it is easy to believe that nothing can stand against the protean power of mystification based on tragedy and religion. Those who reject mystifications of religion find solace in the mysteries of science. The sharp critics of business domination in society are willing to turn control of the community over to politicians. Our businessmen see our poor starving amid affluence, and still argue that the cure for poverty is more, not less, appeal to the profit motive. Our militarists assure us they are really preserving world peace. Architects admit that each new hundred-story building adds to the further deterioration of urban life, yet they design such skyscrapers, and city councils urge that they be built.

Even when the mysteries of heaven, empire, love, war, and money are "revealed" by some "higher source," they must be communicated. No leader ever relied more on revealed truths than Hitler, yet no one struggled harder to attain mastery in the communication of his revelations. *Mein Kampf* contains many terrible lessons (still unheeded!) on how to satisfy the conscious and unconscious longings of people for authority. Hitler, as he himself said, understood that people want to *participate* in community dramas of salvation, not simply to witness them, or to think about them. He created great and moving dramas of struggle and purification in the understanding that the faith in which men can live bravely, and die at peace, must be a certainty, or it is nothing.

The European tragic religious drama of social integration is familiar to us in our American sociodrama of war. The war in Vietnam we have been told (until the late spring of 1968) is a war of salvation. We are saving the world for "Freedom" in an extension of The Great American Crusade to make the world safe for democracy that we began under President Wilson's regime and carried on under President Eisenhower's generalship. Or, a cruder sociodrama of defense is mounted for the American people. The battlefields of Asia are really the battlefields of America. In defending ourselves in Vietnam we are really defending our homes and our sacred "way of life." If bombs must fall, better far that they fall on Vietnam than upon enemies already intrenched upon our own soil. The wounded and dead civilians of Vietnam are suffering only because of their blasphemy against Americans who alone are the sacred guardians of freedom, or they suffer as cunning and terrible enemies who seek to bring war to our shores must suffer.

Until the Depression, American business was mounted as a drama of salvation. The "gospel of service" was the real explanation of the profit motive. Making money was not based in greed but in service to humanity. The Christmas gift, the gift of price, was a sacrifice. Poverty was a punishment for sloth. The high point of business sociodrama still occurs in Christmas shopping. By a symbolic linkage of money and the Nativity, in thirty frenzied shopping days between Thanksgiving and Christmas we are goaded into spending our way to heaven. Within one generation, from 1890 to 1925, the American businessman was deified, and the profit motive transformed into a "gospel of service." In 1925, Americans read Bruce Barton's *The Man Nobody Knows: A Discovery of the Real Jesus*, the most widely read nonfiction book of that year. Barton wrote that if Jesus were to live again we would recognize in him the first businessman.

ART AS THE HOME OF THE CRITICAL SPIRIT

Mystery lurks everywhere in our lives. The great rituals of religion, the incantations of our commercial magicians, the beguiling oratory of our politicians, the "sweet mystery" of romantic love, and now the "conquest" of science, are evidence enough of the power of mystification. And if, as I have implied in these propositions, it is only through the development of open, free, and informed discussion, and the creation and distribution of a free art, that men will be saved, how can this be done? How can we create and maintain criticism as a *constituent,* and, therefore, *necessary,* element in community life? Art makes criticism a constituent and public part of its institutional structure. Even popular art submits to constant, sharp, and widely communicated criticism, in contrast to sacred art, where faith, not aesthetic sensitivity, decides judgment. A new show on television becomes the subject of review in hundreds of publications. Any campus performance of art is reviewed in the campus paper.

But how many sermons are reviewed in Monday morning editions of the press? How many lectures of resident professors are given serious review in the college paper? How often is the conduct of war discussed openly and freely in the press? When does a hospital publish the pathologist's findings on the diagnostic accuracy of its staff members? Seldom, if ever.

Hitler forbade free and open criticism; he introduced what he called "the principle of absolute responsibility," because this, he said, was the only way to combat the "parliamentary madness" of open, free, informed, and sustained discussion.

Only in art, even in popular art where success or failure is measured in profit, is the critic given an honored, necessary, and daily place, and only in art is he encouraged to communicate widely. He is an *integral* part of the social institution of art, for art, above all institutions, is the home of novelty, change, and originality, as it is of classical tradition. Art is not sacred; the truths of art are created, not discovered or revealed. There are many artists, expressing many different views, and often these views are highly critical of those in power. Even in authoritarian societies art, and especially comic art, may be a permissible, and, indeed, an honored and sanctioned form of disrespect. The judgments of art on society are seldom heard in one god-like voice. The courtiers of Versailles heard Racine, but they also heard Molière.

The dark mantle of tragedy, and the mystifications of salvation devices, are balanced in American political life (and business life) by a high sense of comedy. Incongruities between means and ends in political action are exposed through laughter. Political cartoons in which opponents are caricatured mercilessly are given front page space. Campaign jokes increase as the fervor of candidates rises. Candidates joke about themselves before audiences who must be moved to vote for them. Buttons, bumper stickers, and many kinds of emblems appear bearing comic slogans. Ludicrous pictures of candidates are printed. Candidates themselves are pictured in smiles and laughter. News and television commentators poke fun at candidates, as they do at the annual Washington Gridiron Dinner where members of the Press satirize the many incongruities of American political life.

Abraham Lincoln's sanctification as an American political god is well under way, but his deification rests on comedy as much as tragedy. He is a new kind of political god, the laughing god. Lincoln used comedy to solve problems by pointing up the many incongruities of political life, just as he used humor to confront the pain and disorder of daily life. Lincoln stories and jokes have a strong moral, and it is a moral rooted in problems familiar to Americans who speak of politics as a game or contest played in the name of "campaign issues" over social order in democratic society. The American political sociodrama is not only a sacred drama with heroes and villains who become gods and devils. And while it is true that we still elect tragic figures such as generals to high public office, they must go through a process of "demilitarization" before they run for office. Mussolini, Hitler, Stalin, staged themselves as soldiers, as Mao Tse-tung, Marshal Tito, and even de Gaulle, still do. But General Eisenhower, the military hero, died a symbolic death in his rebirth as a civilian university president and—ultimately—political hero.

This use of comedy teaches us that men turn to art, as they do to religion, to learn how to act in the world. The world I have chosen in this book of propositions is the democratic world, where harmony is reached only through the agreement of free men. The form of art selected, the art of dramatic form, as the model for action in society is above all others the form of action and passion. Drama in art, and sociodrama in the community, are the guardians of public reason, because through them we confront the many disrelationships in our lives. The sacrificial victim in religion, like the tragic hero of drama, is beyond hope. He must be destroyed, for in his destruction lies our salvation. The comic hero of art is loaded with our vices and then punished and banished as a scapegoat. But the court of appeal for the comic and tragic hero of art is society, not God or some transcendental power beyond reason. Art *opens* social disrelationships to doubt and question, for the artist believes that whatever men can discuss they can resolve.

The great revolution of our time is the creation of sociodramas in which not few but *all* participate. The study of how these sociodramas give form to community life must begin. Much evil lies behind us, and, no doubt, there is much to come. But there is good, too. Ghandi, Churchill, and Roosevelt stand against Hitler and Mussolini as creators of sociodramas based on compassion and human fellowship. In their voices we hear ringing down the corridors of time great voices of the Renaissance, the springtime of our civilization when so many fair hopes of men were born. As Pico della Mirandola said in his *Oration on the Dignity of Man:*

> Thou constrained by no limits, in accordance with thine own free will in whose hands we have placed thee, shall ordain for thyself the limits of thy nature. We have set thee at the world's center that thou mayest from thence more easily observe whatever is in the world. We have made thee neither of heaven nor of earth, neither mortal nor immortal, so that with freedom of choice and with honor, as though the maker and molder of thyself, thou mayest fashion thyself in whatever shape thou shalt prefer. Thou shalt have the power to degenerate unto the lower forms of life which are brutish. Thou shalt have the power, out of thy soul's judgment to be reborn into the higher forms, which are divine.

But we hear, too, the grim voice of Hobbes. Men who live without other security "than what their own strength, and their own invention shall furnish them," condemn themselves to a life that is "solitary, poor, nasty, brutish, and short." Yet who will say that the surrender of liberty to masters such as Mussolini, Hitler, and Stalin has saved us? We now hunt each other down with a ferocity and skill unknown to past ages, or to what we call "beasts of prey" among animals. We realize in horror that our skill in killing has become absolute. We can destroy the world. Even in "limited" war we can wound, cripple, and kill great numbers in but a few hours. Man, the social beast of prey who wars against his fellow beings in the name of symbols of social order, can will the destruction of his world.

He *knows* he can be a devil. Can he become a god?

Man's freedom is freedom to communicate through symbols of his own creation. This is his glory and his burden. Naming can be either a blessing or a curse. In a democratic society we are committed to open, free, informed, and constant public discussion in which competing sociodramas in religion, business, politics, education, art, and science are staged. Our survival will depend on how well, and how quickly, we learn to mount these dramas for *all* the people. The sociopathology of community life can be studied in the work of Hitler, Stalin, and all the grim tyrants who integrated men in blood, violence, terror, and death. Such study must lead to a better understanding of how to create human communities based on love and fellowship. We have learned in great suffering that we must be our brother's keeper, for if we are not, we become his, and our own, executioner.

The assassination of Senator Robert Kennedy, like the killing of President Kennedy and the Reverend Martin Luther King, Jr., offers fresh and terrible proof that modern sociodramas of violence cannot be considered screens on which "reality" casts its images. Nor can they be considered the sole cause of violence. Images of violence do not leap into the camera by themselves. They are selected, edited, and assembled as popular sociodramas of violence that will interest the publics created and sustained by what we call "news." *What* we communicate about the war in Vietnam is determined by *how* we communicate it, but symbols alone do not create the war, any more than they create riot and pillage in the streets.

How can we expect societies led by those skilled in violence, and by leaders who style themselves in military dress and equipage as masters of violence, not to be violent? When we stage the killing of our enemies as an act of salvation why do we not expect our enemies to do the same to us? And if we do not treat those who differ with us as members of a loyal opposition, but as enemies, why are we so outraged when they turn us into enemies? When we make our opponents villains and scapegoats why are we so shocked when they do the same to us? When we do not tell the people what really happened in war why are we so disturbed when they no longer believe anything we tell them? When we alienate the young, the poor, and those whose race, religion, or way of life differs from ours, *by refusing to communicate with them,* why are we so surprised when they turn to those who will?

The new audiences created by modern means of communication want their voices to be heard, *and to be heard in dialogue.*

Abraham, sacrifice of son, 147

Absurdity in dream and art, 160

Act: action theory and culture theory, 13; studied in American sociology, 13; elements in, 16; institutional forms, 16; reduced to structure by Lévi-Strauss, 20; neglect of symbolic elements in American sociology, 20; perfected, serving as guide to action in present, 29; problematical, 29; determined by communicative forms, 48; infusion of motor phase, 48; contains past, present, and future, 48; of creation, 112; and consummation, 112; measure of reason in society, 128; sociodrama of hierarchy, 155

Action, dramatic structure of, 22

Adam, vicarious sinner, 142

Address: commitment, 101; social covenant, 104; hierarchal communication, 127; clue to distribution of authority, 129; inner forms learned in address to outer selves, 149

Aesthetic experience, consummatory, 223

Aesthetic myths, 235

Aesthetic norms of conduct, 188

Agreement: basis of equality, 37; based on discussion, 38; under rules among equals, 57; necessary in all societies, 58; in discussion among peers, 86; mystique of rules, 91

Alice in Wonderland, 227

Ambiguity, bridge in social experience, 7

American Legion, 98

American Medical Association, 216

Analects, 56, 187, 188

Analogies based in symbolic relatedness, 153

Anxiety: communicative factors, 77; cause of fantasy, 107; in communication, 136

Arbitration, 113

Archaic heritage, in memory-traces, archetypes, and engrams, 46

Architecture, and social staging, 94

Aristophanes, 228; on intervention of gods in Greek drama, 163

Aristotle, 37, 87, 188

Art, 17; C. Wright Mills's view, 10; comic and grotesque, 14; realm of experimentation with forms, 50; and sociodrama, 125; self-address in, compared with that of dreams, 129; source of attitudes in sociodrama, 146; and symbolic victims, 146; human quality of symbols, 146; exercises power, 188; social, 188, 245; realm of change, 190; social meaning, 191; form as order in, 222; shared experience, 223; determines social experience, 223; power of, 223; great, 223; and action, 223; conscious exploration, 223; great, magical, or make-believe, 224; and incongruity, 225, 246; both tragedy and comedy, 225; shifts among tragic, comic, and ironic modes, 228

Art of Courtly Love, 57

Art drama, and purgation, 59

Artist: ally of scientist in Freud's view, 11; role in creation of forms, 164

Athens, 163; in American Middle West, 29

Atonement: vicarious, 141; re-establishment of communication with sacred power, 144

Attitudes: in communication, 48; toward stimulation, 71; in use of forms, 187

Audience: approval necessary to hierarchal position, 58; clues to types in comic drama, 81; types in courtroom and in politics, 81; basic types, 81; "They," "We," "Thou," "Me," and "It," 81; types of address to, 82; difficulty in addressing, 83; inner and outer, 83; in fantasy, 84; negative, 85; reached through delegates, 88; and definition of self, 101; ideal, and the self, 101; search for ideal, 101; power of, in definition of the self, 101; in dreams, 105; mixed nature, 105; public and private, 105; disagreement weakens mystification, 106; father as primal in Freud, 106; parents as authoritarian, 107; ultimate, addressed as supernatural power, 110; multipilicity in address by individuals, 128; internal, 128; real and imagined, 128; "I" to "Me"; selves as, to each other, 128; expiatory power, 141; "seeing and being seen" as member, 162; stratification, 162; staging in sociodrama, 163; address as clue to authority, 171, 172
Audubon, John James, 231
Authority: and symbolic control, 62; longing for, in childhood, 76, 242; parents and other early, 84; confusion over, in childhood, 84; and competition, 85; reliance on, 113; staging in sociodrama, 161; use in ritual, 189
Axioms resembling rules of game, 43

Babbitt, 28
Bacchanalia, 182
Bach's *St. Matthew Passion*, cry of despair, 144
Bacon, Francis: on friend as equal, 56; on friendship as necessary to aristocratic life, 87; on religious bonds, 240
Bagehot, W., 55, 240; on dignification, 219
Barnett, J. H., 11
Beauty, supernatural term, 235
Bebel, A., 204
Beckett, Samuel, 160
Beliefs, grounded in transcendent ultimates, 53
Berelson, Bernard, 9; confusion of science with quantification, 9
Board of Rites, Chinese, 56
Boulding, Kenneth, on money, 15
Burckhardt, J., 13
Bureaucratic communication as mystification, 133
Burke, Kenneth, 13, 14, 16, 18, 19, 30, 40, 156, 170, 189, 217, 220, 225; on four realms of social order, 114; analogies for relationships between words and supernatural, 115; on symbolic nature of rights, 219
Businessmen, waning power in American life of, 133

Cappellanus, Andreas, on love as status address, 57
Carlyle, Thomas, on clothes, 184; in clothes as "emblematic" of social order, 219
Carnival, 182
Cassirer, Ernst, 13
Celestial symbols, 78
Ceremonies: enhancement of social roles, 54; Spencer on power of, 55; problem of form, 55; drama of solidarity, 55; play, 183; sociodrama of rank, 183, 184
Change: sign of strength, 37; institutionalization, 122; attitudes toward, 123; seldom easy, 123; and permanence, 135; threat to tradition, 174; normal under rules, 175; institutionalized in art, 190
Chaplin, Charlie, 175
Chicago, 163, 232
Childhood play a source of rules, 214
Childhood satisfactions as social, 161
Chinese literati, "keepers of the rites," 204
Christ and expiation, 142
Christian sociodrama, Christ as mediator in, 139; Hitler and, 238
Christianity, 234
Christmas: business celebration, 133, 243; fellowship through money in, 181
Cicero, 156; on friendship, 56
Circumlocutions, 193
Civil War, 232
Clay, Henry, on competition, 92
Clothes: and social order, 184; and ceremony, 184
Clown: guardian of social order, 99; and exposure of incongruity, 99; victim, 141
Cochran, Thomas C., 8
Collective unconscious, 46
Comedy: sanctioned doubt, 60; and sin of pride, 60; and reason in society, 60; wards off threats to social bonds, 60; brings incongruity into consciousness, 60; clue to audiences, 82; in

Shriner's conventions, 98; and tragedy as sociodramas, 127; social nature, 127; invokes social principle of reason, 175; confrontation of social problems, 175; and social purgation, 176; confrontation of incongruity, 227; guardian of reason in society, 227; sustains and attacks authority, 227

Comic actor, address to various audiences, 99

Comic art: compared with religious art, 225; sanctioned doubt and disrespect, 227, 244

Comic drama as social corrective, 126

Comic gods, 175

Comic guardians: conservative, 99; open mystifications to reason, 99; lighten burdens of tragedy, 99

Comic hero, address to audiences, 82

Comic victimage: confrontation of social incongruity, 24; compared with tragic, 25; for sin against society, 126

Commemoration, integrative function, 131

Communication: significant symbols, 4; failure to develop theory, 5; prime social data, 7; in Parsons's theory, 15; social *and* physical event, 15; and social order, 16; basic elements, 17; as community, 19; and social integration, 19; and origin of the self, 19; safeguard of American democracy, 28; constituent element in social integration, 31; relationship between *how* and *what*, 32; and public and private self, 32; great modern revolution, 33; not media alone, 33; necessary category of any theory, 44; basic to Dewey's thought, 44; constituent category of experience, 46; social category, 46; laws must be demonstrated, 46; created in human discourse, 46; problem-solving activity, 47; beseechment, 77; basic to communion, 77; sacred, 77; necessary to power of elite, 95; and community, 100; perfected in love, 101; and sociopathology, 130; and guilt, 137; hidden and secret, 138; problem in democracies and tyrannies, 140; of struggle, 148; absurdity in, 159; in economic life, 207; and freedom, 247

Communication and Social Order, 30, 31, 239

Communication gaps: dangerous to social system, 133; caused by irrele-

vance of traditions and utopias, 133; desertion by God in *St. Matthew Passion*, 144

Communicators, source of power, 144

Communism, tragic drama of victimage, 25

Community: created and sustained in role enactment, 63; born in struggle, 64

Community guardians: must communicate, 83; type of audience ("We"), 95; uphold group views, 96; defenders of sacred principles, 96; staging in "reviewing stand," 96; comic guardians as, 97; choric voice in comic drama, 97; voice of tradition and custom, 98; guard principles of order, 99

Competition, 92

Conflicts: inner, between instinctual and cultural needs, 84; originate in role conflict, 84; between sex and status, 84; and parental authority, 84; of audiences, 85; source in role conflict, 85; in outer and inner roles, 105

Confucius, 86, 187, 188, 234; and rite of obeisances, 55; on friends as equals, 56, 57; on manners, 180

Consecration: apogee of "upward way" in religion, 22; social act, 22; negative and positive aspects, 22

Consummatory phase of action in total act, 112

Contemporary Sociological Theories, 3

Content, manifest and latent in symbols, 50

Content analysis: no theory of communicative effect, 5; problem of meaning in literature, 9

Contents of social experience, basic forms of, 17

Conversation among equals, 87

Cooley, C. H., 13, 19, 26; on communication, 44

Corneille, Pierre, 57

Coronation as sociodrama, 164

Courtship: rhetoric of society, 54; of superiors, 55; versus worship, 56; "keepers of the rites," types, 56; sustains and sustained by liturgy, 56; social elements in sexual, 58; address to various audiences in, 127

Creation: shifts in theories, 112; and social order, 217

Crime, an organization of disorder, 137

Crime and Punishment, 11

Criminal not "disorganized," 137
Criticism: free, open, and informed, 27; in free community, 27; method of inquiry, 27; way to truth, 62; taking role of other toward self, 177; use to assess means-end relationships, 191; constituent to social life, 192; open or closed, 192, 244; analysis, 192; and circumlocutions, 193; in primary relationships, 194; in closed groups, 195; problems of, among elites, 195; and general public, 196; sociodrama of, 197; clue to distribution of authority, 197; study of, 198; in art, 244
Critics as craft judges, 196, 244
"Cultural lag," theory of, 13
Culture, in Chicago of 1890, 29
Current Sociological Research, 1962: A Listing of Research in Progress as Reported by Members of the American Sociological Association, 11
Cursing, social value of, 108

Dachau, 28
Darwin, Charles, 28
Death, 218
Debate, and rules, 205
Defense, 17; sociodrama of, 208; paradox of, 209
A Defense of Poetry, 188
Demand, social problem of, 13
Democracy: comic sociodrama, 25; use of comedy in, 25; lives in agreement, 38
"Desanctification," 149
Dewey, John, 13, 16, 26, 39, 40; on communication, 44
Difference, 38
Dilthey, W., 13, 45
Disagreement, among equals, 106
Discontent, necessary, 169; divine, 78
Discussion, *rules* and, 37
Disease, and sociopathology, 216
Dishonor, and status, 89
Disobedience: guilt and, 59; threat to principles of social order, 135; destroys communication, 144
Disorder: "outside" order, 137; personification in scapegoat, 138
Disorganization: not based in hate, 102; originates in indifference, 102
Disraeli, Benjamin, 37
"Do" and "do not," 220, 221
Doctor, staging role of, 216
Dodge, G. M., 231

Don Quixote: death as moment of transformation, 127
Doubt: method of assessing conduct, 8; necessary to social integration, 36; inquiry, 62; method of inquiry, 134; characteristic of hierarchy, 158; uncommon in dreams, 159; sanctioned, 190; and question, 226
Drama of hierarchy, social passage in, 156
Dreams: formal quality, 4; address in, 149
Dress: social identification, 118; communication, 213
Dryden, John, 23
Dueling code: dance of death, 54; glory of honor under rules, 54
Durkheim, Émile, 13, 17, 28, 186, 188, 219, 240, 242

Economics, 17, 206, 207
Edison, Thomas A., 231
Education, 17; tasks, 211; analysis, 211, 212; and tradition, 212
Ego, and resolution of role conflict, 109
Elites, masters of communication, 95
Embarrassment, 136
Emotion: always expressed, 47; learned in communication, 47; form and social reality, 47; social feelings, 47
Ends: "as if," 47; infuse total act, 115; perfected by institutions, 115; "revealed," 124
Enemy, as victim, 65
Engels, Friedrich, 12
Environment: symbolic *and* physical, 16; symbolic nature, 70; organized through perception, 71
Equality: element lacking in European social theory, 28, 239; form of social order, 36; characteristic of societies, 52; determined by rules in games, 57; grounded on rules in democracy, 57; and honor, 57; necessary to societies, 58; agreement basis for authority, 69; necessary to social order, 86; and conversation, 87; and disagreement, 106; learned in childhood, 106; and play, 174; and irony, 179; and joking, 180; in fun and play, 182; under rules, 206
Equalization, in competition, 174
Equals: jealous of rules, 37; do not command or obey, 38; compete under rules, 57; freely given relationships, 56; relations under rules, 58; and

doubt, 86; expose differences, 103; discussion and argument by, 107; and "umpirage," 178

Erotic play, power of symbolic forms in, 121

Eternal return, 189

"Eternalizing," 235

Etiquette: regulation by Board of Rites in China, 56; power of, as form of integration, 119

Excommunication: guilt and, 59; social variants, 107

Expiation: makes fear manageable, 140; social function, 140; inner and outer, 141; social purgation, 141; through sociodrama, 141

Expiatory killings, 141

Extra-symbolic explanations, interpretation, 152

Fables, Ancient and Modern, 23

Fair play, 37; depends on objective forms, 37; and rules, 57; mystery of rules, 91; mystique among equals, 206

Falstaff, 57

Family, 17; first experience of authority, 201; use of, in sociodrama, 201; and communication, 202; miniature community, 202

Fantasy: organization of wishes, 131; and created wants, 131; communication, 138

Fashion, 185

Fastnacht, 182

Fear, noncommunication and, 144

Feasts: of spring, 182; inversion of hierarchy in, 183; saturnalian types, 183

Feasts of Fools, 183

Festival: sacrifice and, 181; form of sociodrama, 181; gives form to social life, 181; and social euphoria, 181; joy and sorrow, 181; and inversion of hierarchy, 182; of folly, 182; celebration of social order, 182

Festivals, 17

Fetishism, social and sexual, 142

Fields, W. C., 175

Firth, A. R., 21

Fool: of God, 127; of the people, 127

Forbidden acts, mysterious appeal of, 221

Force: legitimized, 33; weakness of, 200; public opinion and, 203; rights and, 204; origin of state, 204

Forest Lawn, 194

Form: reduction to content by Freud, 5; and content of the act, 7; determinant of content, 7; need for sociological propositions on, 7; of sociation as power, 48; creation necessary to relationships, 48; created in social life, 49; and interests as basis of act, 49; reality of social relationships, 49; directly observable, 72; makes emotions possible, 160; indication of response, 214; of prayer as sociodrama, 222

Forms of sociation, ultimates in themselves, 212

Frazer, James G., 24, 156, 182, 186, 242

Frederick the Great, on ridicule, 180

Freud, Sigmund, 7, 11, 17, 19, 28, 40, 45, 46, 63, 102, 106, 111, 154, 156, 161, 170, 225; neglect of form, 5; on artist's understanding of social motivation, 17; "combined technique" of interpretation, 32; on public referents of private symbols, 32; on interpretation of dream symbols, 32; high evaluation of Oedipus complex, 45; on words and magic, 45; on Nirvana principle and death instinct, 65; family psychology, 169, 201; on jokes, 226; elitism, 241; on "psychological poverty of groups," 241

Friend: importance to development as individual, 58; talk with, as exploration, 58; other self, 58; second self in talk, 86; audience, 103

Friendship: and social will, 38; ideal type of equality, 56; and honor, 56; "I" speaking to its "Thou," 86; possible only among equals, 87; reciprocal nature of, 102; mutual definition of selves, 103; and problem-solving in human relationships, 103

Frustration, 137; in communication, 136

Function, as social concept, 63

Future: and destruction of past in American life, 25; knowledge of, considered as subjective (like fantasy), 25; source of transcendence, 26; Hitler's use of, as ideal past, 26; image open to criticism, 26; Edenic myth as, 26; tradition of the new, 26; "progress" in American life, 26; must be subject to criticism, 26; forms image to guide action in a present, 29; images of, analyzed as guides to

Future (*Cont.*)
action, 29; always part of act, 48; organization of attitudes, 48; immanence, 113; and past myths of perfection, 171; in socialistic states, 207

Gaiety, submission to others in, 121
Games, 17, 37, 214
Gandhi, 95, 246
General Introduction to Psycho-Analysis, 45
General public ("They"): audience, not "mass," 93; competition for, 93; courted by all, 93; Hitler's courtship, 93; Stalin's courtship, 93; drama of shopping, 93; staging of appeals to, 94; requires sociodrama, 94
Genesis, and governance, 217
Gentleman, and hierarchal observances in China, 187
Glorification, forms of, 205
Glory, in art and sociodrama, 164
Go-between, threatened by open communication, 145
Gods, intervention in classical drama, 163
God-terms, ultimate legitimation of hierarchy, 66
The Golden Bough, 182
"Good form," social order and, 212
Gospels, 144
Government: sociodrama of, 203; symbols of, 203; "way of life," 204; glory of, as sociodrama of dignification, 205
Gracian, B., 56, 145; on friend as second self, 56
The Grammar of Motives, 18
Gridiron dinners, 183
Grotesque, ignorance of social function of, 159
Guernica, 160
Guilt: disobedience, 59; personification in Negro and Jew, 59; in tragedy, 59; purging of, 94; "categorical" or "original," 131, 236; result of offence against principle of order, 135; and communication, 137; absolved in communication, 138; and lack of communication, 138; based on belief we cannot communicate, 139; and fantasy, 159; and need for expiation, 222; sociodramatic forms, 222

Handicaps, and equalization in play, 174

Hate: satisfied through other, 102; creates social bonds, 131
Hawthorne, Nathaniel, 226
Haydn, Franz Joseph, 184
Health: sociodrama of, 215; and symbols of authority, 215
Health and welfare, 17
Hero and villain, interchangeable roles of, 147
Hertzler, J. O., 3, 6
Hierarchy: and social order, 20; fixed and in passage, 52; relations between superiors, inferiors, and equals, 52; positions determined by rights, 58; final leap into faith, 66; purified by appeals to higher authority, 66; perfection of, 80; communicable mystery, 89; types, 156; social and linguistic, 157; "upward way" to perfection, 165; play and, 174; celestial, 219
History: American sense of future in, 28, 86; and change, 123
Hitler, A., 28, 33, 34, 39, 64, 95, 139, 141, 147, 205, 242, 245-7; Jew as scapegoat of, 40; his life as allegory, 53; and dramas of German destiny, 53; staged sociodramas for general publics, 93; use of military dress, 184; use of past in oratory, 26; death camps, 236; on participation, 237
Hobbes, Thomas, 240, 246; on power of the word, 217
Honor: as "status honor" in Weber, 21; before God in Weber, 22; not egalitarian concept, 37; dependence on style, 54; personal versus public, 54; aristocratic concept, 57; not extended to lower classes, 57; defined through dishonor, 89; under rules, 174, 215
Hostility, symbolic, 108
Hsun Tze, 187
Hubert, Henri, 24
Huckleberry Finn, 142, 175, 226, 227
Huckleberry Finn, 225, 227

"I," in address, 172
"Ideal-types": range of explanation, 154; symbolic analysis, 154
Identification, 45, 179, 237; positive and negative, 22, 69; negative, 22; dramatic process, 34; dramatic participation, 34; of public through speech, 93; with those who judge us, 136; acceptance, rejection, or irony, 179; and manners, 179

Imagery in the act: drawn from past and future, 29, 71; consummatory as completed, 71; guide to action, 71; of spirit as mystification, 81; and form, 223
Images of Man, 12
Immanence: and transcendence, 51; and incarnation, 235
Incognito, 174
Incongruity, exposure in comedy, 99; in role playing, 149
Indifference, makes social bond impossible, 104
Individual: action of, 122; community subordination to, 122
Inequality, and communication, 108
Institutions, contradictory appeals of, 105
Integrative symbols, love and hate in, 131
Intention, dependence on form of, 6
The Interpretation of Dreams, 32; discussion of symbolic interpretation in, 32n, 42
Interpretation of forces "beyond" symbols, 50
Irony: and equality, 179; and hierarchy, 179, 180; based on faith in reason, 226; accepts authority, 227; based on reason in society, 227

James, Henry, 225
James, William, 11, 13
Jefferson, Thomas: on rules, 38; on "umpirage," 178
Jesus, 147
Jews: scapegoats for Hitler's Germans, 138, 147; victims who "purified" Aryan blood, 141; "perfected" victims under Hitler, 146
Johnson, A. B., and American semantics, 22
Jokes: open mystery to reason, 61; safe only with peers, 180
Judge as umpire, 73
Judicial process as way to truth, 113
Jung, Carl, 111; theory of engrams, 46

Kennedy, John F., 247
Kennedy, Robert F., 247
King, Martin Luther, Jr., 247
Knowledge of society, "apprehension" or "act," 13
Krafft-Ebing, Baron Richard von: on fetishism, 142; rejection of social explanation of sexual symbolism, 143
Krakodil, and official humor, 60
Ku Klux Klan, 35

Language, 154; cause and effect of social order, 112; affects all grounds for social order, 116
Language and Literature in Society, 30
La Rochefoucauld, Duc François de, 40, 156, 180; on love as "talkative," 101; on self-love, 227
Laughter, 121; reduces mystery, 108; at and with others, 176; at immigrant in America, 227; at contradictions, 228
Law: covenant, 76; transcendence in legal appeals, 112; transcendent factor in the social order, 136; in science, 229; makes crime, 209
Lawyer, arbiter in American life, 54
Legal process, mystifications in, 113
Legitimation: of force, 33; style of life, 34; integrative factor, 53; Weber's use of, 53; and social beliefs, 110; types in social hierarchies, 110; grounded in nature, man, society, language, or God, 116; "service," 199; based on persuasion, 200
Li Chi (Book of Rites), 187
Life cycles, 189
Life histories, narrative forms of, 4
Lincoln, Abraham: on consent, 91; and expiation, 142; laughing god, 245
Lindsay, Vachel, 29
Linkage: of images of social order, 117; clues to meanings in sociodrama, 157
Linkages in sociodrama: stage-act, 166; stage-role, 166; stage-means, 166; act-principle of social order, 167; act-role, 167; stage-principle of social order, 167; act-means, 168; role-principle of social order, 168; means-principle of social order, 168; roll-means, 168
Lippmann, Walter, 12
Liturgy, sustained by social courtship, 56
Lord of Misrule, 183
Louis XIV, 193
Love: sex and symbol, 7; feudal service, 58; ideal communication, 101
Lukács, Georg, 13
Lupercalia, 182
Luther, Martin, 137, 148, 189; on God's silence, 77; on devil as author of evil, 137; on fear of sinning, 148, 210

McLuhan, Marshall, 17, 20
Magic, and religion, 186
Maine, H. S., 25, 55
Make-believe, 128
Malinowski, Bronislaw, 9, 18, 19, 20, 44, 154, 188, 240, 247; on symbolic element in ritual, 186
Man, social beast of prey, 102
Manners: determinants of status, 48; playful, 121; form of social legitimation, 122; ironic and playful, 123; rules, 123; basis of judgment of skill, 179; daily rhetoric of society, 179; purely social bonds, 179; and social distance, 179; and social style, 179; blessing and cursing, 180; Confucius on, 180; form of social integration, 180; and laws, 180; and status, 180; weapon, 180
Manual of Parliamentary Practise, 38
Mark Twain, 226
Martyrdom, and sacred audience, 129
Marx, Karl, 12, 28; on clothes, 184; on capitalistic mystifications, 219
Mary, Mother of Christ, 235
Mauss, Marcel, 24
Mead, George Herbert, 13, 16, 18, 19, 26, 29, 30, 39, 40, 43, 229; on position in games, 37; on communication as basic social bond, 44
Meaning: symbolic interpretation, 5; source in social action, 7; symbolic, 50; in paggage from lower to higher status, 51
The Meaning of Meaning, 18, 20
Mechanistic imagery: prevalence of, 5; spatial not temporal, 5
Medium: one element in communicative act, 16; partial explanation of communication, 17, 74; effect on communication, 73
Mein Kampf, 64, 237, 238, 242
Memory-traces, Freud's theory of, 46
Message, act, not medium, 74
Method, as magic, 35
Methodology: of symbolic interpretation in psychology, 45; interpretation and demonstration, 50; of symbolic interpretation, 50, 151, 153; false combinations of mechanical and dramatic images, 155; linkages of elements of the act, 157; action frame of reference in concept of sociodrama, 165; in clarifying struggle and change, 169; incongruity of, 170; and limitations of

Freudian model, 170; and analysis of sociodrama, 199
Michels, Robert, 13, 28
Mills, C. Wright, 12, 13; on sociological breakthrough, 10
Models: use of non-mechanistic, 5; need for sociolinguistic, 7; false without art, 14; dependence on theory in construction, 16; mixed, 17; of Burke, Ogden and Richards, Malinowski, and Mead, 18; Burke's pentad, 18, 19, 68; adaptation of Burke's pentad, 19; Mead's parliament of selves, 19; problems in deriving sociodrama from art drama, 19; distinction between art and social, 30; game and drama, 30; behavioral as spatial, 31; refining definition of, 31; need for dramatic, 63; ritual, 64; forms of struggle in, 65; Burke's dramatistic, 68; failure to explain change by ritual, 68; Mead's use of play, game, and conversation in, 68; need to express change *in* permanence, 68; based on integrative factors in sociation, 117; criticism and democratic, 197
Military symbols, glory and humility of, 205
Molière, 228, 244
Money: circulation of, as analogy for communication in Parsons's theory, 14; and promise of higher life, 79; spiritualization of, 79; domination of Christmas by, 93; relevance to social order, 134; as sacred principle, 175; as symbol, 207; symbolic properties of, 207; and transformation, 208; and "way of life," 219
Montgomery Ward Catalogue as "Wishing Book," 214
Mosca, Gaetano, 13
Motives, sociological view of, 49
Mystery: in democratic communication, 107; in bureaucratic communication, 133; communicable to many audiences, 133; of enemy reduced, 148; common to all societies, 173; Burke on, 219; and obedience, 220; and the forbidden, 220; negation, 220; and moment of belief, 234
Mystics, technological and religious, 133
Mystification: of means, 36; of technique, 36; many forms of, 80; and immanence, 113; in law, 113; divine attribute, 145; Gracian on, 145; in

priestly hierarchy, 219; terms for, 219; protean power of, 242
Mystique of efficiency, 36
Myth: and ritual, 186; types of, 190

Naming: and social integration, 21; source of social honor, 21; religious grounds, 22; sacred, 22; purification, 22; in struggle over social order, 23, 236; and sociopolitical order, 24; form of social control, 33; magical power, 44; determinant of common actions, 46; fixed social meanings, 103; and relationships, 103; social reference, 103; clues to consubstantiality, 171; identification, 171, 236; title, 171; sacred, 194; source of power, 200
The Nature of Judicial Process, 73
Nazis, personification of Jew as devil by, 138
Negation and sin, 86
Negatives: in conduct, 86; importance in symbolic analysis, 157
Negro, and unfulfilled wants, 131
The Nicomachean Ethics, 37

Obedience: principle of order and, 86; types, 86; resolution of difference, 220
Obeisances, ceremonial nature of, 55
Obscenity as opposition, 158
Oedipus complex, 202
Oedipus legend, 225
Office, man not identified with, 23
Office party, 183
Ogburn, William Fielding, 13
Opposition, institutionalized, 158
Order within and without individual psyche, 65
Origen, on supernatural end in social order, 111
Outline of Psychoanalysis, 45

Pain, enjoyment of, 40
Parents: comic *and* tragic, 106; gods, 161
Pareto, Vilfredo, 6, 13, 28
Park, R. E., 13, 16
Parsons, Talcott: on communication, 14; exchange theory of communication, 14; on relationship between art and society, 14; use of Burke's *Permanence and Change,* 14; neglect of symbolic action, 15; mechanistic equilibrium model, 44
Parties, and social manners, 179

Pascal, Blaise, 40
Passage: existence of social order in, 52; sanctioned, 69; need for sanctions in, 105, 135; transformation, 156
Passion of Christ, 144
Passion of wisdom in academic life, 79
Past: in organic school of social theory, 25; in European and American social thought, 26; recaptured, is symbolic construction, 48; social function in reminiscence, 129
Peer relations, public and private, 58
Perceptions and word presentations in Freud, 46
Perfection of community images, 171
Permanence *in* change, 33
Permanence and Change, 14, 41
Personification in communication, 89
Persuasion, basic element in communication, 221
The Philosophy of the Present, 18, 29
Picasso, Pablo, 160
Plato, 188, 235
Play, 17, 37; random and structured, 173; society a form of, 173; and equality, 174, 182; hierarchy in, 174; and ceremony, 183; and "internalization" of roles, 214; and rules, 214
"Playing society," 173
Political communication, staging in television, 132
Politician, contestant in American politics, 92
Political modes of action, 17
Politics: and glory, 204; sociodrama of contest, 205
Poverty, 243
Power: based on understanding of dramatic power, 25; communicated even when sacred, 145; tyrants' dramatization of, 146
Present, infusion by future, 235
Presidency, role in sociodrama, 164
Priestly office, 235
Principles of Sociology, 55
Propaganda, 17
Proprieties, 179
Protocol, social structure and, 88
Proverbs, public nature of, 4
Psychiatry, neglect of social factors in sex, 144
Psychopathia Sexualis, 142
Public images: basic to action in society, 19; Mead's definition of, 19
Public staging, clues to ultimates, 165

Punishment: and purgation, 59; sign of grace, 76; as communication, 139; bond of, 139; preferred to indifference, 139

Purgation: through tragic victimage, 24; drama of, 59; way to open communication, 145; moment of transformation, 157; naming of, 157

Purges: community purification through, 124; characteristic of societies, 157

Purification: and social order, 23; and community cleansing, 66

Rabelais, François, 228

Racine, Jean Baptiste, 57, 244

Radcliffe-Brown, A. R., 44, 185, 187, 188, 240, 242; on ritual, 186

Rag days, 183

Reason: exists in sociodrama, 190; lives in dialogue, 190

Rejection, and other's awareness of us, 86

Relata, in symbolic theory, 6

Relatedness, in communication, 7

Relationship, as determined by *what* and *how* in conduct, 7

Religion, 17; ritual, 185; commands, 217; sociodrama, 217; and death, 218

Religious rites: paradigm for social ritual, 185, 218; methodological model, 218; crucial moments in, 218

Responses, selected, 71

Restif de la Bretonne, Nicholas-Edmé, shoe fetishism of, 142

Revolutionary, 136

Revolutions and social life, 200

The Rhetoric of Motives, 18

The Rhetoric of Religion, 189, 217, 225

Rhetoric of social life, 128

Richards, I. A., 18

Ridicule: anxiety and, 107; leads to malediction, 180

Riesman, David, 9

Rights, in economic life, 206

Rites: manners and, 121; past and future in, 124; social, 187; comic *and* tragic, 175; symbolic expression, 186; sociodrama in classical China, 187; general form of sociodrama, 187

Ritual: model of symbolic action, 134; model for analysis of communication, 134; and tradition, 174; communication with supernatural power, 185; communication of fixed sentiments; 185; basic questions on, 186; study of

effects, 186; and cosmology, 187; Chinese thought on, 187; study of form as sociodrama, 188; and supernatural principles, 189; action in time, 191

Ritual drama, 140; tragic form of, 126

Ritual form, anthropologists' use of, 185

Ritual idiom, 186

Ritual value, 186

Robert's Rules of Order, 57

Role conflict, 130

Role enactment: as form of sociation, 49; style *and* content determine meaning, 72; before general publics, 93

Role playing: under rules, 88; as address, 176; in childhood, 176

Roles: exist in communication, 7; enactment, 17; glory sustained, 56; community enactment necessary to survival, 60; enactment in community drama, 61; as problem-solving, 74; basic, 123; and tradition of past and future, 124; based in belief in fixed future, 124; based in art, 125; principle of entelechy in, 131; and symbolic integration, 156; organization of responses, 176; and manners, 179; and clothes, 184; power of, 190; and dress, 213; "internalized," 214

Romantic love, feudal drama of, 58

Rourke, Constance, 9

Rule of law, enforced through umpire, referee, arbitrator, or judge, 91

Ruler, representative of transcendent principle of social order, 53

Rules, 17; compared with other forms of integration, 28; basic form of consensus in America, 30; and voluntary associations, 30; regulation of games, 30; determinant of honor in winning, 30; compared with other forms of relatedness, 30; open to discussion, 36; rational test of action, 36; realm of change, 37; ephemeral but binding, 37; weaken appeals to supernatural, 37; experiments with, 37; and form, 37; basis of fair play, 37; and power of form, 37; basic to reason, 37; and discussion, 37; forms of social order, 38; form of authority in America, 38; Jefferson on, 39; and personal honor, 54; of form in art, 57; and equality, 57; and fair play, 57; will of equals, 58; subject to change, 58; permanence *in* change, 59; change by common agreement, 59; and judicial process, 73; community consent, 75; by divine right, 75; and equality in role playing, 88; and discussion, 88; applied by authority, 90; and mystery, 90; bind us as equals, 90; by agreement, 91, 92, 177; form of legitimation, 91; fair play and mystique of, 91, 215; external to players, 91; formal quality, 91, 173; and increase in social energy, 92; and honor in winning, 174; no hierarchy in, 177; and umpire, 177; and authority, 178; analysis, 178; will of equals, 178; and disobedience, 178; of debate, 205; and play, 214; organization of attitudes, 214; not sacred or mysterious, 215; same for all, 215

Sacher-Masoch, Leopold von, 143
Sacred: beyond critical discussion, 113; "beyond" yet within the world, 134; paradox in, 134; Saint Paul on, 134
Sacrifice: integrative power, 24; means of communication between profane and sacred, 24
Sacrifice: Its Nature and Function, 24
Sade, Marquis de, 40
Sanctification and desanctification, 69
Sapir, E., 44
Satan, 148
Saturnalia: Frazer on, 182; inversion of rank in, 182
Scheler, Max, 3
Schumpeter, Joseph, 13
Science, 17, 229; and mystification, 80; of sociology, 229; dialogue, 229; hypothesis, 229; and social change, 230; progress in, 230; and action, 230; questions, 230; problem-solving, 231; way of life, 231; engineering, 232; war, technology, and money, 232; efficiency, 232; quantification, 232; American image of, 232; control of energy, 233; autonomy of, 233; survival of, 233; method as magic, 233; sociodrama of, 234
A Selected Bibliography on Values, Ethics, and Aesthetics in the Behavioral Sciences and Philosophy, 1920-1958, problems of selection in, 12
Self: Mead on emergence in role enactment, 19; determined by address, 128, 176
Self-love, need for audience, 102

Sentiments, fixed in ritual, 185
Sex as social form of expression, 121
Sexual symbolism, 142
Sharing in communication, 106
Shaw, George Bernard, 111, 228
Shelley, Percy Bysshe, 188
Shriner convention, use of comedy in, 98
Sickness, social factors in, 216
Signals, confusion of language with, 18
Significant other ("Thou"), born in dialogue between "I" and "Thou," 100
Significant symbol, form of address, 43
Simmel, Georg, 13, 117; on "playing society," 48
Situation: problematic, 19; in analysis of symbolic act, 70
Slang and ambiguity, 194
Slaves, inversion of rank in Roman Saturnalia, 182
Smith, W. R., 24
Sociability, 17, 37, 120; risk of, 121
Social bond: and euphoria, 17; dependent on form, 213
Social courtship: of superiors, inferiors, and equals, 56; not reducible to worship, 56; regulates hierarchy, 56; sexual courtship determined by, 58
Social euphoria: deepens social bonds, 61; and social communion, 120
Social facts: not limited to economic and political facts, 13; as symbolic facts, 152; as hierarchic symbols, 155
Social grace, "playing society" and, 173
Social hierarchy, stages in, 170
Social identity, response of audiences and, 101
Social institutions: struggle to make local symbols into universals, 22; basic forms of, 71
Social integration: communication and, 19; naming and, 21; based on rules, 28; need for functional terms, 29; Burke and Mead's model, 29; communication and, 31; doubt and, 36; social glory and, 69; appeals to private and public selves, 69; purely social forms, 118; tact and, 119; manners and, 122, 180; dependent on universal symbols, 132; resolution of incongruity, 150; agonistic qualities in, 169; terms for integrative bonds, 219
Social office, 184; as public role, 173; as sacred, 204
Social order: symbolic analysis and, 19; status honor in Weber and, 21; style

Social order (*Cont.*)
of life in Weber, 21; and consecration, 22; personification in hero and villain, 23; purification in popular art (American westerns), 23; naming and, 23; comic victimage a source of, 24; and selection of sociological data, 43; expressed in hierarchy, 51; in passage from one rank to another, 53; inferior and superior bound by principles of, 53; grounded in legitimations, 53; based on mystery or glory, 54; resolution of conflict, 61; drama of struggle, 64; threats to, 66; power of transcendent ultimates in, 67; consummatory function of "god-terms" in, 69; audiences in drama of, 69; depends on passage from old to new, 69; composite of "thou shalt" and "thou shalt not," 75; personification of, 89; dramatization of sacred principle of order, 89; representation of, 92; principles a basis of harmony, 92; arises out of contention, 92; criticism necessary to group survival, 99; linkages among images of, 117; and art, 125; dependence on integrative symbols, 131; the result of solving problems, 134; includes change, 134; and law, 136; as sociodrama, 139; principle of coherence, 170; mystery, 172; and clothes, 184; basic social functions dramatized in, 200; use of sex in, 201; "good form" and, 212; obedience, 218; mystical symbols of, 219
Social process, problems of obtaining data and, 17
Social relations, appeals to others in, 48
Social sciences, 229
Social self: arises in communication, 100; and response of significant other, 100
Social studies, study of incongruity in human relationships, 27
Social theory, theatrical analogies and, 31
Socialization, 39
Sociation: Simmel's pure forms, 117; at party, 120; rules of, 121; play-forms of, 121
Sociodramas: intensity and diversity, 33; new relationship, 33; source of power, 33; and community purification, 34; dramas of war, 34; public dramas of salvation, 34; and victimage, 34; vio-

lence and killing, 34; in war news, 34; of legitimation, 49; both comic and tragic, 59; staging of community roles, 61; common action, 94; in American politics and business, 95; basis for power, 95; new "mass appeal" in Russia, Germany, and America, 95; forms of, 125; of guilt, 140; problems of analysis, 152; versus art drama, 154; communication of glory, 164; model, 170; ceremonies, rites, and dramas, forms of, 174; elements in, 189; source of attitudes, 190; born in dialogue, 190; social context, 191; basic, 199; and art drama, 210; moment of invocation in, 234; as social reality, 237
Sociological jargon, 35
Sociology: failure to deal with meaning in conduct, 5; and humanistic approach to conduct in literature, 9; and art-gap, 10; cult, 11; and arts, 11; on relationships necessary to community survival, 27; failure to create model for study of symbolic action, 38
Sociology of Language, 3; failure to define "social" in social use of symbols, 6
Sociology Today: Problems and Prospects: failure to deal with communicative data, 8; neglect of art, 11
Sociopathology of everyday life: begins in role conflict, 130; breakdown in communication, 130; 247
Sociopolitical order, struggle to purify names in, 23
Socrates: comic god of Athenian democracy, 142; sacrifice as salvation, 147; god of irony, 227
Soliloquy: symbolization of role conflict, 105; role rehearsal in imagination, 105; in social life, 108; and role conflict, 109; sanctioned in society, 129
Solitude and communication, 160
Sorel, G., 28
Sorokin, P., 3, 13
Spencer, H., 12, 25, 55, 205; on ceremonial obeisances, 55, 219
Spending, guilt over, 149
Spiller, R. E., 8, 9
Spirits of the Corn and the Wild, 182
Stage of social action: design as clue to hierarchy, 94, 161, 162
Stalin, 39, 64, 93, 95, 205, 238, 245-7
Standard of living, 189

Status: style in Weber's theory of legitimation, 5; act of socil consecration, 22; enactment involves passage as well as fixity of position, 105; honor in, as style of life, 204

Streicher, J., 146; preparation of Jew as scapegoat, 138

Structure of social action: form of relatedness, 49; mechanical concepts, 67; elements in sociodramatic model, 67; social function, 155

Struggle: between good and evil, 65; forms in various models of the psyche, 65; and hierarchal purification, 65

Style: Weber's failure to develop "style of life" concept, 5; as positive and negative identification with social order, 22, 57, 123; as legitimation, 49; power of, 213

Style of life: as basis for social order in Weber, 21, 57; as goad to action, 21; as form, 118

Sumner, W. G., 25

Superiors, 53

Sullivan, Harry Stack , 220

Sumptuary laws, 70; as related to money, 78

Supernaturals: often invoked in hierarchy, 66; appeals to, 66; "beyond" reason, 80; model for social ends, 111; and invocation of ends, 111; in daily communication, 114; types of, 115; in tragic ritual, 126

Swift, Jonathan, 40, 228

Symbols: as masks, 6; interpretation by extra-symbolic reality, 6; obscurity and ambiguity, 7; "meaningless," 7; study of, 10; and "true" source of social order, 22; sociological analysis, 30; meaning, 31; public referents of private symbols, 32; and society, 44; as directly observable data, 50, 152; as universals, 51; laws of, 71; celestialization of, 78; attempts to maximize mystery of, 79; names in address, 104; social interaction, 116; element in relationship between self and other, 214

Symbols of order, hierarchy and, 156

Symbols of transcendence: reached through final leap into faith, 132; upward and downward way in, 132; methodology as transcendence, 133

Symbolic action: and development of social theory, 14; reduction to act of cognition, 20; and identification with principles of social order, 22; structure and function in, 22

Symbolic systems, stability in, 44

Symbolic analysis, basis of psychoanalytic technique, 45

Symbolic forms, 3

Symbolic function, and social order in sociology, 19

Symbolic integration, in birth and rebirth of roles, 156

Symbolic interactionists, use of mechanical models by, 5

Symbolic personification, 6

Symbolic purification, 23

Symbolic theory, and integrative factors, 20

Symbolization and consciousness, 126

Synchronic linguistics and sociolinguistic theory, 20

Table Talk, 78, 137

Taboo, 186

Tact: and social integration, 119; touchstone of manners, 119; in sociodrama, 213

Thomas, W. I., 13

Thoreau, Henry David, on consent, 91

Time, in American social thought, 25

Tocqueville, Alexis de, on voluntary associations in America, 30

Tönnies, F., 25, 28

Total sacrifice, 147

Tradition, and problem-solving, 47

Tragedy: and guilt and fear, 59; power of, 59; and mystery, 60; and victimage, 127

Tragic sense of life, lack of, in America, 27

Traitor, as stock figure in Soviet literature, 64

Transcendence, as resolution of struggle in sociodrama, 169

A Treatise on Language: or the Relation Words Bear to Things, 21

Truth, of drama and ritual, 190

Tyranny, study of, necessary to democracy's survival, 247

Ultimate symbols: metaphors for social order, 115; social incarnation, 165; of order, 234

Umpire, 57, 91; guardian of rules, 37; Jefferson on, 89; personification of rules, 90; dignity of role, 90; applies rules, 90, 97; necessary to rules, 90

"Upward way" of symbols, 79, 80
Utopias: relation to present, 47; Edenic past or future, 139

Veblen, Thorstein, 207, 232
Venus in Furs, 143
Vice, as excess of virtue, 175
Victimage: necessary to social order, 23; comic victim, 24; categorical, 25; symbolic, 34; in sociodrama, 34, 237; human need for, 35, 39; purge of fear and guilt, 39; scapegoat, 40; in popular art, 40; within the self, 40; in tragedy, 59; in comedy, 126; and guilt, 136; basic form of expiation, 144; purgation, 145; and torture, 145; in art, 146; perfected, 146; and total purgation, 146; perfect and imperfect, 147; of self, 147; private and public, 149; of Jew in Nazi Germany, 149; sanctioned, 150; need for total victims, 150; social catharsis, 157; on television, 141; source of, 210
Violence, as community drama, 237
Voltaire, François Marie Arouet, 180; on need for friendship, 87
Voluntary associations: and rules, 30; determined by rules, 57

Wach, Joachim, on typology of religious roles, 114
Waiting for Godot, 160
War as sociodrama, 209, 237, 243, 246
Ward, L., 26
Warner, L., 45
"We," social existence of "I" and "You," 104
Weber, M., 5, 13, 28, 30, 53, 55, 56, 91, 118, 154, 204, 240; on dignity as "being," 21; on status honor, 21; on style of life, 57, 74, 219; on legitimation of power, 91; types of legitimation, 114
Wesley, John, 149
Wilhelm (Kaiser), and use of military dress, 184
Word presentations, Freud's theory of, 46
Worship, as persuasion, 221
Wright, Frank Lloyd, 29

"You," public other, 128

Ziegfield musicals, 163
Znaniecki, F., 13